"The Theology of Work project is providir
pastors and the entire church on what th
hope that every pastor will preach regularly on how the gospel changes the
way we work and sometimes the work that we do. And I hope that every Christian will see the ways their work connects to God's work!"

Tim Keller, Senior Pastor
Redeemer Presbyterian Church, New York City
author of *Every Good Endeavor:
Connecting Your Work to God's Work*

"From the very beginning, God designed us to work. We each have gifts and callings intended to reflect his glory and to bring us fulfillment, even as we serve
others. While there are various resources addressing this subject, this unique
commentary offers a comprehensive survey of an important biblical theme.
With its added online availability, it is an invaluable resource for pastors and
business professionals alike."

Ravi Zacharias, author and speaker

"Did you ever wonder what your work has to do with your faith? The short answer is everything, and now you can read all about it in this *Theology of Work
Bible Commentary*, now in print for the first time. Heartily recommended."

Eric Metaxas, *New York Times* best-selling author of
Bonhoeffer: Pastor, Martyr, Prophet, Spy

"When it comes to biblical preaching and teaching, the church today has an
elephant-in-the-room problem. We spend the least amount of time addressing the very thing that people spend their waking hours doing the most: work
and career. The result is that people assume, perhaps unconsciously, that the
Bible doesn't address their actual lived experience. But it does, and between
these pages you will find the resources to help you connect the dots between
faith and work."

Gregory Alan Thornbury, PhD
President, The King's College, New York City

"The Bible encourages us to 'follow hard' after the Lord (Psalm 63:8). Now, a
new resource helps us daily on that quest, especially in our work. Crafted by
experts who love God's Word, the Theology of Work team's robust scholarship,
timely insights, and wisdom are a gift for the ages."

John D. Beckett, Chairman
The Beckett Companies, North Ridgeville, Ohio
author of *Loving Monday* and *Mastering Monday*

"Recapturing the power of vocation in daily work is completely dependent on understanding how Scripture speaks into our labors. The *Theology of Work Bible Commentary* is an invaluable resource for pastors who want to connect themselves and their churches to the Lord's creative callings on our everyday lives."

Daniel M. Harrell, PhD, Senior Minister
Colonial Church, Edina, Minnesota

"The *Theology of Work Bible Commentary* states its thesis quite succinctly in its introduction to the Gospel of Matthew, 'The workplace consequences of living in God's kingdom are profound.' As a layman, I am always on the lookout for Bible research tools that illumine God's word in a way that offers practical guidance for my life and work. This commentary fits the bill. Look no further than the excellent treatment of Matthew 6:19–34 to see an example of guidance on the ways in which our treasure profoundly transforms us. I highly recommend this resource to my fellow laypersons."

Scott Griffin, Founder and Chief Architect
Pro Bono Publico, Seattle, Washington

"The Bible is full of business lessons and leadership principles that are often missed. The *Theology of Work Bible Commentary* provides valuable insights and a provocative, yet practical guide to incorporating those lessons into our everyday lives, as well as simple tips and tools to follow. The *Theology of Work Bible Commentary* is simply incredible!"

Gloria S. Nelund, Chair and CEO, TriLinc Global
Former CEO, Deutsche Bank North America
Private Wealth Management, Manhattan Beach, California

"The *Theology of Work Bible Commentary* is an excellent and vital addition to a growing interest surrounding the integration of calling, vocation, and mission. Whether you are a business owner, barista, mechanic, policymaker, or aid worker, The *Theology of Work Bible Commentary* is a tool you will want to have as you navigate your role as a leader—regardless of your position—in the work God has given you."

Travis Vaughn, Director of Cultural Renewal
Perimeter Church, Johns Creek, Georgia

"This commentary provides a unique resource for the person who wants to better understand God's purpose for work and how our work, whatever it may be, can be a ministry for the kingdom of God as we learn to integrate the claims of our faith with the demands of our work."

C. William Pollard, Chairman Emeritus
The ServiceMaster Company, Wheaton, Illinois

"The *Theology of Work Bible Commentary* is a long-awaited and welcome re-source for pastors and serious Christians seeking to make Jesus the Lord of their work lives. It is the product of a diverse team including 'in the trenches' business leaders alongside first rate biblical scholars. As valuable as the in-sights and comments of the authors themselves is the constant, implicit chal-lenge to readers to listen carefully for themselves to what God might be saying about work on every page of Scripture."

David W. Gill, PhD, Mockler-Phillips Professor of
Workplace Theology & Business Ethics
Director, Mockler Center for Faith & Ethics in the Workplace
Gordon-Conwell Theological Seminary
South Hamilton, Massachusetts

"As a longtime advocate for a theology of work, I have urged people to see the Bible as a guidebook for our working lives. Reading these marvelous commen-taries, however, has given me inspiring new insights into how rich a guidebook God's Word really is!"

Richard J. Mouw
President Emeritus and Professor of Faith and Public Life
Fuller Theological Seminary, Pasadena, California

"I struggled for the first decade of my business career, mostly alone and in the middle of the night, to find meaning in my work and gradually came to see that I was looking at work all wrong. I was trying to derive meaning *from* my work, instead of bringing meaning *to* my work. The *Theology of Work Bible Commen-tary* skillfully articulates God's perspective—the source of our work's ultimate meaning. This book is the helpful guide I never had, and I hope that as you read it your work life will come alive!"

Barry Rowan
Executive Vice President and Chief Financial Officer
Cool Planet Energy Systems, Greenwood Village, Colorado

"This commentary is a revolutionary document! It does what no other commen-tary has done, which is to turn us around and to see what the Bible actually says about work. Human enterprise is the main thing we do with our waking hours. It is about time we saw that the Word of God gives meaning, purpose, perspective, and practical guidelines for daily work. It is hard not to be enthusiastic about something that is just plain wonderful and transformative. This commentary can turn the church inside out as the people of God serve God full time from Monday to Friday."

R. Paul Stevens
Professor Emeritus, Marketplace Theology
Regent College, Vancouver, BC

"My calling is to form Christian leaders for their callings, so I am always looking for resources that help followers of Jesus truly hear God's voice the real world. The *Theology of Work Bible Commentary* is the right tool for the job. Bringing together serious biblical scholarship with keen pastoral perspective and the insights of a wise mentor, this commentary helps us read the scriptures with a Monday-through-Friday lens. Work, calling, career, relationships, family, friendships, and all that shapes our ability to hear and heed the voice of God in a world where we struggle to slow down even for Sundays. I'll be recommending this commentary to seminarians, pastors and 'fellow-workers' all."

Tod Bolsinger, PhD
Vice President for Vocation and Formation
Assistant Professor of Practical Theology
Fuller Theological Seminary, Pasadena, California

"An elucidating exploration of an issue that is relevant to all believers, this is a wonderful resource for anyone who wants Scripture to inform their life at work. This tremendous commentary has my wholehearted recommendation."

D. Michael Lindsay, President
Gordon College, Wenham, Massachusetts

"In this unique commentary, the Gospels and Acts are discussed through the lens of work—how why we work informs how we work, the example of Jesus Christ as a worker, and God's principles applied to the workplace. A great guide for clergy and laity alike; either a surface or detailed examination point out the Bible's relevance for everyday life, including work. This commentary is a gift to the Church."

Bob Doll, Chief Equity Strategist
Nuveen Asset Management, New York City

"An easily readable book that will give you much to think about, on every conceivable topic related to the world of work. Even if you end up disagreeing with some of the positions taken or views shared, overall this book will enlighten you on your way to work, and in your day at work."

Prabhu Guptara, Distinguished Professor of
Global Business, Management and Public Policy
William Carey University, India
Member of the Board, Institute of Management
University of St. Gallen, Switzerland
Chairman, Relational Thinking Network

"The *Theology of Work Bible Commentary* is an exceptional resource for not only Christians in the marketplace, but for everyone who works, period. The design and layout are brilliant! It's easy to access material by subject and topic. I'm impressed by the contributors and know others will feel inspired and encouraged by their collective wisdom, too."

Nancy Matheson Burns, Chief Executive Officer
Dole & Bailey Inc., Woburn, Massachusetts

"Some suggest that modern industrial society made work a pervasive concern of modern humankind. But in the creation accounts God is presented as a worker who labors six days and takes a 'breather' on the seventh day, and is represented as a potter in his making of man and as a temple builder in his making of woman. Moreover, humankind's first obligation in the Bible after being fruitful is to 'work' the Garden of Eden. Indeed, the subject of work pervades the Bible. There are many popular books on the doctrine of work and a few on the theology of work. But this *Theology of Work Bible Commentary* is the first to investigate the biblical text book by book in order to glean insights into work from God's perspective. Unfortunately, work pervades much of the Christian's life apart from God and rules it. But this book helps Christian workers to relate their labor to God and thereby make their work holy and meaningful."

Bruce Waltke, Professor Emeritus of Biblical Studies
Regent College, Vancouver, Canada

"This series is a magnificent contribution to one of the most neglected themes in Christian ethics. Avoiding the easy anachronism of finding a few proof-texts that might apply to modern work, the authors let the distinctive voices and broader themes of Scripture illuminate our working life. The conversation about faith and work is deeper and richer thanks to the Theology of Work Project."

Andy Crouch, Executive Editor, *Christianity Today*
author of *Culture Making* and *Playing God*

"This commentary was written exactly for those of us who aim to integrate our faith and work on a daily basis, and is an excellent reminder that God hasn't called the world to go to church, but has called the Church to go to the world (and there is no place we do that more than at our place of work!). Having served for more than thirty-five years in global leadership roles in both the for-profit and, now, the nonprofit sectors, I only wish I had had access to the insights shared in the *Theology of Work Bible Commentary* many years ago."

Bonnie Wurzbacher, Chief Resource Development Officer
World Vision International, London
Sr. Vice President, Global Customer Leadership
The Coca-Cola Company (retired)

GENESIS THROUGH DEUTERONOMY

THEOLOGY OF WORK
BIBLE
COMMENTARY

GENESIS THROUGH DEUTERONOMY
VOLUME 1

THEOLOGY OF WORK ▶ PROJECT

THEOLOGY OF WORK BIBLE COMMENTARY, VOLUME 1:
GENESIS THROUGH DEUTERONOMY

Copyright © 2015 by the Theology of Work Project, Inc.

Print edition published by Hendrickson Publishers Marketing, LLC, P.O. Box 3473, Peabody, Massachusetts 01961-3473 under license from the Theology of Work Project, Inc.

No part of the print edition may be reproduced or transmitted in any form or by any means, electronic or mechanical, including photocopying, recording, or by any information storage and retrieval system, without permission in writing from the publisher.

Online edition copy permission is governed by a Creative Commons 4.0 license available at http://www.theologyofwork.org/about/cc-license/.

ISBN 978-1-61970-660-6

Unless otherwise noted, the Scripture quotations contained herein are from the New Revised Standard Version Bible, Copyright © 1989, Division of Christian Education of the National Council of the Churches of Christ in the U.S.A., and are used by permission. All rights reserved.

Scripture quotations marked (NIV) are taken from the Holy Bible, New International Version®, NIV®. Copyright © 1973, 1978, 1984, 2011 by Biblica, Inc.™ Used by permission of Zondervan. All rights reserved worldwide. www.zondervan.com. The "NIV" and "New International Version" are trademarks registered in the United States Patent and Trademark Office by Biblica, Inc.™

Scripture quotations marked (NLT) are taken from the *Holy Bible*, New Living Translation, copyright © 1996, 2004, 2007 by Tyndale House Foundation. Used by permission of Tyndale House Publishers, Inc., Carol Stream, Illinois 60188. All rights reserved.

Printed in the United States of America

First Printing — August 2015

Library of Congress Cataloging-in-Publication Data

Theology of work Bible commentary / by the Theology of Work Project ;
   William Messenger, executive editor.
      volumes cm
   Includes bibliographical references and index.
      Contents: volume 4. Matthew through Acts — 1. Work—Religious aspects—
   Christianity. 2. Work—Biblical teaching. I. Messenger, William, 1960- editor.
   II. Theology of Work Project (Boston, Mass.)
      BT738.5.T45 2014
      220.8'331—dc23
                    2014022025

Table of Contents

Abbreviations

Old Testament

Gen.	Genesis	Eccl.	Ecclesiastes
Exod.	Exodus	Song	Song of Songs
Lev.	Leviticus	Isa.	Isaiah
Num.	Numbers	Jer.	Jeremiah
Deut.	Deuteronomy	Lam.	Lamentations
Josh.	Joshua	Ezek.	Ezekiel
Judg.	Judges	Dan.	Daniel
Ruth	Ruth	Hos.	Hosea
1 Sam.	1 Samuel	Joel	Joel
2 Sam.	2 Samuel	Amos	Amos
1 Kgs.	1 Kings	Obad.	Obadiah
2 Kgs.	2 Kings	Jonah	Jonah
1 Chr.	1 Chronicles	Mic.	Micah
2 Chr.	2 Chronicles	Nah.	Nahum
Ezra	Ezra	Hab.	Habakkuk
Neh.	Nehemiah	Zeph.	Zephaniah
Est.	Esther	Hag.	Haggai
Job	Job	Zech.	Zechariah
Ps(s).	Psalm(s)	Mal.	Malachi
Prov.	Proverbs		

New Testament

Matt.	Matthew	Acts	Acts
Mark	Mark	Rom.	Romans
Luke	Luke	1 Cor.	1 Corinthians
John	John	2 Cor.	2 Corinthians

Gal.	Galatians	Heb.	Hebrews
Eph.	Ephesians	James	James
Phil.	Philippians	1 Pet.	1 Peter
Col.	Colossians	2 Pet.	2 Peter
1 Thess.	1 Thessalonians	1 John	1 John
2 Thess.	2 Thessalonians	2 John	2 John
1 Tim.	1 Timothy	3 John	3 John
2 Tim.	2 Timothy	Jude	Jude
Titus	Titus	Rev.	Revelation
Philem.	Philemon		

Any commentary references not in this particular volume can be found at the Theology of Work website (www.theologyofwork.org), along with video interviews and sidebars on people in the work world.

Foreword

The *Theology of Work Bible Commentary* is unique in that it explores what the entire Bible says about work. It represents more than five years of research by 140 contributors from sixteen countries, guided by an international steering committee of twenty scholars, pastors, and Christians from a variety of workplaces. We are thankful to God for this opportunity to present it to you in this volume.

Why does anyone need a theology of work? When we talk about a "theology," it can sound as stuffy as a tomb. Theology is often considered the domain of scholars who are wrestling with questions that no one ever asks, or solving problems that have never really arisen. When we talk about theology, however, we are really talking about what we know or do not know about God. Everyone does theology. Atheists who say they don't believe in God are already dealing with theology. Wars are fought over theology by people who are convinced that they are doing God's will. Agree with them or not, everyone everywhere does theology. People in the workplace who may never attend church are dealing with theology in some way every day. Ultimately, the questions we ask about God are not merely religious, they are life altering. In fact, what you believe about God may be the most important thing you ever think about. That's theology!

When it comes to work, theology is seldom practiced out loud. During my early years as president at Denver Seminary, I hosted a morning Bible study for business people. After class, over breakfast, we discussed the myriad dilemmas these workers and leaders faced in the workplace. Again and again, I heard, "You're the first pastoral person to actively address how my faith relates to my work." It was then that I realized there was a great divide between the leadership of the church and the everyday lives of the people they are called to equip.

At its heart, the perceived distance between God and everyday work is a theological issue. Most Christians believe that God cares about how we relate to others, how we relate to him, and whether we cheat, steal, lie, or break the Ten Commandments. However, it would surprise a lot of us to learn that our work matters to God. God cares what we do for a living, how we do it, and how we use our resources. As it turns out, the Bible has much to say about work. In fact, work is a major topic in the Bible, beginning with the surprising statement in Genesis 2:15 that God created people to work—not as a punishment, but as a pleasure and a way of relating to God himself.

The Scriptures provide principles that both give *meaning* to work and tell us *how* to work. Unfortunately, there is not a book in the Bible called First and Second Executive or Letter to the Christian Plumbers. Instead, what the Bible teaches about God's view of work is embedded in the Scriptures. Only a few of the biblical writers speak directly about the work that people do. They simply assume it. For instance, one of the Ten Commandments declares, "Remember the sabbath day and keep it holy" (Exod. 20:8), as if the only day God cared about was the Sabbath. But the command also says, "Six days you shall labor and do all your work" (Exod. 20:9). So the command deals not only with a special day when we can rest, but with the other days of the week designed for work.

The *Theology of Work Bible Commentary* goes through the Bible book by book to bring to the surface what we might not have seen about work at first blush. For example, consider the last book of the Bible, Revelation. It is possible to be so caught up in the visions in Revelation and questions about when they will occur, that we do not see that the Scripture also tells us about work now and in the future. You might be surprised that the Song of Solomon, a love poem, has quite a bit to say about workers and work. This book attempts through a study of the Scriptures to answer the question, "Does the work we do matter to God?"

This commentary deals with the theology of *work*. In that sense, it is limited. And in another sense, it is very broad. It is limited to work, but work is as diverse as are the people in the world. One question that may come to mind is, "What is work?" The answer to that question seems obvious. Work is what we do to make a living. Saying that, however, implies that people work for forty or fifty hours a week in order to live for the other hours of the week. There is more to work than that. A farmer, for example, doesn't "work to make a living." Plowing a field, planting a crop, bringing in a harvest is really his life. Or when we say that people "work to make a living," we imply that they work to receive a salary or a wage. But what about volunteers who travel to another country at their own expense to help people who have suffered in an earthquake or a flood? What about the person who raises children, cooks meals, and takes care of the family home? Certainly these people work, and work hard, but do not receive a salary. What, then, do we mean when we talk about their "work"?

Others might insist that the opposite of work is play. These are the folks who say, "TGIF: Thank God, it's Friday and the weekend is coming!" The recreation we enjoy on the weekend stands in contrast to the labor we put in during the week. But what about the professional basketball or tennis player? Do they work? How does their "work" differ from recreation?

If you own a business, what responsibility do you have to the people who work for you and to the people who buy your products or services? If you're an employee, does God care about the products you make or the way your company advertises them? Is what you talk about when you're having coffee with co-workers important to God? Does God have anything to do with the work that consumes a major part of your life?

If you're a pastor reading this material on a theology of work, do you find yourself thinking about a woman in the eighth row, three seats from the end, who works in financial services, or the man behind her who is a nurse? Or a couple on the other side of the sanctuary who has recently invested everything they have to open a restaurant? Do you think about yourself as a pastor? Do you work? Perhaps you are tempted to respond, "Of course I do, but it's really not the same thing. I have a special calling from God." That leads to another question: What do you mean by a "call"? Is it reserved for missionaries, teachers at a Bible college or a seminary, or translators of the Bible? How about the executive, the vice president of an insurance company, or the bus driver who attends your church? Do they have a call from God? Does God call men and women in business, government, or nonprofit organizations to their positions? Can you imagine God "calling" a pastor to go back into the world of work? Is that whole way of thinking true to the Bible?

So you see, there is a flood of questions about the simple concept of work. In fact, we are barraged by questions about work that have to be answered. This commentary will not answer these sticky issues by providing a set of rules, but it will give you direction in coming to your own conclusions. After all, the Scriptures resemble a compass rather than a road map. But when you're on the journey, a compass can be very helpful. The *Theology of Work Bible Commentary* helps us plumb the depths of God's word, so that we can hear and respond to Jesus' voice in the calling of our everyday work.

Haddon W. Robinson
President
Theology of Work Project

Harold John Ockenga Distinguished Professor of Preaching
Gordon-Conwell Theological Seminary
Hamilton, Massachusetts, USA

Introduction to the Theology of Work

Work is not only a human calling, but also a divine one. "In the beginning God created the heavens and the earth." God worked to create us and created us to work. "The LORD God took the man and put him in the garden of Eden to till it and keep it" (Gen. 2:15). God also created work to be good, even if it's hard to see in a fallen world. To this day, God calls us to work to support ourselves and to serve others (Eph. 4:28).

Work can accomplish many of God's purposes for our lives—the basic necessities of food and shelter, as well as a sense of fulfillment and joy. Our work can create ways to help people thrive; it can discover the depths of God's creation; and it can bring us into wonderful relationships with co-workers and those who benefit from our work (customers, clients, patients, and so forth).

Yet many people face drudgery, boredom, or exploitation at work. We have bad bosses, hostile relationships, and unfriendly work environments. Our work seems useless, unappreciated, faulty, frustrating. We don't get paid enough. We get stuck in dead-end jobs or laid off or fired. We fail. Our skills become obsolete. It's a struggle just to make ends meet. But how can this be if God created work to be good—and what can we do about it? God's answers for these questions must be somewhere in the Bible, but where?

The Theology of Work Project's mission has been to study what the Bible says about work and to develop resources to apply the Christian faith to our work. It turns out that every book of the Bible gives practical, relevant guidance that can help us do our jobs better, improve our relationships at work, support ourselves, serve others more effectively, and find meaning and value in our work. The Bible shows us how to live all of life—including work—in Christ. Only in Jesus can we and our work be transformed to become the blessing it was always meant to be.

To put it another way, if we are not following Christ during the 100,000 hours of our lives that we spend at work, are we really following Christ? Our lives are more than just one day a week at church. The fact is that God cares about our life *every day of the week*. But how do we become equipped to follow Jesus at work? In the same ways we become equipped for every aspect of life in Christ—listening to sermons, modeling our lives on others' examples, praying for God's guidance, and most of all by studying the Bible and putting it into practice.

This Theology of Work series contains a variety of books to help you apply the Scriptures and Christian faith to your work. This book is one volume in the multivolume *Theology of Work Bible Commentary*, examining what the Gospels and the book of Acts say about work. These commentaries are intended to assist those with theological training or interest to conduct in-depth research into passages or books of Scripture.

Pastors will find these volumes helpful as they consider the Bible's perspective on work when teaching on particular passages or topics. Professors may use the commentary to help prepare classes or as a textbook for students. Laypeople may find practical help for workplace decisions (the topical index could be helpful in this regard), or they may read it as part of their personal or group Bible study. Other books in the Theology of Work series include Bible studies adapted from the *Theology of Work Commentary* and additional materials to help apply the Christian faith to daily work.

Christians today recognize God's calling to us in and through our work—for ourselves and for those whom we serve. May God use this book to help you follow Christ in every sphere of life and work.

Will Messenger, Executive Editor
Theology of Work Project

Genesis 1–11 and Work

Introduction to Genesis 1–11

The book of Genesis is the foundation for the theology of work. Any discussion of work in biblical perspective eventually finds itself grounded on passages in this book. Genesis is incomparably significant for the theology of work because it tells the story of God's work of creation, the first work of all and the prototype for all work that follows. God is not dreaming an illusion but creating a reality. The created universe that God brings into existence then provides the material of human work—space, time, matter, and energy. Within the created universe, God is present in relationship with his creatures and especially with people. Laboring in God's image, we work *in* creation, *on* creation, *with* creation and—if we work as God's intends—*for* creation.

In Genesis we see God at work, and we learn how God intends us to work. We both obey and disobey God in our work, and we discover that God is at work in both our obedience and disobedience. The other sixty-five books of the Bible each have their own unique contributions to add to the theology of work. Yet they all spring from the source found here, in Genesis, the first book of the Bible.

God Creates the World (Genesis 1:1–2:3)

The first thing the Bible tells us is that God is a creator. "In the beginning God created the heavens and the earth" (Gen. 1:1, NRSV alternate reading). God speaks and things come into being that were not there before, beginning with the universe itself. Creation is solely an act of God. It is not an accident, a mistake, or the product of an inferior deity, but the self-expression of God.

God Works to Create the World (Genesis 1:1–25)

God Brings the Material World into Being (Genesis 1:2)

Genesis continues by emphasizing the materiality of the world. "The earth was a formless void and darkness covered the face of the deep, while a wind from God swept over the face of the waters" (Gen. 1:2). The nascent creation, though still "formless," has the material dimensions of space ("the deep") and matter ("waters"), and God is fully engaged with this materiality ("a wind from God swept over the face of the waters"). Later, in chapter 2, we even see God working the dirt of his creation. "The LORD God formed man from the dust of the ground" (Gen. 2:7). Throughout chapters 1 and 2, we see God engrossed in the physicality of his creation.

Any theology of work must begin with a theology of creation. Do we regard the material world, the stuff we work with, as God's first-rate stuff, imbued with lasting value? Or do we dismiss it as a temporary job site, a testing ground, a sinking ship from which we must escape to get to God's true location in an immaterial "heaven." Genesis argues against any notion that the material world is any less important to God than the spiritual world. Or putting it more precisely, in Genesis there is no sharp distinction between the material and the spiritual. The *ruah* of God in Genesis 1:2 is simultaneously "breath," "wind," and "spirit" (see footnote b in the NRSV or compare NRSV, NASB, NIV, and KJV).

"The heavens and the earth" (Gen. 1:1; 2:1) are not two separate realms, but a Hebrew figure of speech meaning "the universe"[1] in the same way that the English phrase "kith and kin" means "relatives."

Most significantly, the Bible ends where it begins—on earth. Humanity does not depart the earth to join God in heaven. Instead, God perfects his kingdom on earth and calls into being "the holy city, the new Jerusalem, coming down out of heaven from God" (Rev. 21:2). God's dwelling with humanity is here, in the renewed creation. "See, the home of God is among mortals" (Rev. 21:3). This is why Jesus told his disciples to pray in the words, "Your kingdom come. Your will be done, on earth as it is in heaven" (Matt. 6:10). During the time between Genesis 2 and

---

[1]Gordon J. Wenham, *Genesis 1–15*, vol. 1, *Word Biblical Commentary* (Dallas: Word, 1998), 15.

Revelation 21, the earth is corrupted, broken, out of kilter, and filled with people and forces that work against God's purposes. (More on this in Genesis 3 and following.) Not everything in the world goes according to God's design. But the world is still God's creation, which he calls "good." (For more on the new heaven and new earth, see "Revelation 17–22" in *Revelation and Work*.)

Many Christians, who work mostly with material objects, say it seems that their work matters less to the church—and even to God—than work centering on people, ideas, or religion. A sermon praising good work is more likely to use the example of a missionary, social worker, or teacher than a miner, auto mechanic, or chemist. Fellow Christians are more likely to recognize a call to become a minister or doctor than a call to become an inventory manager or sculptor. But does this have any biblical basis? Leaving aside the fact that working with people *is* working with material objects, it is wise to remember that God gave people the tasks both of working with people (Gen. 2:18) and working with things (Gen. 2:15). God seems to take the creation very seriously indeed.

God's Creation Takes Work (Genesis 1:3–25; 2:7)

Creating a world is work. In Genesis 1 the power of God's work is undeniable. God speaks worlds into existence, and step by step we see the primordial example of the right use of power. Note the order of creation. The first three of God's creative acts separate the formless chaos into realms of heavens (or sky), water, and land. On day one, God creates light and separates it from darkness, forming day and night (Gen. 1:3–5). On day two, he separates the waters and creates the sky (Gen. 1:6–8). On the first part of day three, he separates dry land from the sea (Gen. 1:9–10). All are essential to the survival of what follows. Next, God begins filling the realms he has created. On the remainder of day three, he creates plant life (Gen. 1:11–13). On day four he creates the sun, moon, and stars (Gen. 1:14–19) in the sky. The terms "greater light" and "lesser light" are used rather than the names "sun" and "moon," thus discouraging the worship of these created objects and reminding us that we are still in danger of worshiping the creation instead of the Creator. The lights are beautiful in themselves and also essential for plant life, with its need for sunshine, nighttime, and seasons. On day five, God fills the water and sky with fish and birds that could not have survived without the plant life created earlier (Gen. 1:20–23). Finally, on day six, he creates the animals (Gen. 1:24–25) and—the apex of creation—humanity to populate the land (Gen. 1:26–31).[2]

In chapter 1, God accomplishes all his work by speaking. "God said . . ." and everything happened. This lets us know that God's power is more than sufficient to create and maintain the creation. We need not worry that God is running out of gas or that the creation is in a precarious state of existence. God's creation is robust, its existence secure. God does not need help from anyone or anything to create or maintain the world. No battle with the forces of chaos threatens to undo the creation. Later, when God chooses to share creative responsibility with human beings, we know that this is God's choice, not a necessity. Whatever people may do to mar the creation or render the earth unfit for life's fullness, God has infinitely greater power to redeem and restore.

The display of God's infinite power in the text does *not* mean that God's creation is not work, any more than writing a computer program or acting in a play is not work. If the transcendent majesty of God's work in Genesis 1 nonetheless tempts us to think it is not actually work, Genesis 2 leaves us no doubt. God works immanently with his hands to sculpt human bodies (Gen. 2:7, 21), dig a garden (Gen. 2:8), plant an orchard (Gen. 2:9), and—a bit later—tailor "garments of skin" (Gen. 3:21). These are only the beginnings of God's physical work in a Bible full of divine labor.[3]

Creation Is of God, but Is Not Identical with God (Genesis 1:11)

God is the source of everything in creation. Yet creation is not identical with God. God gives his creation what Colin Gunton calls *Selbständig-*

---

[2] For a helpful discussion of the interpretation of the "Days" of creation, see Bruce K. Waltke, *Genesis: A Commentary* (Grand Rapids: Zondervan, 2001), 74–78.

[3] For a long list of the many kinds of work God does in the Bible, see R. Paul Stevens, *The Other Six Days* (Grand Rapids: Wm. B. Eerdmans, 2000), 18–123; and Robert Banks, *God the Worker: Journeys into the Mind, Heart, and Imagination of God* (Eugene, OR: Wipf & Stock, 2008).

keit or a "proper independence." This is not the absolute independence imagined by the atheists or Deists, but rather the meaningful existence of the creation as distinct from God himself. This is best captured in the description of God's creation of the plants. "God said, 'Let the earth put forth vegetation: plants yielding seed, and fruit trees of every kind on earth that bear fruit with the seed in it.' And it was so" (Gen. 1:11). God creates everything, but he also literally sows the seed for the perpetuation of creation through the ages. The creation is forever dependent on God—"In him we live and move and have our being" (Acts 17:28)—yet it remains distinct. This gives our work a beauty and value above the value of a ticking clock or a prancing puppet. Our work has its source in God, yet it also has its own weight and dignity.

God Sees that His Work Is Good (Genesis 1:4, 10, 12, 18, 21, 25, 31)

Against any dualistic notion that heaven is good while earth is bad, Genesis declares on each day of creation that "God saw that it was good" (Gen. 1:4, 10, 12, 18, 21, 25). On the sixth day, with the creation of humanity, God saw that it was "very good" (Gen. 1:31). People—the agents through whom sin is soon to enter God's creation—are nonetheless "very good." There is simply no support in Genesis for the notion, which somehow entered Christian imagination, that the world is irredeemably evil and the only salvation is an escape into an immaterial spiritual world, much less for the notion that while we are on earth we should spend our time in "spiritual" tasks rather than "material" ones. There is no divorce of the spiritual from the material in God's good world.

God Works Relationally (Genesis 1:26a)

Even before God creates people, he speaks in the plural, "Let *us* make humankind in our image" (Gen. 1:26; emphasis added). While scholars differ on whether "us" refers to a divine assembly of angelic beings or to a unique plurality-in-unity of God, either view implies that God is inherently relational.[4] It is difficult to be sure exactly what the ancient Israelites would have understood the plural to mean here. For our purposes it seems best to follow the traditional Christian interpretation

---

[4] Waltke, 64–65.

that it refers to the Trinity. In any case, we know from the New Testament that God is indeed in relationship with himself—and with his creation—in a Trinity of love. In John's Gospel we learn that the Son—"the Word [who] became flesh" (John 1:14)—is present and active in creation from the beginning.

> In the beginning was the Word, and the Word was with God and the Word was God. He was in the beginning with God. All things came into being through him, and without him not one thing came into being. What has come into being in him was life, and the life was the light of all people. (John 1:1–4)

Thus Christians acknowledge our Trinitarian God, the unique Three-Persons-in-One-Being, God the Father, God the Son, and God the Holy Spirit, all personally active in creation.

God Limits His Work (Genesis 2:1–3)

At the end of six days, God's creation of the world is finished. This doesn't mean that God ceases working, for as Jesus said, "My Father is still working, and I also am working" (John 5:17). Nor does it mean that the creation is complete, for, as we will see, God leaves plenty of work for people to do to bring the creation further along. But chaos had been turned into an inhabitable environment, now supporting plants, fish, birds, animals, and human beings.

> God saw everything that he had made, and indeed, it was very good. And there was evening and there was morning, the sixth day. Thus the heavens and the earth were finished, and all their multitude. And on the seventh day God finished the *work* that he had done, and he rested on the seventh day from all the work that he had done. (Gen. 1:31–2:2; emphasis added)

God crowns his six days of work with a day of rest. While creating humanity was the climax of God's creative work, resting on the seventh day was the climax of God's creative week. Why does God rest? The majesty of God's creation by word alone in chapter 1 makes it clear that God is not tired. He doesn't *need* to rest. But he chooses to limit his creation in time as well as in space. The universe is not infinite. It has a beginning, attested by Genesis, which science has learned how to observe in light of the big bang theory. Whether it has an end in time is not unambiguously clear, in either the Bible or science, but God gives time a limit *within* the world as we know it. As long as time is running, God blesses six days for work and one for rest. This is a limit that God himself observes, and it later becomes his command to people as well (Exod. 20:8–11).

God Creates and Equips People to Work (Genesis 1:26–2:25)

People are Created in God's Image (Genesis 1:26, 27; 5:1)

Having told the story of God's work of creation, Genesis moves on to tell the story of human work. Everything is grounded on God's creation of people in his own image.

> God said, "Let us make humankind in our image, according to our likeness." (Gen. 1:26)

> So God created humankind in his image, in the image of God he created them; male and female he created them. (Gen. 1:27)

> When God created humankind, he made them in the likeness of God. (Gen. 5:1)

All creation displays God's design, power, and goodness, but only human beings are said to be made in God's image. A full theology of the image of God is beyond our scope here, so let us simply note that something about us is uniquely like him. It would be ridiculous to believe that we are *exactly* like God. We can't create worlds out of pure chaos, and we shouldn't try to do everything God does. "Beloved, never avenge yourselves, but leave room for the wrath of God; for it is written, 'Vengeance is mine, I will repay, says the Lord'" (Rom. 12:19). But the chief thing we know about God, so far in the narrative, is that God is a creator who works in the material world, who works in relationship, and whose work observes limits. We have the ability to do the same.

The rest of Genesis 1 and 2 develops human work in five specific categories: dominion, relationships, fruitfulness/growth, provision, and limits. The development occurs in two cycles, one in Genesis 1:26–2:4 and the other in Genesis 2:4–25. The order of the categories is not exactly in the same order both times, but all the categories are present in both cycles. The first cycle develops what it means to *work* in God's image. The second cycle describes how God *equips* Adam and Eve for their work as they begin life in the Garden of Eden.

The language in the first cycle is more abstract and therefore well suited for developing principles of human labor. The language in the second cycle is earthier, speaking of God forming things out of dirt and other elements, and is well suited for practical instruction for Adam and Eve in their particular work in the garden. This shift of language—with similar shifts throughout the first four books of the Bible—has attracted uncounted volumes of research, hypothesis, debate, and even division among scholars. Any general purpose commentary will provide a wealth of details. Most of these debates, however, have little impact on what the book of Genesis contributes to understanding work, workers, and workplaces, and we will not attempt to take a position on them here. What is relevant to our discussion is that chapter 2 repeats five themes developed earlier—in the order of dominion, provision, fruitfulness/growth, limits, and relationships—by describing how God equips people to fulfill the work we are created to do in his image. In order to make it easier to follow these themes, we will explore Genesis 1:26–2:25 category by category, rather than verse by verse.

Dominion (Genesis 1:26; 2:5)

To Work in God's Image Is to Exercise Dominion (Genesis 1:26)

A consequence we see in Genesis of being created in God's image is that we are to "have dominion over the fish of the sea, and over the birds of the air, and over the cattle, and over all the wild animals of the earth, and over every creeping thing that creeps upon the earth" (Gen. 1:26). As Ian Hart puts it, "Exercising royal dominion over the earth as God's representative is the basic purpose for which God created man. . . . Man is appointed king over creation, responsible to God the ultimate king, and as such expected to manage and develop and care for creation, this task to include actual physical work."[5] Our work in God's image begins with faithfully representing God.

As we exercise dominion over the created world, we do it knowing that we mirror God. We are not the originals but the images, and our duty is to use the original—God—as our pattern, not ourselves. Our work is meant to serve God's purposes more than our own, which prevents us from domineering all that God has put under our control.

Think about the implications of this in our workplaces. How would God go about doing our job? What values would God bring to it? What products would God make? Which people would God serve? What organizations would God build? What standards would God use? In what ways, as image-bearers of God, should our work display the God we represent? When we finish a job, are the results such that we can say, "Thank you, God, for using me to accomplish this?"

God Equips People for the Work of Dominion (Genesis 2:5)

The cycle begins again with dominion, although it may not be immediately recognizable as such. "No plant of the field was yet in the earth and no herb of the field had yet sprung up—for the LORD God had not caused it to rain upon the earth, and *there was no one to till the ground*" (Gen. 2:5; emphasis added). The key phrase is "there was no one to till the ground." God chose not to bring his creation to a close until he created people to work with (or under) him. Meredith Kline puts it this way, "God's making the world was like a king's planting a farm or park or orchard, into which God put humanity to 'serve' the ground and to 'serve' and 'look after' the estate."[6]

Thus the work of exercising dominion begins with tilling the ground. From this we see that God's use of the words *subdue*[7] and *dominion* in

---

[5] Ian Hart, "Genesis 1:1–2:3 as a Prologue to the Book of Genesis," *TynBul* 46, no. 2 (1995): 322.

[6] Meredith G. Kline, *Kingdom Prologue: Genesis Foundations for a Covenantal Worldview* (Eugene, OR: Wipf & Stock, 2006), 69.

[7] "Subdue" (*kavash*) applies to cultivation (farming), domestication (shepherding), even mining, "making use of all the economic and cultural potential

chapter 1 do not give us permission to run roughshod over any part of his creation. Quite the opposite. We are to act as if we ourselves had the same relationship of love with his creatures that God does. Subduing the earth includes harnessing its various resources as well as protecting them. Dominion over all living creatures is not a license to abuse them, but a contract from God to care for them. We are to serve the best interests of all whose lives touch ours; our employers, our customers, our colleagues or fellow workers, or those who work for us or who we meet even casually. That does not mean that we will allow people to run over us, but it does mean that we will not allow our self-interest, our self-esteem, or our self-aggrandizement to give us a license to run over others. The later unfolding story in Genesis focuses attention on precisely that temptation and its consequences.

Today we have become especially aware of how the pursuit of human self-interest threatens the natural environment. We were meant to tend and care for the garden (Gen. 2:15). Creation is meant for our use, but not *only* for our use. Remembering that the air, water, land, plants, and animals are good (Gen. 1:4–31) reminds us that we are meant to sustain and preserve the environment. Our work can either preserve or destroy the clean air, water, and land, the biodiversity, the ecosystems, and biomes, and even the climate with which God has blessed his creation. Dominion is not the authority to work *against* God's creation, but the ability to work *for* it.

Relationships (Genesis 1:27; 2:18, 21–25)

To Work in God's Image Is to Work in Relationship with Others (Genesis 1:27)

A consequence we see in Genesis of being created in God's image is that we work in relationship with God and one another. We have already seen that God is inherently relational (Gen. 1:26), so as images of a relational God, we are inherently relational. The second part of Genesis 1:27 makes the point again, for it speaks of us not individually but in

---

associated with the concept of 'land,'" according to Robert B. Chisholm Jr., *From Exegesis to Exposition: A Practical Guide to Using Biblical Hebrew* (Grand Rapids: Baker, 1998), 46.

twos, "Male and female he created them." We are in relationship with our creator and with our fellow creatures. These relationships are not left as philosophical abstractions in Genesis. We see God talking and working with Adam in naming the animals (Gen. 2:19). We see God visiting Adam and Eve "in the garden at the time of the evening breeze" (Gen. 3:8).

How does this reality impact us in our places of work? Above all, we are called to love the people we work with, among, and for. The God of relationship is the God of love (1 John 4:7). One could merely say that "God loves," but Scripture goes deeper to the very core of God's *being* as Love, a love flowing back and forth among the Father, the Son (John 17:24), and the Holy Spirit. This love also flows out of God's being to us, doing nothing that is not in our best interest (*agape* love in contrast to human loves situated in our emotions).

Francis Schaeffer explores further the idea that because we are made in God's image and because God is personal, we can have a personal relationship with God. He notes that this makes genuine love possible, stating that machines can't love. As a result, we have a responsibility to care consciously for all that God has put in our care. Being a relational creature carries moral responsibility.[8]

God Equips People to Work in Relationship with Others (Genesis 2:18, 21–25)

Because we are made in the image of a relational God, we are inherently relational ourselves. We are made for relationships with God himself and also with other people. God says, "It is not good that the man should be alone; I will make him a helper as his partner" (Gen. 2:18). All of his creative acts had been called "good" or "very good," and this is the first time that God pronounces something "not good." So God makes a woman out of the flesh and bone of Adam himself. When Eve arrives, Adam is filled with joy. "This at last is bone of my bones and flesh of my flesh" (Gen. 2:23). (After this one instance, all new people will continue to come out of the flesh of other human beings, but born by women rather than men.) Adam and Eve embark on a relationship so close that "they become one flesh" (Gen. 1:24). Although this may sound

---

[8] Francis A. Schaeffer, *Genesis in Space and Time* (Downers Grove, IL: InterVarsity Press, 1972), 47–48.

like a purely erotic or family matter, it is also a working relationship. Eve is created as Adam's "helper" and "partner" who will join him in working the Garden of Eden. The word *helper* indicates that, like Adam, she will be tending the garden. To be a helper means to work. Someone who is not working is not helping. To be a partner means to work *with* someone, in relationship.

When God calls Eve a "helper," he is not saying she will be Adam's inferior or that her work will be less important, less creative, less *anything*, than his. The word translated as "helper" here (Hebrew *ezer*) is a word used elsewhere in the Old Testament to refer to God himself. "God is my helper [*ezer*]" (Ps. 54:4). "Lord, be my helper [*ezer*]" (Ps. 30:10). Clearly, an *ezer* is not a subordinate. Moreover, Genesis 2:18 describes Eve not only as a "helper" but also as a "partner." The English word most often used today for someone who is both a helper and a partner is "co-worker." This is indeed the sense already given in Genesis 1:27, "male and female he created them," which makes no distinction of priority or dominance. Domination of women by men—or vice versa—is not in accordance with God's good creation. It is a tragic consequence of the Fall (Gen. 3:16).

Relationships are not incidental to work; they are essential. Work serves as a place of deep and meaningful relationships, under the proper conditions at least. Jesus described our relationship with himself as a kind of work, "Take my yoke upon you, and learn from me; for I am gentle and humble in heart, and you will find rest for your souls" (Matt. 11:29). A yoke is what makes it possible for two oxen to work together. In Christ, people may truly work together as God intended when he made Eve and Adam as co-workers. While our minds and bodies work in relationship with other people and God, our souls "find rest." When we don't work with others towards a common goal, we become spiritually restless. For more on yoking, see the section on 2 Corinthians 6:14–18 in the *Theology of Work Bible Commentary*.

A crucial aspect of relationship modeled by God himself is delegation of authority. God delegated the naming of the animals to Adam, and the transfer of authority was genuine. "Whatever the man called every living creature, that was its name" (Gen. 2:19). In delegation, as in any other form of relationship, we give up some measure of our power and independence and take the risk of letting others' work affect us. Much of the past fifty years of development in the fields of leadership and management has come in the form of delegating authority, empowering workers, and fostering teamwork. The foundation of this kind of development has been in Genesis all along, though Christians have not always noticed it.

Many people form their closest relationships when some kind of work—whether paid or not—provides a common purpose and goal. In turn, working relationships make it possible to create the vast, complex array of goods and services beyond the capacity of any individual to produce. Without relationships at work, there are no automobiles, no computers, no postal services, no legislatures, no stores, no schools, no hunting for game larger than one person can bring down. And without the intimate relationship between a man and a woman, there are no future people to do the work God gives. Our work and our community are thoroughly intertwined gifts from God. Together they provide the means for us to be fruitful and multiply in every sense of the words.

Fruitfulness/Growth (Genesis 1:28; 2:15, 19–20)

To Work in God's Image Is to Bear Fruit and Multiply (Genesis 1:28)

Since we are created in God's image, we are to be fruitful, or creative. This is often called the "creation mandate" or "cultural mandate." God brought into being a flawless creation, an ideal platform, and then created humanity to continue the creation project. "God blessed them, and God said to them, 'Be fruitful and multiply, and fill the earth'" (Gen. 1:28a). God could have created everything imaginable and filled the earth himself. But he chose to create humanity to work alongside him to actualize the universe's potential, to participate in God's own work. It is remarkable that God trusts us to carry out this amazing task of building on the good earth he has given us. Through our work God brings forth food and drink, products and services, knowledge and beauty, organizations and communities, growth and health, and praise and glory to himself.

A word about beauty is in order. God's work is not only productive, but it is also a "delight to the eyes" (Gen. 3:6). This is not surprising, since people, being in the image of God, are inherently beautiful. Like any other good, beauty can become an idol, but Christians have often been too worried about the dangers of beauty and too unappreciative of beauty's value in God's eyes. Inherently, beauty is not a waste of resources, or a distraction from more important work, or a flower doomed to fade away at the end of the age. Beauty is a work in the image of God, and the kingdom of God is filled with beauty "like a very rare jewel" (Rev. 21:11). Christian communities do well at appreciating the beauty of music with words about Jesus. Perhaps we could do better at valuing all kinds of true beauty.

A good question to ask ourselves is whether we *are* working more productively and beautifully. History is full of examples of people whose Christian faith resulted in amazing accomplishments. If our work feels fruitless next to theirs, the answer lies not in self-judgment, but in hope, prayer, and growth in the company of the people of God. No matter what barriers we face—from within or without—by the power of God we can do more good than we could ever imagine.

God Equips People to Bear Fruit and Multiply (Genesis 2:15, 19–20)

"The LORD God took the man and put him in the Garden of Eden to till it and keep it" (Gen. 2:15). These two words in Hebrew, *avad* ("work" or "till") and *shamar* ("keep"), are also used for the worship of God and keeping his commandments, respectively.[9] Work done according to God's purpose has an unmistakable holiness.

Adam and Eve are given two specific kinds of work in Genesis 2:15–20, gardening (a kind of physical work) and giving names to the animals (a kind of cultural/scientific/intellectual work). Both are creative enterprises that give specific activities to people created in the image of the Creator. By growing things and developing culture, we are indeed fruitful. We bring forth the resources needed to support a growing population and to increase the productivity of creation. We develop the means to fill, yet not overfill, the earth. We need not imagine that gardening and naming animals are the *only* tasks suitable for human beings. Rather the human task is to extend the creative work of God in a multitude of ways limited only by God's gifts of imagination and skill, and the limits God sets. Work is forever rooted in God's design for human life. It is an

---

[9] R. Laird Harris, Gleason L. Archer, Jr., and Bruce K. Waltke, eds., *Theological Wordbook of the Old Testament* (Chicago: Moody Press, 1999), 639, 939.

avenue to contribute to the common good and as a means of providing for ourselves, our families, and those we can bless with our generosity.

An important (though sometimes overlooked) aspect of God at work in creation is the vast imagination that could create everything from exotic sea life to elephants and rhinoceroses. While theologians have created varying lists of those characteristics of God that have been given to us that bear the divine image, imagination is surely a gift from God we see at work all around us in our workspaces as well as in our homes.

Much of the work we do uses our imagination in some way. We tighten bolts on an assembly line truck and we imagine that truck out on the open road. We open a document on our laptop and imagine the story we're about to write. Mozart imagined a sonata and Beethoven imagined a symphony. Picasso imagined *Guernica* before picking up his brushes to work on that painting. Tesla and Edison imagined harnessing electricity, and today we have light in the darkness and myriad appliances, electronics, and equipment. Someone somewhere imagined virtually everything surrounding us. Most of the jobs people hold exist because someone could imagine a job-creating product or process in the workplace.

Yet imagination takes work to realize, and after imagination comes the work of bringing the product into being. Actually, in practice the imagination and the realization often occur in intertwined processes. Picasso said of his *Guernica*, "A painting is not thought out and settled in advance. While it is being done, it changes as one's thoughts change. And when it's finished, it goes on changing, according to the state of mind of whoever is looking at it."[10] The work of bringing imagination into reality brings its own inescapable creativity.

Provision (Genesis 1:29–30; 2:8–14)

To Work in God's Image Is to Receive God's Provision (Genesis 1:29–30)

Since we are created in God's image, God provides for our needs. This is one of the ways in which those made in God's image are not God himself. God has no needs, or if he does he has the power to meet them all on his own. We don't. Therefore:

---

[10] While this quote is widely repeated, its source is elusive. Whether or not it is genuine, it expresses a reality well known to artists of all kinds.

God said, "See, I have given you every plant yielding seed that is upon the face of all the earth, and every tree with seed in its fruit; you shall have them for food. And to every beast of the earth, and to every bird of the air, and to everything that creeps on the earth, everything that has the breath of life, I have given every green plant for food." And it was so. (Gen. 1:29–30)

On the one hand, acknowledging God's provision warns us not to fall into hubris. Without him, our work is nothing. We cannot bring ourselves to life. We cannot even provide for our own maintenance. We need God's continuing provision of air, water, earth, sunshine, and the miraculous growth of living things for food for our bodies and minds. On the other hand, acknowledging God's provision gives us confidence in our work. We do not have to depend on our own ability or on the vagaries of circumstance to meet our need. God's power makes our work fruitful.

God Equips People with Provision for Their Needs (Genesis 2:8–14)

The second cycle of the creation account shows us something of *how* God provides for our needs. He prepares the earth to be productive when we apply our work to it. "The LORD God planted a garden in Eden, in the east; and there he put the man whom he had formed" (Gen. 2:8). Though we till, God is the original planter. In addition to food, God has created the earth with resources to support everything we need to be fruitful and multiply. He gives us a multitude of rivers providing water, ores yielding stone and metal materials, and precursors to the means of economic exchange (Gen. 2:10–14). "There is gold, and the gold of that land is good" (Gen. 2:11–12). Even when we synthesize new elements and molecules or when we reshuffle DNA among organisms or create artificial cells, we are working with the matter and energy that God brought into being for us.

Limits (Genesis 2:3; 2:17)

To Work in God's Image Is to Be Blessed by the Limits God Sets (Genesis 2:3)

Since we are created in God's image, we are to obey limits in our work. "God blessed the seventh day and hallowed it, because on it God rested from all the work that he had done in creation" (Gen. 2:3). Did

God rest because he was exhausted, or did he rest to offer us image-bearers a model cycle of work and rest? The fourth of the Ten Commandments tells us that God's rest is meant as an example for us to follow.

> Remember the sabbath day, and keep it holy. Six days you shall labor and do all your work. But the seventh day is a sabbath to the LORD your God; you shall not do any work—you, your son or your daughter, your male or female slave, your livestock, or the alien resident in your towns. For in six days the LORD made heaven and earth, the sea, and all that is in them, but rested the seventh day; therefore the Lord blessed the sabbath day and consecrated it. (Exod. 20:8–11)

While religious people over the centuries tended to pile up regulations defining what constituted keeping the Sabbath, Jesus said clearly that God made the Sabbath for us—for our benefit (Mark 2:27). What are we to learn from this?

When, like God, we stop our work on whatever is our seventh day, we acknowledge that our life is not defined only by work or productivity. Walter Brueggemann put it this way, "Sabbath provides a visible testimony that God is at the center of life—that human production and consumption take place in a world ordered, blessed, and restrained by the God of all creation."[11] In a sense, we renounce some part of our autonomy, embracing our dependence on God our Creator. Otherwise, we live with the illusion that life is completely under human control. Part of making Sabbath a regular part of our work life acknowledges that God is ultimately at the center of life. (Further discussions of Sabbath, rest, and work can be found in the sections on "Mark 1:21–45," "Mark 2:23–3:6," "Luke 6:1–11," and "Luke 13:10–17" in the *Theology of Work Bible Commentary*.)

God Equips People to Work within Limits (Genesis 2:17)

Having blessed human beings by his own example of observing workdays and Sabbaths, God equips Adam and Eve with specific instructions about the limits of their work. In the midst of the Garden of Eden, God plants two trees, the tree of life and the tree of the knowledge of good

---

[11] Walter Brueggemann, "Sabbath," in *Reverberations of Faith: A Theological Handbook of Old Testament Themes* (Louisville: Westminster John Knox Press, 2002), 180.

and evil (Gen. 2:9). The latter tree is off limits. God tells Adam, "You may freely eat of every tree of the garden; but of the tree of the knowledge of good and evil you shall not eat, for in the day that you eat of it you shall die" (Gen. 2:16–17).

Theologians have speculated at length about why God would put a tree in the Garden of Eden that he didn't want the inhabitants to use. Various hypotheses are found in the general commentaries, and we need not settle on an answer here. For our purposes, it is enough to observe that not everything that *can* be done *should* be done. Human imagination and skill can work with the resources of God's creation in ways inimical to God's intents, purposes, and commands. If we want to work *with* God, rather than *against* him, we must choose to observe the limits God sets, rather than realizing everything possible in creation.

Francis Schaeffer has pointed out that God didn't give Adam and Eve a choice between a good tree and an evil tree, but a choice whether or not to acquire the knowledge of evil. (They already knew good, of course.) In making that tree, God opened up the possibility of evil, but in doing so God validated choice. All love is bound up in choice; without choice the word *love* is meaningless.[12] Could Adam and Eve love and trust God sufficiently to obey his command about the tree? God expects that those in relationship with him will be capable of respecting the limits that bring about good in creation.

In today's places of work, some limits continue to bless us when we observe them. Human creativity, for example, arises as much from limits as from opportunities. Architects find inspiration from the limits of time, money, space, materials, and purpose imposed by the client. Painters find creative expression by accepting the limits of the media with which they choose to work, beginning with the limitations of representing three-dimensional space on a two-dimensional canvas. Writers find brilliance when they face page and word limits.

All good work respects God's limits. There are limits to the earth's capacity for resource extraction, pollution, habitat modification, and the use of plants and animals for food, clothing, and other purposes. The human body has great yet limited strength, endurance, and capacity to

---

[12] Schaeffer, 71–72.

work. There are limits to healthy eating and exercise. There are limits by which we distinguish beauty from vulgarity, criticism from abuse, profit from greed, friendship from exploitation, service from slavery, liberty from irresponsibility, and authority from dictatorship. In practice it may be hard to know exactly where the line is, and it must be admitted that Christians have often erred on the side of conformity, legalism, prejudice, and a stifling dreariness, especially when proclaiming what other people should or should not do. Nonetheless, the art of living as God's image-bearers requires learning to discern where blessings are to be found in observing the limits set by God and that are evident in his creation.

The Work of the "Creation Mandate" (Genesis 1:28, 2:15)

In describing God's creation of humanity in his image (Gen. 1:1–2:3) and equipping humanity to live according to that image (Gen. 2:4–25), we have explored God's creation of people to exercise dominion, to be fruitful and multiply, to receive God's provision, to work in relationships, and to observe the limits of creation. We noted that these have often been called the "creation mandate" or "cultural mandate," with Genesis 1:28 and 2:15 standing out in particular:

> God blessed them, and God said to them, "Be fruitful and multiply, and fill the earth and subdue it; and have dominion over the fish of the sea and over the birds of the air and over every living thing that moves upon the earth." (Gen. 1:28)

> The Lord God took the man and put him in the garden of Eden to till it and keep it. (Gen. 2:15)

The use of this terminology is not essential, but the idea it stands for seems clear in Genesis 1 and 2. From the beginning God intended and created human beings to be his junior partners in the work of bringing his creation to fulfillment. It is not in our nature to be satisfied with things as they are, to receive provision for our needs without working, to endure idleness for long, to toil in a system of uncreative regimentation, or to work in social isolation. To recap, we are created to work as sub-creators in relationship with other people and with God, depending on God's provision to make our work fruitful and respecting the limits given in his Word and evident in his creation.

People Fall into Sin in Work (Genesis 3:1–24)

Until this point, we have been discussing work in its ideal form, under the perfect conditions of the Garden of Eden. But then we come to Genesis 3:1–6.

> Now the serpent was more crafty than any other wild animal that the LORD God had made. He said to the woman, "Did God say, 'You shall not eat from any tree in the garden'?" The woman said to the serpent, "We may eat of the fruit of the trees in the garden; but God said, 'You shall not eat of the fruit of the tree that is in the middle of the garden, nor shall you touch it, or you shall die.'" But the serpent said to the woman, "You will not die; for God knows that when you eat of it your eyes will be opened, and *you will be like God*, knowing good and evil." So when the woman saw that the tree was good for food, and that it was a delight to the eyes, and that the tree was to be desired to make one wise, she took of its fruit and ate; and she also gave some to her husband, who was with her, and he ate. (emphasis added)

The serpent represents anti-god, the adversary of God. Bruce Waltke notes that God's adversary is malevolent and wiser than human beings. He's shrewd as he draws attention to Adam and Eve's vulnerability even as he distorts God's command. He maneuvers Eve into what looks like a sincere theological discussion, but distorts it by emphasizing God's prohibition instead of his provision of the rest of the fruit trees in the garden. In essence, he wants God's word to sound harsh and restrictive.

The serpent's plan succeeds, and first Eve, then Adam, eats the fruit of the forbidden tree. They break the limits God had set for them, in a vain attempt to become "like God" in some way beyond what they already had as God's image-bearers (Gen. 3:5). Already knowing from experience the goodness of God's creation, they choose to become "wise" in the ways of evil (Gen. 3:4–6). Eve's and Adam's decisions to eat the fruit are choices to favor their own pragmatic, aesthetic, and sensual tastes over God's word. "Good" is no longer rooted in what God says enhances life but in what people think is desirable to elevate life. In short, they turn what is good into evil.[13]

By choosing to disobey God, they break the relationships inherent in their own being. First, their relationship together—"bone of my bones and flesh of my flesh," as it had previously been (Gen. 2:23)—is riven apart as they hide from each other under the cover of fig leaves (Gen. 3:7). Next to go is their relationship with God, as they no longer talk with him in the evening breeze, but hide themselves from his presence (Gen. 3:8). Adam further breaks the relationship between himself and Eve by blaming her for his decision to eat the fruit, and getting in a dig at God at the same time. "The woman whom you gave to be with me, she gave me fruit from the tree, and I ate" (Gen. 3:12). Eve likewise breaks humanity's relationship with the creatures of the earth by blaming the serpent for her own decision (Gen. 3:13).

Adam's and Eve's decisions that day had disastrous results that stretch all the way to the modern workplace. God speaks judgment against their sin and declares consequences that result in difficult toil. The serpent will have to crawl on its belly all its days (Gen. 3:14). The woman will face hard labor in delivering children, and also feel conflict over her desire for the man (Gen. 3:16). The man will have to toil to wrest a living from the soil, and it will produce "thorns and thistles" at the expense of the desired grain (Gen. 3:17–18). All in all, human beings will still do the work they were created to do, and God will still provide for their needs (Gen. 3:17–19). But work will become more difficult, unpleasant, and liable to failure and unintended consequences.

It is important to note that when work became toil, it was not the beginning of work. Some people see the curse as the origin of work, but Adam and Eve had already worked the garden. Work is not inherently a curse, but the curse affects work. In fact, work becomes more important as a result of the Fall, not less, because more work is required now to yield the necessary results. Furthermore, the source materials from which Adam and Eve sprang in God's freedom and pleasure now become sources of subjugation. Adam, made from dirt, will now struggle to till the soil until his body returns to dirt at his death (Gen. 3:19); Eve, made

---

[13] Waltke, 90–91.

from a rib in Adam's side, will now be subject to Adam's domination, rather than taking her place beside him (Gen. 3:16). Domination of one person over another in marriage and work was not part of God's original plan, but sinful people made it a new way of relating when they broke the relationships that God had given them (Gen. 3:12, 13).

Two forms of evil confront us daily. The first is natural evil, the physical conditions on earth that are hostile to the life God intends for us. Floods and droughts, earthquakes, tsunamis, excessive heat and cold, disease, vermin, and the like cause harm that was absent from the garden. The second is moral evil, when people act with wills that are hostile to God's intentions. By acting in evil ways, we mar the creation and distance ourselves from God, and we mar the relationships we have with other people.

We live in a fallen, broken world and we cannot expect life without toil. We were made for work, but in this life that work is stained by all that was broken that day in the Garden of Eden. This too is often the result of failing to respect the limits God sets for our relationships, whether personal, corporate, or social. The Fall created alienation between people and God, among people, and between people and the earth that was to support them. Suspicion of one another replaced trust and love. In the generations that followed, alienation nourished jealousy, rage, even murder. All workplaces today reflect that alienation between workers—to greater or lesser extent—making our work even more toilsome and less productive.

People Work in a Fallen Creation (Genesis 4–8)

When God drives Adam and Eve from the Garden of Eden (Gen. 3:23–24), they bring with them their fractured relationships and toilsome work, scratching out an existence in resistant soil. Nonetheless, God continues to provide for them, even to the point of sewing clothes for them when they lack the skill themselves (Gen. 3:21). The curse has not destroyed their ability to multiply (Gen. 4:1–2), or to attain a measure of prosperity (Gen. 4:3–4).

The work of Genesis 1 and 2 continues. There is still ground to be tilled and phenomena of nature to be studied, described, and named.

Men and women must still be fruitful, must still multiply, must still govern. But now, a second layer of work must also be accomplished—the work of healing, repairing, and restoring the things that go wrong and the evils that are committed. To put it in a contemporary context, the work of farmers, scientists, midwives, parents, leaders, and everyone in creative enterprises is still needed. But so is the work of exterminators, doctors, funeral directors, corrections officers, forensic auditors, and everyone in professions that restrain evil, forestall disaster, repair damage, and restore health. In truth, everyone's work is a mixture of creation and repair, encouragement and frustration, success and failure, joy and sorrow. Roughly speaking, there is twice as much work to do now than there was in the garden. Work is not less important to God's plan, but more.

The First Murder (Genesis 4:1–25)

Genesis 4 details the first murder when Cain kills his brother Abel in a fit of angry jealousy. Both brothers bring the fruit of their work as offerings to God. Cain is a farmer, and he brings some of the fruit of the ground, with no indication in the biblical text that this is the first or the best of his produce (Gen. 4:3). Abel is a shepherd and brings the "firstlings," the best, the "fat portions" of his flock (Gen. 4:4). Although both are producing food, they are neither working nor worshiping together. Work is no longer a place of good relationships.

God looks with favor on the offering of Abel but not on that of Cain. In this first mention of anger in the Bible, God warns Cain not to give into despair, but to master his resentment and work for a better result in the future. "If you do well, will you not be accepted?" the Lord asks him (Gen. 4:7). But Cain gives way to his anger instead and kills his brother (Gen. 4:8; cf. 1 John 3:12; Jude 11). God responds to the deed in these words:

> "Listen; your brother's blood is crying out to me from the ground! And now you are cursed from the ground, which has opened its mouth to receive your brother's blood from your hand. When you till the ground, it will no longer yield to you its strength; you will be a fugitive and a wanderer on the earth." (Gen. 4:10–12)

Adam's sin did not bring God's curse upon people, but only upon the ground (Gen. 3:17). Cain's sin brings the ground's curse on Cain himself

(Gen. 4:11). He can no longer till the ground, and Cain the farmer be-comes a wanderer, finally settling in the land of Nod, east of Eden, where he builds the first city mentioned in the Bible (Gen. 4:16–17). (See Gen. 10–11 for more on the topic of cities.)

The remainder of chapter 4 follows Cain's descendants for seven generations to Lamech, whose tyrannical deeds make his ancestor Cain seem tame. Lamech shows us a progressive hardening in sin. First comes polygamy (Gen. 4:19), violating God's purpose in marriage in Genesis 2:24 (cf. Matt. 19:5–6). Then, a vendetta that leads him to kill someone who had merely struck him (Gen. 4:23–24). Yet in Lamech we also see the beginnings of civilization. Division of labor—which spelled trouble between Cain and Abel—brings a specialization here that makes certain advances possible. Some of Lamech's sons create musical instruments and ply crafts using bronze and iron tools (Gen. 4:21–22). The ability to create music, to craft the instruments for playing it, and to develop technological advances in metallurgy are all within the scope of the cre-ators we are created to be in God's image. The arts and sciences are a worthy outworking of the creation mandate, but Lamech's crowing about his vicious deeds points to the dangers that accompany technology in a depraved culture bent on violence. The first human poet after the Fall celebrates human pride and abuse of power. Yet the harp and the flute can be redeemed and used in the praise of God (1 Sam. 16:23), as can the metallurgy that went into the construction of the Hebrew tabernacle (Exod. 35:4–19, 30–35).

As people multiply, they diverge. Through Seth, Adam had hope of a godly seed, which includes Enoch and Noah. But in time there arises a group of people who stray far from God's ways.

> When people began to multiply on the face of the ground, and daughters were born to them, the sons of God saw that they were fair, and they took wives for themselves of all that they chose. . . . The Nephilim [giants, he-roes, fierce warriors—the meaning is unclear] were on the earth in those days—and also afterward—when the sons of God went in to the daughters of humans, who bore children to them. These were the heroes that were of old, warriors of renown. The LORD saw that the wickedness of humankind was great in the earth, and that every inclination of the thoughts of their hearts was only evil continually. (Gen. 6:1–5)

What could the godly line of Seth—narrowed eventually to only Noah and his family—do against a culture so depraved that God would eventually decide to destroy it utterly?

A major workplace issue for many Christians today is how to observe the principles that we believe reflect God's will and purposes for us as his image-bearers or representatives. How can we do this in cases where our work puts us under pressure toward dishonesty, disloyalty, low-quality workmanship, unlivable wages and working conditions, exploitation of vulnerable co-workers, customers, suppliers, or the community at large? We know from Seth's example—and many others in Scripture—that there is room in the world for people to work according to God's design and mandate.

When others may fall into fear, uncertainty, and doubt, or succumb to unbounded desire for power, wealth, or human recognition, God's people can remain steadfast in ethical, purposeful, compassionate work because we trust God to bring us through the hardships that may prove too much to master without God's grace. When people are abused or harmed by greed, injustice, hatred, or neglect, we can stand up for them, work justice, and heal hurts and divisions because we have access to Christ's redeeming power. Christians, of all people, can afford to push back against the sin we meet at our places of work, whether it arises from others' actions or within our own hearts. God quashed the project at Babel because "nothing that they propose to do will now be impossible for them" (Gen 11:6), for people did not refer to our actual abilities but to our hubris. Yet by God's grace we actually do have the power to accomplish all God has in store for us in Christ, who declares that "nothing will be impossible for you" (Matt. 17:20) and "nothing will be impossible with God" (Luke 1:37).

Do we actually work as if we believe in God's power? Or do we fritter away God's promises by simply trying to get by without causing any fuss?

God Says "Enough!" and Creates a New World (Genesis 6:9–8:19)

Some situations may be redeemable. Others may be beyond redemption. In Genesis 6:6–8, we hear God's lament about the state of the pre-flood world and culture, and his decision to start over:

The LORD was sorry that he had made humankind on the earth, and it grieved him to his heart. So the LORD said, "I will blot out from the earth the human beings I have created—people together with animals and creeping things and birds of the air, for I am sorry that I have made them." But Noah found favor in the sight of the LORD.

From Adam to us, God looks for persons who can stand against the culture of sin when needed. Adam failed the test but sired the line of Noah, "a righteous man, blameless in his generation; Noah walked with God" (Gen. 6:9). Noah is the first person whose work is primarily redemptive. Unlike others, who are busy wringing a living from the ground, Noah is called to save humanity and nature from destruction. In him we see the progenitor of priests, prophets, and apostles, who are called to the work of reconciliation with God, and those who care for the environment, who are called to the work of redeeming nature. To greater or lesser degrees, all workers since Noah are called to the work of redemption and reconciliation.

But what a building project the ark is! Against the jeers of neighbors, Noah and his sons must fell thousands of cypress trees, then hand plane them into planks enough to build a floating zoo. This three-deck vessel needs the capacity to carry the various species of animals and to store the food and water required for an indefinite period. Despite the hardship, the text assures us that "Noah did this; he did all that God commanded him" (Gen. 6:13–22).

In the business world, entrepreneurs are used to taking risks, working against conventional wisdom in order to come up with new products or processes. A long-term view is required, rather than attention to short-term results. Noah faces what must at times have seemed to be an impossible task, and some biblical scholars suggest that the actual building of the ark took a hundred years. It also takes faith, tenacity, and careful planning in the face of skeptics and critics. Perhaps we should add project management to the list of Noah's pioneering developments. Today innovators, entrepreneurs, and those who challenge the prevailing opinions and systems in our places of work still need a source of inner strength and conviction. The answer is not to talk ourselves into taking foolish risks, of course, but to turn to prayer and the counsel of those wise in God when we are confronted with opposition and discouragement. Perhaps we need a flowering of Christians gifted and trained for the work of encouraging and helping refine the creativity of innovators in business, science, academia, arts, government, and the other spheres of work.

The story of the flood, found in Genesis 7:1–8:19, is well known. For more than half a year Noah, his family, and all of the animals bounce around inside the ark as the floods rage, swirling the ark in water covering the mountaintops. When at last the flood subsides, the ground is dry and new vegetation is springing up. The occupants of the ark once again step on dry land. The text echoes Genesis 1, emphasizing the continuity of creation. God blows a "wind" over "the deep" and "the waters" recede (Gen. 8:1–3). Yet it is, in a sense, a new world, reshaped by the force of the flood. God was giving human culture a new opportunity to start from scratch and get it right. For Christians, this foreshadows the new heaven and new earth in Revelation 21–22, when human life and work are brought to perfection *within* the cosmos healed from the effects of the Fall, as we discussed in "God brings the material world into being" (Gen. 1:1–2).

What may be less apparent is that this, humanity's first large-scale engineering work, is an environmental project. Despite—or perhaps as a result of—humanity's broken relationship with the serpent and all creatures (Gen. 3:15), God assigns a human being the task of saving the animals and trusts him to do it faithfully. People have not been released from God's call to "have dominion over the fish of the sea and over the birds of the air and over every living thing that moves upon the earth" (Gen. 1:28). God is always at work to restore what was lost in the Fall, and he uses fallen-but-being-restored humanity as his chief instrument.

God Works to Keep His Promise (Genesis 9–11)

God's Covenant with Noah (Genesis 9:1–19)

Once again on dry land with this new beginning, Noah's first act is to build an altar to the Lord (Gen. 8:20). Here he offers sacrifices that please God, who resolves never again to destroy humanity "as long as the earth endures, seedtime and harvest, cold and heat, summer and winter, day and night, shall not cease" (Gen. 8:22). God binds himself to a covenant with Noah and his descendants, promising never to destroy the earth by flood (Gen. 9:8–17). God gives the rainbow as a sign of his promise. Although the earth has radically changed again, God's purposes for work remain the same. He repeats his blessing and promises that Noah and his sons will "be fruitful and multiply, and fill the earth" (Gen. 9:1). He affirms his promise of provision of food through their work (Gen. 9:3). In return he sets requirements for justice among humans and for the protection of all creatures (Gen. 9:4–6).

The Hebrew word translated "rainbow" actually omits the sense of "rain." It refers simply to a bow—a battle and hunting tool. Waltke notes that in ancient Near East mythologies, stars in the shape of a bow were associated with the anger or hostility of the god, but that "here the warrior's bow is hung up, pointed away from the earth."[14] Meredith Kline observes that "the symbol of divine bellicosity and hostility has been transformed into a token of reconciliation between God and man."[15] The relaxed bow stretches from earth to heaven, from horizon to horizon. An instrument of war has become a symbol of peace through God's covenant with Noah.

Noah's Fall (Genesis 9:20–29)

After his heroic work on behalf of humanity, Noah falls into a troubling domestic incident. It begins—as so many domestic and workplace tragedies do—with substance abuse, in this case alcohol. (Add alcoholic beverage production to the list of Noah's innovations; Gen. 9:20.) After becoming drunk, Noah passes out naked in his tent. His son Ham bursts in and sees him in this state, but his other sons—alerted by Ham—circumspectly enter the tent backwards and cover up their father without looking upon him in the raw. Exactly what is so shameful or immoral about this situation is hard for most modern readers to understand, but he and his sons clearly understand it to be a family disaster. When Noah regains consciousness and finds out, his response permanently destroys the family's tranquility. Noah curses Ham's descendants via Canaan and

---

[14] Waltke, 146.
[15] Kline, 152.

makes them slaves to the other two sons' branches. This sets the stage for thousands of years of enmity, war, and atrocity among Noah's family.

Noah may be the first person of great stature to come crashing down into disgrace, but he was not the last. Something about greatness seems to make people vulnerable to moral failure—especially, it seems, in our personal and family lives. In an instant, all of us could name a dozen examples on the world stage. The phenomenon is common enough to spawn proverbs, whether biblical—"Pride goes before destruction, and a haughty spirit before a fall" (Prov. 16:18)—or colloquial—"The bigger they come, the harder they fall."

Noah is undoubtedly one of the great figures of the Bible (Heb. 11:7), so our best response is not to judge Noah but to ask God's grace for ourselves. If we find ourselves seeking greatness, it's better to seek humility first. If we have become great, it's best to beg God for the grace to escape Noah's fate. If we have fallen, similarly to Noah, let us confess swiftly and ask those around us to prevent us from turning a fall into a disaster through our self-justifying responses.

Noah's Descendants and the Tower of Babel (Genesis 10:1–11:32)

In what is called the Table of Nations, Genesis 10 traces first the descendants of Japheth (Gen. 10:2–5), then the descendants of Ham (Gen. 10:6–20), and finally the descendants of Shem (Gen. 10:21–31). Among them, Ham's grandson Nimrod stands out for his significance to the theology of work. Nimrod founds an empire of naked aggression based in Babylon. He is a tyrant, a mighty hunter to be feared, and most significantly a builder of cities (Gen. 10:8–12).

With Nimrod, the tyrannical city-builder, fresh in our memory, we come to the building of the tower of Babel (Gen. 11:1–9). Babel, like many cities in the ancient Near East is designed as a walled enclosure of a great temple or ziggurat, a mud-brick stair tower designed to reach to the realm of the gods. With such a tower, people could ascend to the gods, and the gods could descend to earth. Although God does not condemn this drive to reach the heavens, we see in it the self-aggrandizing ambition and escalating sin of pride that drives these people to begin building such a mighty tower. "Let us build ourselves a city, and a tower with its top in the heavens, and let us make a name for ourselves; otherwise we shall be scattered abroad upon the face of the whole earth" (Gen. 11:4). What did they want? Fame. What did they fear? Being scattered without the security of numbers. The tower they envisioned building seemed huge to them, but the Genesis narrator smiles while telling us that it was so puny that God "came down to see the city and the tower" (Gen. 11:5). How different from the city of peace, order, and virtue that are God's purposes for the world.[16]

God's objection to the tower is that it will give people the expectation that "nothing that they propose to do will now be impossible for them" (Gen. 11:6). Like Adam and Eve before them, they intend to use the creative power they possess as image-bearers of God to act against God's purposes. In this case, they plan to do the opposite of what God commanded in the cultural mandate. Instead of filling the earth, they intend to concentrate themselves here in one location. Instead of exploring the fullness of the name God gave them—*adam*, "humankind" (Gen. 5:2)—they decide to make a name for themselves. God sees that their arrogance and ambition are out of bounds and says, "Let us go down and confuse their language there, so that they will not understand one another's speech" (Gen. 11:7). Then "the LORD scattered them abroad from there over the face of all the earth, and they left off building the city. Therefore it was called Babel, because there the LORD confused the language of all the earth; and from there the LORD scattered them abroad over the face of all the earth" (Gen. 11:8–9).

These people were originally of one blood, all descended from Noah through his three sons. But after God destroyed the Tower of Babel, the descendants of these sons migrated to different parts of the Middle East: Japheth's descendants moved west into Anatolia (Turkey) and Greece; Ham's descendants went south into Arabia and Egypt; and Shem's descendants remained in the east in what we know today as Iraq. From these three genealogies in Genesis 10, we discover where the tribal and national divisions of the ancient Near East developed.

We might be tempted to conclude from this study that cities are inherently bad, but this is not so. God gave Israel their capital city of

---

[16] Augustine, *City of God*, Book XIX.

Jerusalem, and the ultimate abode of God's people is God's holy city coming down from heaven (Rev. 21:2). The concept of "city" is not evil, but the pride that we may come to attach to cities is what displeases God (Gen. 19:12–14). We sin when we look to civic triumph and culture, in place of God, as our source of meaning and direction. Bruce Waltke concludes his analysis of Genesis 11 in these words:

> Society apart from God is totally unstable. On the one hand, people earnestly seek existential meaning and security in their collective unity. On the other hand, they have an insatiable appetite to consume what others possess. . . . At the heart of the city of man is love for self and hatred for God. The city reveals that the human spirit will not stop at anything short of usurping God's throne in heaven.[17]

While it might appear that God's scattering of the peoples is a punishment, in fact it is also a means of redemption. From the beginning, God intended people to disperse across the world. "Be fruitful and multiply, and fill the earth" (Gen. 1:28). By scattering people after the fall of the tower, God put people back on the path of filling the earth, ultimately resulting in the beautiful array of peoples and cultures that populate it today. If people had completed the tower under a singularity of malicious intent and social tyranny, with the result that "nothing that they propose to do will now be impossible for them" (Gen. 11:6), we can only imagine the horrors they would have worked in their pride and strength of sin. The scale of evil worked by humanity in the twentieth and twenty-first centuries gives a mere glimpse of what people might do if all things were possible without dependence on God. As Dostoevsky put it, "Without God and the future life, it means everything is permitted."[18] Sometimes God will not give us our way because his mercy toward us is too great.

What can we learn from the incident of the Tower of Babel for our work today? The specific offense the builders committed was disobeying God's command to spread out and fill the earth. They centralized not only their geographical dwellings, but also their culture, language, and

---

[17] Waltke, 182–183.

[18] Fyodor Dostoevsky, *The Brothers Karamazov*, trans. Richard Pevear and Larissa Volokhonsky (San Francisco: North Point Press, 1990), 589.

institutions. In their ambition to do one great thing ("make a name for ourselves" [Gen. 11:4]), they stifled the breadth of endeavor that ought to come with the varieties of gifts, services, activities, and functions with which God endows people (1 Cor. 12:4–11). Although God wants people to work together for the common good (Gen. 2:18; 1 Cor. 12:7), he has not created us to accomplish it through centralization and accumulation of power. He warned the people of Israel against the dangers of concentrating power in a king (1 Sam. 8:10–18). God has prepared for us a divine king, Christ our Lord, and under him there is no place for great concentration of power in human individuals, institutions, or governments.

So, then, we could expect Christian leaders and institutions to be careful to disperse authority and to favor coordination, common goals and values, and democratic decision-making instead of concentration of power. But in many cases Christians have sought something different, the same kind of concentration of power that tyrants and authoritarians seek, though with more benevolent goals. In this mode, Christian legislators seek just as much control over the populace, though with the object of enforcing piety or morality. In this mode, Christian businesspeople seek as much oligopoly as others, though for the purpose of enhancing quality, customer service, or ethical behavior. In this mode, Christian educators seek as little freedom of thought as authoritarian educators do, though with the intent of enforcing moral expression, kindness, and sound doctrine.

As laudable as all these goals are, the events of the Tower of Babel suggest they are often dangerously misguided (God's later warning to Israel about the dangers of having a king echo this suggestion; see 1 Sam. 8:10–18). In a world where even those in Christ still struggle with sin, God's idea of good dominion (by humans) seems to be to disperse people, power, authority, and capabilities, rather than concentrating it in one person, institution, party, or movement. Of course, some situations demand decisive exercise of power by one person or a small group. A pilot would be foolish to take a passenger vote about which runway to land on. But could it be that more often than we realize, when we are in positions of power, God is calling us to disperse, delegate, authorize, and train others, rather than exercising it all ourselves? Doing so is messy, inefficient, hard to measure, risky, and anxiety-inducing. But it may be exactly what God calls Christian leaders to do in many situations.

Conclusions from Genesis 1–11

In the opening chapters of the Bible, God creates the world and brings us forth to join him in further creativity. He creates us in his image to exercise dominion, to be fruitful and multiply, to receive his provision, to work in relationship with him and with other people, and to observe the limits of his creation. He equips us with resources, abilities, and communities to fulfill these tasks, and gives us the pattern of working toward them six days out of seven. He gives us the freedom to do these things out of love for him and his creation, which also gives us the freedom to *not* do the things for which he created us. To our lasting injury, the first human beings chose to violate God's mandate, and people have continued to choose disobedience—to a greater or lesser degree—to the present day. As a result, our work has become less productive, more toilsome, and less satisfying, and our relationships and work are diminished and at times even destructive.

Nonetheless, God continues to call us to work, equipping us and providing for our needs. And many people have the opportunity to do good, creative, fulfilling work that provides for their needs and contributes to a thriving community. The Fall has made the work that began in the Garden of Eden more necessary, not less. Although Christians have sometimes misunderstood this, God did not respond to the Fall by withdrawing from the material world and confining his interests to the spiritual, nor is it possible to divorce the material and the spiritual anyway. Work, including the relationships that pervade it and the limits that bless it, remains God's gift to us, even if it is severely marred by the conditions of existence after the Fall.

At the same time, God is always at work to redeem his creation from the effects of the Fall. Genesis 4–11 begins the story of how God's power is working to order and reorder the world and its inhabitants. God is sovereign over the created world and over every living creature, human and otherwise. He continues to tend to his own image in humanity. But he does not tolerate human efforts to "be like God" (Gen. 3:5) in order either to acquire excessive power or to substitute self-sufficiency for relationship with God. Those, like Noah, who receive work as a gift from God and do their best to work according to his direction, find blessing and fruitfulness in their work. Those like the builders of the tower of Babel, who try to grasp power and success on their own terms, find violence and frustration, especially when their work turns toward harming others. Like all the characters in these chapters of Genesis, we face the choice of whether to work with God or in opposition to him. How the story of God's work to redeem his creation will turn out is not told in the book of Genesis, but we know that it ultimately leads to the restoration of creation—including the work of God's creatures—as God has intended from the beginning.

Genesis 12–50 and Work

Introduction to Genesis 12–50 and Work

Genesis chapters 12 through 50 tell about the life and work of Abraham, Sarah, and their descendants. God called Abraham, Sarah, and their family to leave their homeland for the new country that God would show them. Along the way, God promised to make them into a great nation: "In you all the families of the earth shall be blessed" (Gen. 12:3). As Abraham's spiritual descendants, blessed by this great family and brought to faith through their descendant Jesus Christ, we are called to follow in the footsteps of the faith of the father and mother of all who truly believe (Rom. 4:11; Gal. 3:7, 29).

The story of Abraham and Sarah's family is perfused with work. Their work encompasses nearly every facet of the work of seminomadic peoples in the ancient Near East. At every point, they face crucial questions about *how* to live and work in faithful observance of God's covenant. They struggle to make a living, endure social upheaval, raise children in safety, and remain faithful to God in the midst of a broken world, much as we do today. They find that God is faithful to his promise to bless them in all circumstances, although they themselves prove faithless again and again.

But the purpose of God's covenant is not merely to bless Abraham's family in a hostile world. Instead, he intends to bless the whole world through these people. This task is beyond the abilities of Abraham's family, who fall again and again into pride, self-centeredness, foolhardiness, anger, and every other malady to which fallen people are apt. We recognize ourselves in them in this aspect too. Yet by God's grace, they retain a core of faithfulness to the covenant, and God works through the work of these people, beset with faults, to bring unimaginable blessings to the world. Like theirs, our work also brings blessings to those around us because in our work we participate in God's work in the world.

When seen from beginning to end, it is clear that Genesis is a literary whole, yet it falls into two distinct parts. The first part (Gen. 1–11) deals with God's creation of the universe, then traces the development of humanity from the original couple in the Garden of Eden to the three sons of Noah and their families who spread out into the world. This section closes on a low note when people from the whole world gather in unity to construct a city to make a name for themselves and instead experience defeat, confusion, and scattering as judgment from God. The second part (Gen. 12–50) opens with the Lord's call to the particular man, Abraham.[1] God called him to leave his homeland and family to set out for a new life and land, which he did. The rest of the book follows the life of this man and the next three generations who begin to experience the fulfillment of the divine promises made to their father Abraham.

Abraham (Genesis 12:1–25:11)

Abraham's Faithfulness Contrasted with the Faithlessness of Babel (Genesis 12:1–3)

God called Abraham into a covenant of faithful service, as is told at the beginning of Genesis 12. By leaving the territory of his faithless extended family and following God's call, Abraham distinguished himself sharply from his distant relatives who stayed in Mesopotamia and attempted to build the Tower of Babel, as was told at the close of Genesis 11. The comparison between Abraham's immediate family in chapter 12 and Noah's other descendants in chapter 11 highlights five contrasts.

First, Abraham puts his trust in God's guidance, rather than on human device. In contrast, the tower builders believed that by their own skill and ingenuity, they could devise a tower "with its top in the heavens" (Gen. 11:4), and in so doing achieve significance and security in a way that usurped God's authority.[2]

---

[1] God's changing of Abram's name to Abraham (17:5) is important in the book of Genesis, but not particularly relevant to the topic of work. We will refer to him throughout by his familiar name, Abraham, and likewise, for Sarai/Sarah.

[2] Bruce K. Waltke, *Genesis: A Commentary* (Grand Rapids: Zondervan, 2001), 182–83.

Second, the builders sought to make a name for themselves (Gen. 11:4), but Abraham trusted God's promise that *he* would make Abraham's name great (Gen. 12:2). The difference was not the desire to achieve greatness, per se, but the desire to pursue fame on one's own terms. God did indeed make Abraham famous, not for his own sake but in order that "all the families of the earth shall be blessed" (Gen. 12:3). The builders sought fame for their own sake, yet they remain anonymous to this day.

Third, Abraham was willing to go wherever God led him, while the builders attempted to huddle together in their accustomed space. They created their project out of fear that they would be scattered across the earth (Gen. 11:4). In doing so, they rejected God's purpose for humanity to "fill the earth" (Gen. 1:28). They seem to have feared that spreading out in an apparently hostile world would be too difficult for them. They were creative and technologically innovative (Gen. 11:3), but they were unwilling to fully embrace God's purpose for them to "be fruitful and multiply" (Gen. 1:28). Their fear of engaging the fullness of creation coincided with their decision to substitute human ingenuity for God's guidance and grace. When we cease to aspire for more than we can attain on our own, our aspirations become insignificant.

By contrast, God made Abraham into the original entrepreneur, always moving on to fresh endeavors in new locations. God called him away from the city of Haran toward the land of Canaan where Abraham would never settle into a fixed address. He was known as a "wandering Aramean" (Deut. 26:5). This lifestyle was inherently more God-centered in that Abraham would have to depend on God's word and leadership in order to find his significance, security, and success. As Hebrews 11:8 puts it, he had to "set out, not knowing where he was going." In the world of work, believers must perceive the contrast in these two fundamental orientations. All work entails planning and building. Ungodly work stems from the desire to depend on no one but ourselves, and it restricts itself narrowly to benefit only ourselves and the few who may be close to us. Godly work is willing to depend on God's guidance and authority, and it desires to grow widely as a blessing to all the world.

Fourth, Abraham was willing to let God lead him into new relationships. While the tower builders sought to close themselves off in a guarded fortress, Abraham trusted God's promise that his family would grow into a great nation (Gen. 12:2; 15:5). Though they lived among strangers in the land of Canaan (Gen. 17:8), they had good relationships with those they came in contact with (Gen. 21:22–34; 23:1–12). This is the gift of community. Another key theme thus emerges for the theology of work: God's design is for people to work in healthy networks of relationship.

Finally, Abraham was blessed with the patience to take a long-term view. God's promises were to be realized in the time of Abraham's offspring, not in the time of Abraham himself. The Apostle Paul interpreted the "offspring" to be Jesus (Gal. 3:19), meaning that the payoff date was more than a thousand years in the future. In fact, the promise to Abraham will not be fulfilled completely until the return of Christ (Matt. 24:30–31). Its progress cannot be adequately measured by quarterly reports! The tower builders, in comparison, took no thought for how their project would affect future generations, and God criticized them explicitly for this lapse (Gen. 11:6).

In sum, God promised Abraham fame, fruitfulness, and good relationships, by which meant he and his family would bless the whole world, and in due course be blessed themselves beyond imagining (Gen. 22:17). Unlike others, Abraham realized that an attempt to grasp such things on his own power would be futile, or worse. Instead, he trusted God and depended every day on God's guidance and provision (Gen. 22:8–14). Although these promises were not fully realized by the end of Genesis, they initiated the covenant between God and the people of God through which the redemption of the world will come to completion in the day of Christ (Phil. 1:10).

God promised a new land to Abraham's family. Making use of land requires many kinds of work, so a gift of land reiterates that work is an essential sphere of God's concern. Working the land would require occupational skills of shepherding, tent-making, military protection, and the production of a wide array of goods and services. Moreover, Abraham's descendants would become a populous nation whose members would be as innumerable as the stars in the sky. This would require the work of developing personal relationships, parenting, politics, diplomacy and administration, education, the healing arts, and other social occupations. To bring such blessings to all the earth, God called Abraham and his descendants to "walk before me, and be blameless" (Gen. 17:1). This required the work of worship, atonement, discipleship, and other religious occupations. Joseph's work was to create a solution responding to the impact of the famine, and sometimes our work is to heal brokenness. All these types of work, and the workers who engage in them, come under God's authority, guidance, and provision.

The Pastoral Lifestyle of Abraham and His Family (Genesis 12:4–7)

When Abraham left his home in Haran and set out for the land of Canaan, his family was probably already quite large by modern standards. We know that his wife Sarah and his nephew Lot came with him, but so did an unspecified number of people and possessions (Gen. 12:5). Soon Abraham would become very wealthy, having acquired servants and livestock as well as silver and gold (Gen. 12:16; 13:2). He received people and animals from Pharaoh during his stay in Egypt, and the precious metals would have been the result of commercial transactions, indicating the Lord as the ultimate one to bestow blessing.[3] Evidence that both Abraham and Lot had become successful lies in the quarreling that broke out between the herders for each family over the inability of the land to support so many grazing animals. Eventually, the two had to part company in order to support their business activities (Gen. 13:11).

Anthropological studies of this period and region suggest the families in these narratives practiced a mix of seminomadic pastoralism and herdsman husbandry (Gen. 13:5–12; 21:25–34; 26:17–33; 29:1–10; 37:12–17).[4] These families needed seasonal mobility and thus lived in tents of leather, felt, and wool. They owned property that could be borne by donkeys or, if one was wealthy enough, also camels. Finding the balance between the optimal availability of usable pasture land and water required good judgment and intimate knowledge of weather and geography. The wetter months of October through March afforded grazing on the lower plains, while in the warmer and drier months of April through September the shepherds would take their flocks to higher

---

[3] Waltke, 216.

[4] Victor H. Matthews, "Nomadism, Pastoralism" in *Eerdmans Dictionary of the Bible*, eds. David Noel Freedman, Allen C. Myers, and Astrid B. Beck (Grand Rapids: Wm. B. Eerdmans, 2000), 972.

elevations for greener vegetation and flowing springs.[5] Because a family could not be entirely supported through shepherding, it was necessary to practice local agriculture and trade with those living in more settled communities.[6]

Pastoral nomads cared for sheep and goats to obtain milk and meat (Gen. 18:7–8; 27:9; 31:38), wool, and other goods made from animal products such as leather. Donkeys carried loads (Gen. 42:26), and camels were especially suited for long-range travel (Gen. 24:10, 64; 31:17). The skills required to maintain these herds would have involved grazing and watering, birthing, treating the sick and injured, protecting animals from predators and thieves, as well as locating strays.

Fluctuations in weather and the size of growth in the population of the flocks and herds would have affected the economy of the region. Weaker groups of shepherds could easily become displaced or assimilated at the expense of those who needed more territory for their expanding holdings.[7] Profit from shepherding was not stored as accumulated savings or investments on behalf of the owners and managers, but shared throughout the family. By the same token, the effects of hardship due to famine conditions would have been felt by all. While individuals certainly had their own responsibilities and were accountable for their actions, the communal nature of the family business generally stands apart from our contemporary culture of personal achievement and the expectation to show ever-increasing profits. Social responsibility would have been a daily concern, not an option.

In this way of life, shared values were essential for survival. Mutual dependence among the members of a family or tribe and awareness of their common ancestry would have resulted in great solidarity, as well as vengeful hostility toward anyone who would disrupt it (Gen. 34:25–31).[8]

---

[5] John H. Walton, Victor H. Matthews, and Mark W. Chavalas, *The IVP Bible Background Commentary: Old Testament* (Downers Grove, IL: IVP Academic, 2000), 44.

[6] Matthews, "Nomadism, Pastoralism," 971.

[7] T. C. Mitchell, "Nomads," in *New Bible Dictionary*, 3rd ed., eds. I. Howard Marshall, A. R. Millard, J. I. Packer, and D. J. Wiseman (Downers Grove, IL: InterVarsity Press, 1996), 828–31.

[8] Mitchell, 829.

Leaders had to know how to tap the wisdom of the group in order to make sound decisions about where to travel, how long to stay, and how to divide the herds.[9] They must have had ways of communicating with shepherds who took the flocks away at some distance (Gen. 37:12–14). Conflict-resolution skills were necessary to settle inevitable disputes over grazing land and water rights to wells and springs (Gen. 26:19–22). The high mobility of life in the country and one's vulnerability to marauders made hospitality much more than a courtesy. It was generally considered a requirement of decent people to offer refreshment, food, and lodging.[10]

The patriarchal narratives repeatedly mention the great wealth of Abraham, Isaac, and Jacob (Gen. 13:2; 26:13; 31:1). Shepherding and animal husbandry were honorable fields of work and could be lucrative, and Abraham's family became very wealthy. For example, to soften the attitude of his offended brother Esau prior to their meeting after a long time, Jacob was able to select from his property a gift of at least 550 animals: 200 female goats with 20 males, 200 ewes with 20 rams, 30 female camels with their calves, 40 cows with 10 bulls, and 20 female donkeys with 10 males (Gen. 32:13–15). It is therefore fitting that at the end of his life when Jacob conferred blessings on his sons, he testified that the God of his fathers had been "my shepherd all my life to this day" (Gen. 48:15). Although many passages in the Bible warn that wealth is often inimical to faithfulness (e.g., Jer. 17:11, Hab. 2:5, Matt. 6:24), Abraham's experience shows that God's faithfulness can be expressed in prosperity as well. As we shall see, this is by no means a promise that God's people should expect prosperity on a continuous basis.

Abraham's Journey Begins with Disaster in Egypt (Genesis 12:8–13:2)

The initial results of Abraham's journeys were not promising. There was fierce competition for the land (Gen. 12:6), and Abraham spent a long time trying to find a niche to occupy (Gen. 12:8–9). Eventually,

---

[9] Matthews, "Nomadism, Pastoralism," 972.

[10] Julian Pitt-Rivers, "The Stranger, the Guest, and the Hostile Host: Introduction to the Study of the Laws of Hospitality," in *Contributions to Mediterranean Sociology*, ed. John G. Peristiany (Paris: Mouton, 1968), 13–30.

deteriorating economic conditions forced him to pull out entirely and take his family to Egypt, hundreds of miles away from the land of God's promise (Gen. 12:10).

As an economic migrant to Egypt, Abraham's vulnerable position made him fearful. He feared that the Egyptians might murder him to obtain his beautiful wife, Sarah. To prevent this, Abraham told Sarah to claim that she was his sister rather than his wife. As Abraham anticipated, one of the Egyptians—Pharaoh, in fact—did desire Sarah and she "was taken into Pharaoh's house" (Gen 12:15). As a result, "the Lord afflicted Pharaoh and his house with great plagues" (Gen. 12:17). When Pharaoh found out the reason—that he had taken another man's wife—he returned Sarah to Abraham and immediately ordered them both to depart his country (Gen. 12:18–19). Nevertheless, Pharaoh enriched them with sheep and cattle, male and female donkeys, male and female servants as well as camels (Gen. 12:16), and silver and gold (Gen. 13:2), a further indication that Abraham's wealth (Gen. 13:2) was due to royal gifts.[11]

This incident dramatically indicates both the moral quandaries posed by great disparities in wealth and poverty and the dangers of losing faith in the face of such problems. Abraham and Sarah were fleeing starvation. It may be hard to imagine being so desperately poor or afraid that a family would subject its female members to sexual liaisons in order to survive economically, but even today millions face this choice. Pharaoh berates Abraham for taking this course of action, yet God's response to a later, similar incident (Gen. 20:7, 17) shows more of compassion than judgment.

On the other hand, Abraham had received God's direct promise, "I will make of you a great nation" (Gen. 12:2). Did his faith in God to make good on his promises fail so quickly? Did survival really require him to lie and allow his wife to become a concubine, or would God have provided another way? Abraham's fears seem to have made him forget his trust in God's faithfulness. Similarly, people in difficult situations often convince themselves that they have no choice but to do something they regard as wrong. However, unpleasant choices, no matter our feelings about them, are not the same as having no choice at all.

---

[11] Waltke, 216.

Abraham and Lot Parted (Genesis 13:3–18)

When Abraham and his family reentered Canaan and came to the region around Bethel, the friction that erupted between the herders of Abraham and those of his nephew Lot posed Abraham with a choice regarding the scarcity of land. A division had to be made, and Abraham took the risk of offering Lot first choice of the real estate. The central ridge of land in Canaan is rocky and does support much vegetation for grazing. Lot's eye fell to the east and the plain around the Jordan River, which he regarded as "like the garden of the LORD," so he chose this better portion for himself (Gen. 13:10). Abraham's trust in God released him from the anxiety of looking out for himself. No matter how Abraham and Lot would prosper in the future, the fact that Abraham let Lot make the choice displayed generosity and established trust between him and Lot.

Generosity is a positive trait in both personal and business relationships. Perhaps nothing establishes trust and good relationships as solidly as generosity. Colleagues, customers, suppliers, even adversaries, respond strongly to generosity and remember it for a long time. When Zacchaeus the tax collector welcomed Jesus into his home and promised to give half of his possessions to the poor and to repay fourfold those he had cheated, Jesus called him a "son of Abraham" for his generosity and fruit of repentance (Luke 19:9). Zacchaeus was responding, of course, to the relational generosity of Jesus, who had unexpectedly, and uncharacteristically for the people of that time, opened his heart to a detested tax collector.

Abraham and Sarah's Hospitality (Genesis 18:1–15)

The story of Abraham and Sarah's generous hospitality to three visitors who came to them by the oaks of Mamre is told in Genesis 18. Seminomadic life in the country would often bring people from different families into contact with one another, and the character of Canaan as a natural land bridge between Asia and Africa made it a popular trade route. In the absence of a formal industry of hospitality, people living in cities and encampments had a social obligation to welcome strangers. From Old Testament descriptions and other Ancient Near Eastern texts, Matthews derived seven codes of conduct defining what counts for good hospitality that maintains the honor of persons, their households, and communities by receiving and offering protection to strangers.[12] Around a settlement was a zone in which the individuals and the town were obliged to show hospitality.

1. In this zone, the villagers were responsible to offer hospitality to strangers.

2. The stranger must be transformed from being a potential threat to becoming an ally by the offer of hospitality.

3. Only the male head of household or a male citizen of a town or village may offer the invitation of hospitality.

4. The invitation may include a time span statement for the period of hospitality, but this can then be extended, if agreeable to both parties, on the renewed invitation of the host.

5. The stranger has the right of refusal, but this could be considered an affront to the honor of the host and could be a cause for immediate hostilities or conflict.

6. Once the invitation is accepted, the roles of the host and the guest are set by the rules of custom. The guest must not ask for anything. The host provides the best he has available, despite what may be modestly offered in the initial offer of hospitality. The guest is expected to reciprocate immediately with news, predictions of good fortune, or expressions of gratitude for what he has been given, and praise of the host's generosity and honor. The host must not ask personal questions of the guest. These matters can only be volunteered by the guest.

7. The guest remains under the protection of the host until the guest has left the zone of obligation of the host.

---

[12] Abstracted from Victor H. Matthews, "Hospitality and Hostility in Judges 4," *Biblical Theology Bulletin* 21, no. 1 (1991): 13–15.

This episode provides the background for the New Testament command, "Do not neglect to show hospitality to strangers, for by doing that some have entertained angels without knowing it" (Heb. 13:2).

Hospitality and generosity are often underappreciated in Christian circles. Yet the Bible pictures the kingdom of heaven as a generous, even extravagant, banquet (Isa. 25:6–9; Matt. 22:2–4). Hospitality fosters good relationships, and Abraham and Sarah's hospitality provides an early biblical insight to the way relationships and sharing a meal go hand in hand. These strangers reaped a deeper understanding of each other by sharing a meal and an extended encounter. This remains true today. When people break bread together, or enjoy recreation or entertainment, they often grow to understand and appreciate each other better. Better working relationships and more effective communication are often fruits of hospitality.

In Abraham and Sarah's time, hospitality was almost always offered in the host's home. Today, this is not always possible, or even desirable, and the hospitality industry has come into being to facilitate and offer hospitality in a wide variety of ways. If you want to offer hospitality and your home is too small or your cooking skills too limited, you might take someone to a restaurant or hotel and enjoy camaraderie and deepening relationships there. Hospitality workers would assist you in offering hospitality. Moreover, hospitality workers have in their own right the opportunity to refresh people, create good relationships, provide shelter, and serve others much as Jesus did when he made wine (John 2:1–11) and washed feet (John 13:3–11). The hospitality industry accounts for 9 percent of the world gross domestic product and employs 98 million people,[13] including many of the less-skilled and immigrant workers who represent a rapidly growing portion of the Christian church. Even more engage in unpaid hospitality, offering it to others as an act of love, friendship, compassion, and social engagement. The example of Abraham and Sarah shows that this work can be profoundly important as a service to God and humanity. How could we do more to encourage each other to be generous in hospitality, no matter what our professions are?

---

[13] World Travel and Tourism Council, *Travel and Tourism Economic Impact 2012, World* (London: 2012), 1.

Abraham's Dispute with Abimelech (Genesis 20:1–16; 21:22–34)

When Abraham and Sarah entered the country of King Abimelech, Abimelech inadvertently violated the rules of hospitality, and as restitution awarded Abraham free grazing rights to whatever land he wanted (Gen. 20:1–16). Subsequently, a dispute erupted over a certain well of water that Abraham had originally dug but Abimelech's servants later seized (Gen. 21:25). Seemingly unaware of the situation, when Abimelech heard of the complaint he entered into a sworn agreement initiated by Abraham, a treaty that publicly acknowledged Abraham's right to the well and therefore his continued business activity in the region (Gen. 21:27–31).

Elsewhere we have seen Abraham give up what was rightfully his to keep (Gen. 14:22–24). Yet here, Abraham doggedly protects what is his. The narrator does not imply that Abraham is again wavering in faith, for the account concludes with worship (Gen. 21:33). Rather, he is a model of a wise and hard-working person who conducts his business openly and makes fair use of appropriate legal protections. In the business of shepherding, access to water was essential. Abraham could not have continued to provide for his animals, workers, and family without it. The fact of Abraham's protection of water rights is therefore important, as well as the means by which he secured those rights.

Like Abraham, people in every kind of work have to discern when to act generously to benefit others, and when to protect resources and rights for the benefit of themselves or their organizations. There is no set of rules and regulations that can lead us to a mechanical answer. In all situations, we are stewards of God's resources, though it may not always be clear whether God's purposes are better served by giving away resources or by protecting them. But Abraham's example highlights an aspect that is easy to forget. The decision is not only a matter of who is in the right, but also of how the decision will affect our relationships with those around us. In the earlier case of dividing the land with Lot, Abraham's willing surrender of first choice to Lot laid the ground work for a good long-term working relationship. In the present case of his demanding access to the well according to his treaty rights, Abraham ensured the resources needed to keep his enterprise functioning. In addition, it seems that Abraham's forcefulness actually improved relationships between himself and Abimelech. Remember that the dispute between them arose because Abraham *didn't* assert his position when first encountering Abimelech (Gen. 20).

A Burial Plot for Sarah (Genesis 23:1–20)

When Sarah died, Abraham engaged in an exemplary negotiation to buy a burial plot for her. He conducted the negotiations openly and honestly in the presence of witnesses, taking due care for the needs of both himself and the seller (Gen. 23:10–13, 16, 18). The property in question is clearly identified (Gen. 23:9), and Abraham's intended use as a burial site is mentioned several times (Gen. 23:4, 6, 9, 11, 13, 15, 20). The dialogue of the negotiation is exceptionally clear, socially proper, and transparent. It takes place at the gate of the city where business was done in public. Abraham initiates the request for a real-estate transaction. The local Hittites freely offer a choice tomb. Abraham demurs, asking them to contact a certain owner of a field with a cave appropriate for a burial site so that he could buy it for the "full price." Ephron, the owner, overheard the request and offered the field as a gift. Because this would not have resulted in Abraham having permanent claim, he politely offered to pay market value for it. Contrary to the staged bargaining that was typical of business transactions (Prov. 20:14), Abraham immediately agreed to Ephron's price and paid it "according to the weights current among the merchants" (Gen. 23:16). This expression meant that the deal conformed to the standard for silver used in real-estate sales.[14] Abraham could have been so wealthy that he did not need to bargain, and/or he could have been wishing to buy a measure of good will along with the land. Additionally, he could have wished to forestall any questioning of the sale and of his right to the land. In the end, he received the title deed to the property with its cave and trees (Gen. 23:17–20). It was the important burial site of Sarah and later Abraham himself, as well as that of Isaac and Rebekah, and Jacob and Leah.

In this matter, Abraham's actions modeled core values of integrity, transparency, and business acumen. He honored his wife by mourning

---

[14] Walton, Matthews, and Chavalas, 55.

and properly caring for her remains. He understood his status in the land and treated its long-term residents with respect. He transacted business openly and honestly, doing so in front of witnesses. He communicated clearly. He was sensitive to the negotiating process and politely avoided accepting the land as a gift. He swiftly paid the agreed amount. He used the site only for the purpose he stated during the negotiations. He thus maintained good relationships with everyone involved.

Isaac (Genesis 21:1–35:29)

Isaac was the son of a great father and the father of a great son, but he himself left a mixed record. In contrast to the sustained prominence that Genesis gives to Abraham, the life of Isaac is split apart and told as attachments to the stories of Abraham and Jacob. The characterization of Isaac's life falls into two parts: one decidedly positive and one negative. Lessons regarding work may be derived from each.

On the positive side, Isaac's life was a gift from God. Abraham and Sarah treasured him and passed on their faith and values, and God reiterated Abrahamic promises to him. Isaac's faith and obedience when Abraham bound him as a sacrifice is exemplary, for he must have truly believed what his father had told him: "God himself will provide the lamb for a burnt offering, my son" (Gen. 22:8). Throughout most of his life, Isaac followed in Abraham's footsteps. Expressing the same faith, Isaac prayed for his childless wife (Gen. 25:21). Just as Abraham gave an honorable burial to Sarah, together Isaac and Ishmael buried their father (Gen. 25:9). Isaac became such a successful farmer and shepherd that the local population envied him and asked him to move away (Gen. 26:12–16). He reopened the wells that had been dug during the time of his father, which again became subjects of disputes with the people of Gerar concerning water rights (Gen. 26:17–21). Like Abraham, Isaac entered into a sworn agreement with Abimelech about treating one another fairly (Gen. 26:26–31). The writer of Hebrews noted that by faith Isaac lived in tents and blessed both Jacob and Esau (Heb. 11:8–10, 20). In short, Isaac had inherited a large family business and considerable wealth. Like his father, he did not hoard it, but fulfilled the role that God had chosen for him to pass on the blessing that would extend to all nations.

In these positive events, Isaac was a responsible son who learned how to lead the family and to manage its business in a way that honored the example of his capable and godly father. Abraham's diligence in preparing a successor and instituting long-lasting values brought blessing to his enterprise once again. When Isaac was a hundred years old, it became his turn to designate his successor by passing on the family blessing. Although he would live another eighty years, this bestowal of the blessing was the last meaningful thing about Isaac recorded in the book of Genesis. Regrettably, he nearly failed in this task. Somehow he remained oblivious to God's revelation to his wife that, contrary to normal custom, the younger son, Jacob, was to become head of the family instead of the older (Gen. 25:23). It took a clever ploy by Rebecca and Jacob to put Isaac back on track to fulfill God's purposes.

Maintaining the family business meant that the fundamental structure of the family had to be intact. It was the father's job to secure this. Foreign to most of us today, two related customs were prominent in Isaac's family, the birthright (Gen. 25:31) and the blessing (Gen. 27:4). The birthright conferred the right to inherit a larger share of the father's estate both in terms of goods and land. Though sometimes the birthright was transferred, it was typically reserved for the firstborn son. The specific laws concerning it varied, but it seems to have been a stable feature of Ancient Near Eastern culture. The blessing was the corresponding invocation of prosperity from God and succession of leadership in the household. Esau wrongly believed that he could surrender the birthright yet still get the blessing (Heb. 12:16–17). Jacob recognized that they were inseparable. With both in his possession, Jacob would assume the right to carry on the heritage of the family economically, socially, and in terms of its faith as well. Central to the unfolding plot of Genesis, the blessing entailed not only receiving the covenantal promises that God had made to Abraham but also mediating them to the next generation.

Isaac's failure to recognize that Jacob should receive the birthright and the blessing arose from Isaac putting his personal comfort above the needs of the family organization. He preferred Esau because he loved the wild game that Esau the hunter got for him. Although Esau did not value the birthright as much as a single meal—meaning that he was neither fit for nor interested in the position of leading the enterprise—Isaac wanted Esau to have it. The private circumstances under which Isaac gave the blessing suggests that he knew such an act would invite criticism. The only positive aspect of this episode is that Isaac's faith led him to recognize that the divine blessing he had mistakenly given to Jacob was irrevocable. Generously, this is what the writer of Hebrews remembered him for. "By faith Isaac invoked blessings for the future on Jacob and Esau" (Heb. 11:20). God had chosen Isaac to perpetuate this blessing and tenaciously worked his will through him, despite Isaac's ill-informed intentions.

Isaac's example reminds us that immersing ourselves in our private perspective too deeply can lead us into serious errors of judgment. Each of us is tempted by personal comforts, prejudices, and private interests to lose sight of the wider importance of our work. Our weakness may be for accolades, financial security, conflict avoidance, inappropriate relationships, short-term rewards, or other personal benefits that may be at odds with doing our work to fulfill God's purposes. There are both individual and systemic factors involved. On the individual level, Isaac's bias toward Esau is repeated today when those in power choose to promote people based on bias, whether recognized or not. On the systemic level, there are still many organizations that enable leaders to hire, fire, and promote people at their own whim, rather than developing successors and subordinates in a long-term, coordinated, accountable process. Whether the abuses are individual or systemic, merely resolving to do better or to change organizational processes is not an effective solution. Instead, both individuals and organizations need to be transformed by God's grace to put the truly important ahead of the personally beneficial.

Jacob (Genesis 25:19–49:33)

The names Abraham, Isaac, and Jacob appear often as a group, because they all received covenantal promises from God and shared the same faith. But Jacob was far different from his grandfather Abraham. Ever wily, Jacob lived much of his life according to his craftiness and ingenious wit. No stranger to conflict, Jacob was driven by a passion to get what he wanted for himself. This struggle was hard work indeed and eventually led him to the signature point of his existence, a wrestling match with a mysterious man in whom Jacob saw God face to face (Gen. 32:24, 30). Out of his weakness, Jacob called out in faith for God's blessing and was transformed by grace.

Jacob's occupational life as a shepherd is of interest to the theology of work. It takes on added significance, however, when set in the larger context of his life that moves in broad stokes from alienation to reconciliation. We have seen with Abraham that the work he did was an inseparable part of his sense of purpose stemming from his relationship with God. The same is true of Jacob, and the lesson holds for us as well.

Jacob's Unethical Procurement of Esau's Birthright and Blessing (Genesis 25:19–34; 26:34–28:9)

Although it was God's plan for Jacob to succeed Isaac (Gen. 25:23), Rebekah and Jacob's use of deception and theft to obtain it put the family in serious jeopardy. Their unethical treatment of husband and brother in order to secure their future at the expense of trusting God resulted in a deep and long-lived alienation in the family enterprise.

God's covenantal blessings were gifts to be received, not grasped. They carried the responsibility that they be used for others, not hoarded. This was lost on Jacob. Though Jacob had faith (unlike his brother Esau), he depended on his own abilities to secure the rights he valued. Jacob exploited hungry Esau into selling him the birthright (Gen. 25:29–34). It is good that Jacob valued the birthright, but deeply faithless for him to secure it for himself, especially in the manner he did so. Following the advice of his mother Rebekah (who also pursued right ends by wrong means), Jacob deceived his father. His life as a fugitive from the family testifies to the odious nature of his behavior.

Jacob began a long period of genuine belief in God's covenantal promises, yet he fails to live in confidence of what God will do for him. Mature, godly people who have learned to let their faith transform their choices (and not the other way around) are in a position to serve out of their strength. Courageous and astute decisions that result in success may be rightly praised for their sheer effectiveness. But when profit comes at the expense of exploiting and deceiving others, something is wrong. Beyond the fact that unethical methods are wrong in themselves, they also may reveal the fundamental fears of those who employ them. Jacob's relentless drive to gain benefits for himself reveals how his fears made him resistant to God's transforming grace. To the extent we come to believe in God's promises, we will be less inclined toward manipulating circumstances to benefit ourselves; we always need to be aware of how readily we can fool even ourselves about the purity of our motives.

Jacob Gains His Fortune (Genesis 30–31)

In escaping from Esau, Jacob ended up at the family farm of Laban, his mother's brother. Jacob worked for Laban for twenty-one frustrating years, during which Laban broke a string of promises to him. Despite this, Jacob succeeded in marrying two of Laban's daughters and starting a family. Jacob wanted to return home, but Laban convinced him to stay on and work for him with the promise that he could "name [his own] wages" (Gen. 30:28). Clearly Jacob had been a good worker, and Laban had been blessed through his association with Jacob.

During this time Jacob had learned the trade of breeding animals, and he used this skill to get back at Laban. Through his breeding techniques, he was able to gain a great deal of wealth at Laban's expense. It got to the point that Laban's sons were complaining that "Jacob has taken all that was our father's; he has gained all this wealth from what belonged to our father" (Gen. 31:1–2). Jacob noticed that Laban's attitude toward him was not what it had been. Yet Jacob claimed the gain as a gift from God, saying, "If the God of my father, the God of Abraham and the Fear of Isaac, had not been on my side, surely now you would have sent me away empty-handed" (Gen. 31:42).

Jacob felt that he had been dealt with poorly by Laban. His response, through his schemes, was to make yet another enemy, similar to the way he had exploited Esau. This is a repeated pattern in Jacob's life. It seems that anything was fair game, and although he ostensibly gave God the credit, it is clear that he did these things as a schemer. We don't see much integration of his faith with his work at this point, and it is interesting that when Hebrews recognizes Jacob as a man of faith, it mentions only his actions at the end of his life (Heb. 11:21).

Jacob's Transformation and Reconciliation with Esau (Genesis 32–33)

After increasing tension with his father-in-law and a business separation in which both men acted less than admirably, Jacob left Laban. Having obtained his position by Laban's dirty trick years ago, Jacob now saw an opportunity to legitimize his position by coming to an agreement with his estranged brother Esau. But he expected the negotiations to be tense. Wracked with fear that Esau would come to the meeting with his four hundred armed men, Jacob split his family and animals into two groups to help ensure some measure of survival. He prayed for protection and sent an enormous gift of animals on ahead of him to pacify Esau before the encounter. But the night before he arrived at the meeting point, the trickster Jacob was visited by a shadowy figure out to play a surprise on *him*. God himself attacked him in the form of a strongman, against whom Jacob was forced to wrestle all night. God, it turns out, is not only the God of worship and religion, but the God of work and family enterprises, and he is not above turning the tables on a slippery operator like Jacob. He pressed his advantage to the point of permanently injuring Jacob's hip, yet Jacob in his weakness said that he would not give up until his attacker had blessed him.

This became the turning point of Jacob's life. He had known years of struggling with people, yet all along Jacob had also been struggling in his relationship with God. Here at last, he met God and received his blessing amid the struggle. Jacob received a new name, Israel, and even renamed the location to honor the fact that there he had seen God face to face (Gen. 32:30). The once-ominous meeting with Esau followed in the morning and contradicted Jacob's fearful expectation in the most delightful way imaginable. Esau ran to Jacob and embraced him. Esau graciously tried to refuse Jacob's gifts, though Jacob insisted he take them. A transformed Jacob said to Esau, "Truly to see your face is like seeing the face of God" (Gen. 33:10).

The ambiguous identity of Jacob's wrestling opponent is a deliberate feature of the story. It highlights the inseparable elements of Jacob's struggling with both God and man.[15] Jacob models for us a truth at the core of our faith: our relationships with God and people are linked. Our reconciliation with God makes possible our reconciliation with others. Likewise, in that human reconciliation, we come to see and know God better. The work of reconciliation applies to families, friends, churches, companies, even people groups and nations. Christ alone can be our peace, but we are his ambassadors for it. Springing from God's initial promise to Abraham, this is a blessing that ought to touch the whole world.

Joseph (Genesis 37:2–50:26)

Recall that God accompanied his call to Abraham with core promises (Gen. 12:2–3). First, God would multiply his descendants into a great nation. Second, God would bless him. Third, God would make Abraham's name great, meaning that Abraham would be worthy of his renown. Fourth, Abraham would be a blessing. This last item pertains to the future generations of Abraham's family and beyond them, to all the families of the earth. God would bless those who blessed Abraham and curse those who cursed him. The book of Genesis traces the partial fulfillment of these promises through the chosen lines of Abraham's descendants, Isaac, Jacob, and Jacob's sons. Among them all, it is in Joseph that God most directly fulfills his promise to bless the nations through the people of Abraham. Indeed, people from "all the world" were sustained by the food system that Joseph managed (Gen. 41:57). Joseph understood this mission and articulated the purpose of his life in line with God's intention: "the saving of many lives" (Gen. 50:20 New International Version).

Joseph Rejected and Sold into Slavery by His Brothers (Genesis 37:2–36)

From a young age, Joseph believed God had destined him for greatness. In dreams, God assured Joseph that he would rise to a position of

---

[15] Kenneth A. Kitchen, "Cupbearer," in *New Bible Dictionary*, 3rd ed., eds. I. Howard Marshall, A. R. Millard, J. I. Packer, and D. J. Wiseman (Downers Grove, IL: InterVarsity Press, 1996), 248.

leadership over his parents and brothers (Gen. 37:5–11). From Joseph's point of view, these dreams were evidence of divine blessing, rather than his own ambition. From his brothers' point of view, however, the dreams were further manifestations of the unfair privilege that Joseph enjoyed as the favorite son of their father, Jacob (Gen. 37:3–4). Being sure that we are in the right does not absolve us from empathizing with others who may not share that same view. Good leaders strive to foster cooperation rather than envy. Joseph's failure to recognize this put him at severe odds with his brothers. After initially plotting murder against him, his brothers settled for selling him to a caravan of traders bearing goods through Canaan to Egypt. The merchants, in turn, sold Joseph to Potiphar, "the captain of the guard" who was "an officer of Pharaoh" in Egypt (Gen. 37:36; 39:1).

The Schemes of Potiphar's Wife and Joseph's Imprisonment (Genesis 39:1–20)

Joseph's stint in Potiphar's employ gave him a wide range of fiduciary responsibilities. At first, Joseph was merely "in" his master's house. We don't know in what capacity he served, but when Potiphar recognized Joseph's general competence, he promoted him to be his personal steward and "put him in charge of all that he had" (Gen. 39:4).

After a time, Potiphar's wife took a sexual interest in Joseph (Gen. 39:7). Joseph's refusal of the wife's advances was articulate and reasonable. He reminded her of the broad trust that Potiphar had placed in him and described the relationship she sought in the moral/religious terms "wickedness" and "sin" (Gen. 39:9). He was sensitive to both the social and theological dimensions. Furthermore, he offered his verbal resistance repeatedly, and he even avoided being in her presence. When physically assaulted, Joseph made the choice to flee half-naked rather than to submit.

The sexual harassment by this woman took place in a power relationship that disadvantaged Joseph. Although she believed that she had the right and power to use Joseph in this way, her words and contact were clearly unwelcome to him. Joseph's work required him to be at home where she was, yet he could not call the matter to Potiphar's attention without interfering in their marital relationship. Even after his escape and arrest on false charges, Joseph seems to have had no legal recourse.

The facets of this episode touch closely on the issues of sexual harassment in the workplace today. People have different standards of what counts for inappropriate speech and physical contact, but the whims of those in power are what often count in practice. Workers are often expected to report incidences of potential harassment to their superiors, but often are reluctant to do so because they know the risk of obfuscation and retaliation. To compound this, even when harassment can be documented, workers may suffer for having come forward. Joseph's godliness did not rescue him from false accusation and imprisonment. If we find ourselves in a parallel situation, our godliness is no guarantee that we will escape unscathed. But Joseph did leave an instructive testimony to Potiphar's wife and possibly others in the household. Knowing that we belong to the Lord and that he defends the weak will certainly help us to face difficult situations without giving up. This story is a realistic recognition that standing up to sexual harassment in the workplace may have devastating consequences. Yet it is also a story of hope that by God's grace, good may eventually prevail in the situation. Joseph also provides a model for us, that even when we are falsely accused and wrongly treated, we carry on with the work God has given us, allowing God to make it right in the end.

Joseph's Interpretation of Dreams in Prison (Genesis 39:20–40:23)

Joseph's service in prison was marked by the Lord's presence, the jailer's favor, and Joseph's promotion to leadership (Gen. 39:21–23). In prison, Joseph met two of Pharaoh's officials who were incarcerated, the chief cupbearer and the chief baker. Many Egyptian texts mention the role of cupbearers, who not only tasted wine for quality and to detect poison but also who enjoyed proximity to those with political power. They often became confidants who were valued for their counsel (see Neh. 2:1–4).[16] Like chief cupbearers, chief bakers were also trusted officials

---

[16] Roland K. Harrison, "Baker," in *The International Standard Bible Encyclopedia*, ed. Geoffrey W. Bromiley (Grand Rapids: Eerdmans, 1979), 1:404.

who had open access to the highest persons in the government and who may have performed duties that extended beyond the preparation of food.[17] In prison, Joseph did the work of interpreting dreams for these politically connected individuals.

Interpreting dreams in the ancient world was a sophisticated profession involving technical "dream books" that listed elements of dreams and their meanings. Records of the veracity of past dreams and their interpretations provided empirical evidence to support the interpreter's predictions.[18] Joseph, however, was not schooled in this tradition and credited God with providing the interpretations that eventually proved true (Gen. 40:8). In this case, the cupbearer was restored to his former post, where he promptly forgot about Joseph.

The dynamics present in this story are still present today. We may invest in the success of another who rises beyond our reach, only to be discarded when our usefulness has been spent. Does this mean that our work has been for nothing and that we would have been better off to focus on our own position and promotion? What's more, Joseph had no way of independently verifying the stories of the two officials in prison. "The one who first states a case seems right, until the other comes and cross-examines" (Prov. 18:17). After sentencing, however, any prisoner can assert his or her own innocence.

We may have doubts about how our investment in others may eventually benefit us or our organizations. We may wonder about the character and motives of the people we help. We may disapprove of what they do afterward and how that might reflect on us. These matters can be varied and complex. They call for prayer and discernment, but must they paralyze us? The Apostle Paul wrote, "Whenever we have an opportunity, let us work for the good of all" (Gal. 6:10). If we start with a commitment to work for God above all others, then it is easier to move ahead, believing that "in all things God works for the good of those who love him, who have been called according to his purpose" (Rom. 8:28 NIV).

---

[17] John H. Walton, *Genesis*, NIV Application Commentary (Grand Rapids: Zondervan, 2001), 672–73.

[18] Waltke, 565–66.

Joseph's Promotion by Pharaoh (Genesis 41:1–45)

Two more years passed until Joseph gained an opportunity for release from his misery in prison. Pharaoh had begun to have disturbing dreams, and the chief cupbearer remembered the skill of the young Hebrew in prison. Pharaoh's dreams about cows and stalks of grain befuddled his most skilled counselors. Joseph testified to God's ability to provide interpretations and his own role as merely the mediator of this revelation (Gen. 41:16). Before Pharaoh, Joseph did not use the covenant name of God exclusive to his own people. Instead, he consistently referred to God with the more general term *elohim*. In so doing, Joseph avoided making any unnecessary offense, a point supported by the fact that Pharaoh credited God with revealing to Joseph the meaning of Pharaoh's dreams (Gen. 41:39). In the workplace, sometimes believers can give God credit for their success in a shallow manner that ends up putting people off. Joseph's way of doing it impressed Pharaoh, showing that publicly giving God credit can be done in a believable way.

God's presence with Joseph was so obvious that Pharaoh promoted Joseph to second-in-command of Egypt, especially to take charge of preparations for the coming famine (Gen. 41:37–45). God's word to Abraham was bearing fruit: "I will bless those who bless you . . . and in you all the families of the earth shall be blessed" (Gen. 12:3). Like Joseph, when we confess our own inability to meet the challenges we face and find appropriate ways to attribute success to God, we forge a powerful defense against the pride that often accompanies public acclaim.

Joseph's promotion brought him significant accoutrements of leadership: a royal signet ring and gold chain, fine clothing appropriate to his high office, official transportation, a new Egyptian name, and an Egyptian wife from an upper class family (Gen. 41:41–45). If ever there was a lure to leave his Hebrew heritage behind, this was it. God helps us deal with failure and defeat, yet we may need his help even more when dealing with success. The text presents several indications of how Joseph handled his promotion in a godly way. Part of this had to do with Joseph's preparation before his promotion.

Back in his father's home, the dreams of leadership that God gave him convinced Joseph that he had a divinely ordained purpose and destiny that he never forgot. His personal nature was basically trusting of people. He seems to have held no grudge against his jealous brothers or the forgetful cupbearer. Before Pharaoh promoted him, Joseph knew that the Lord was with him and he had tangible evidence to prove it. Repeatedly giving God credit was not only the right thing to do, but it also reminded Joseph himself that his skills were from the Lord. Joseph was courteous and humble, showing a desire to do whatever he could to help Pharaoh and the Egyptian people. Even when the Egyptians were bereft of currency and livestock, Joseph earned the trust of the Egyptian people and of Pharaoh himself (Gen. 41:55). Throughout the rest of his life as an administrator, Joseph consistently devoted himself to effective management for the good of others.

Joseph's story to this point reminds us that in our broken world, God's response to our prayers doesn't necessarily come quickly. Joseph was seventeen years old when his brothers sold him into slavery (Gen. 37:2). His final release from captivity came when he was thirty (Gen. 41:46), thirteen long years later.

Joseph's Successful Management of the Food Crisis (Genesis 41:46–57; 47:13–26)

Joseph Creates a Long-term Agricultural Policy and Infrastructure (Genesis 41:46–57)

Joseph immediately went about the work to which Pharaoh had appointed him. His primary interest was in getting the job done for others, rather than taking personal advantage of his new position at the head of the royal court. He maintained his faith in God, giving his children names that credited God with healing his emotional pain and making him fruitful (Gen. 41:51–52). He recognized that his wisdom and discernment were gifts from God, but nevertheless that he still had much to learn about the land of Egypt, its agricultural industry in particular. As the senior administrator, Joseph's work touched on nearly every practical area of the nation's life. His office would have required that he learn much about legislation, communication, negotiation, transportation, safe and efficient methods of food storage, building, economic strategizing and forecasting, record-keeping, payroll, the handling of transactions both by means of currency and through bartering, human resources, and the acquisition of real estate. His extraordinary abilities with respect to God and people did not operate in separate domains. The genius of Joseph's success lay in the effective integration of his divine gifts and acquired competencies. For Joseph, all of this was godly work.

Pharaoh had already characterized Joseph as "discerning and wise" (Gen. 41:39), and these characteristics enabled Joseph to do the work of strategic planning and administration. The Hebrew words for *wise* and *wisdom* (*hakham* and *hokhmah*) denote a high level of mental perceptivity, but also are used of a wide range of practical skills including craftsmanship of wood, precious stones, and metal (Exod. 31:3–5; 35:31–33), tailoring (Exod. 28:3; 35:26, 35), as well as administration (Deut. 34:9; 2 Chr. 1:10) and legal justice (1 Kgs. 3:28). These skills are found among unbelievers as well, but the wise in the Bible enjoy the special blessing of God who intends Israel to display God's ways to the nations (Deut. 4:6).

As his first act, "Joseph . . . went through all the land of Egypt" (Gen. 41:46) on an inspection tour. He would have to become familiar with the people who managed agriculture, the locations and conditions of the fields, the crops, the roads, and means of transportation. It is inconceivable that Joseph could have accomplished all of this on a personal level. He would have had to establish and oversee the training of what amounted to a Department of Agriculture and Revenue. During the seven years of abundant harvest, Joseph had the grain stored in cities (Gen. 41:48–49). During the seven lean years that followed, Joseph dispensed grain to the Egyptians and other people who were affected by the widespread famine. To create and administer all this, while surviving the political intrigue of an absolute monarchy, required exceptional talent.

Joseph Relieves the Poverty of Egypt's People (Genesis 47:13–26)

After the people ran out of money, Joseph allowed them to barter their livestock for food. This plan lasted for one year during which Joseph collected horses, sheep, goats, cattle, and donkeys (Gen. 47:15–17). He would have had to determine the value of these animals and establish an equitable system for exchange. When food is scarce, people are especially concerned for the survival of themselves and their loved ones. Providing access to points of food distribution and treating people evenhandedly become acutely important administrative matters.

When all of the livestock had been traded, people willingly sold themselves into slavery to Pharaoh and sold him the ownership of their lands as well (Gen. 47:18–21). From the perspective of leadership, this must have been awful to witness. Joseph, however, allowed the people to sell their land and to enter into servitude, but he did not take advantage of them in their powerlessness. Joseph would have had to see that these properties were valued correctly in exchange for seed for planting (Gen. 47:23). He enacted an enduring law that people return 20 percent of the harvest to Pharaoh. This entailed creating a system to monitor and enforce the people's compliance with the law and establishing a department dedicated to managing the revenue. In all of this, Joseph exempted the priestly families from selling their land because Pharaoh supplied them with a fixed allotment of food to meet their needs adequately (Gen. 47:22, 26). Handling this special population would have entailed having a smaller, distinct system of distribution that was tailored for them.

Poverty and its consequences are economic realities. Our first duty is to help eliminate them, but we cannot expect complete success until God's kingdom is fulfilled. Believers may not have the power to eliminate the circumstances that require people to make hard choices, but we can find ways to support people as they—or perhaps we ourselves—cope. Choosing the lesser of two evils may be necessary work and can be emotionally devastating. In our work, we may experience tension arising from feeling empathy for the needy, yet bearing responsibility to do what is good for the people and organizations we work for. Joseph experienced God's guidance in these difficult tasks, and we also have received God's promise that "I will never leave you or forsake you" (Heb. 13:5).

Happily, by applying his God-given skill and wisdom, Joseph successfully brought Egypt through the agricultural catastrophe. When the seven years of good harvests came, Joseph developed a stockpiling system to store the grain for use during the coming drought. When the seven years of drought arrived, "Joseph opened the storehouses" and provided enough food to bring the nation through the famine. His wise strategy and effective implementation of the plan even allowed Egypt to supply grain to the rest of the world during the famine (Gen. 41:57). In this case, God's fulfillment of his promise that Abraham's descendants would be a blessing to the world occurred not only for the benefit of foreign nations, but even through the industry of a foreign nation, Egypt. In fact, God's blessing for the people of Israel came only after and through his blessing of foreigners. God did not raise up an Israelite in the land of Israel to provide for Israel's relief during the famine. Instead God enabled Joseph, working in and through the Egyptian government, to provide for the needs of the people of Israel (Gen. 47:11–12). Nonetheless, we shouldn't idealize Joseph. As an official in a sometimes repressive society, he became part of its power structure, and he personally imposed slavery on uncounted numbers of people (Gen. 47:21).

Applications from Joseph's Management Experience (Genesis 41:46–57; 47:13–26)

Genesis's interest in Joseph's management of the food crisis lies more in its effect on the family of Israel than in developing principles for effective management. Nonetheless, to the degree that Joseph's extraordinary leadership can serve as an example for leaders today, we can derive some practical applications from his work:

1. Become as familiar as possible with the state of affairs as they exist at the beginning of your service.

2. Pray for discernment regarding the future so that you can make wise plans.

3. Commit yourself to God first and then expect him to direct and establish your plans.

4. Gratefully and appropriately acknowledge the gifts God has given you.

5. Even though others recognize God's presence in your life and the special talents you have, do not broadcast these in a self-serving effort to gain respect.

6. Educate yourself about how to do your job and carry it out with excellence.

7. Seek the practical good for others, knowing that God has placed you where you are to be a blessing.

8. Be fair in all of your dealings, especially when the circumstances are grim and deeply problematical.

9. Although your exemplary service may propel you to prominence, remember your founding mission as God's servant. Your life does not consist in what you gain for yourself.

10. Value the godliness of the myriad types of honorable work that society needs.

11. Generously extend the fruit of your labor as widely as possible to those who truly need it, regardless of what you think of them as individuals.

12. Accept the fact that God may bring you into a particular field of work under extremely challenging conditions. This does not mean that something has gone terribly wrong or that you are out of God's will.

13. Have courage that God will fit you for the task.

14. Accept the fact that sometimes people must choose what they regard as the better of two unpleasant yet unavoidable situations.

15. Believe that what you do will not only benefit those whom you see and meet, but also that your work has the potential to touch lives for many generations to come. God is able to accomplish abundantly far more than we can ask or imagine (Eph. 3:20).

Joseph's Dealings with His Brothers (Genesis 42–43)

In the midst of the crisis in Egypt, Joseph's brothers arrived from Canaan, seeking to buy food, as the famine severely affected their land also. They did not recognize Joseph, and he did not reveal himself to them. He dealt with his brothers largely through the language of commerce.

The word *silver* (*kesef*) appears twenty times in chapters 42 through 45 and the word for *grain* (*shever*) nineteen. Trading in this commodity provided the framework on which the intricate personal dynamics hung.

Joseph's behavior in this situation became quite shrewd. First, he concealed his identity from his brothers, which—while not necessarily rising to the level of open deceit (Hebrew *mirmah*, as with Jacob in Gen. 27:35)—certainly was less than forthright. Second, he spoke harshly to his brothers with accusations he knew were unfounded (Gen. 42:7, 9, 14, 16; 44:3–5). In short, Joseph took advantage of his power to deal with a group he knew could be untrustworthy because of their earlier treatment of him.[19] His motive was to discern the present character of the people he was dealing with. He had suffered greatly at their hands over twenty years prior, and had every reason to distrust their words, actions, and commitment to the family.

Joseph's methods verged on deception. He withheld critical information and manipulated events in various ways. Joseph acted in the role of a detective conducting a tough interrogation. He could not proceed with full transparency and expect to get reliable information from them. The biblical concept for this tactic is shrewdness. Shrewdness may be exercised for good or for ill. On the one hand the serpent was "the shrewdest of all the wild animals" (Gen. 3:1 New Living Translation), and employed shrewd methods for disastrously evil purposes. (The NLT's consistent use of "shrewd" makes it clear that the same Hebrew word is being translated. The NRSV uses "crafty" here.) The Hebrew word for shrewdness (*ormah* and cognates) is also translated as "good judgment," "prudence," and "clever" (Prov. 12:23; 13:16; 14:8; 22:3; 27:12), indicating it may take foresight and skill to make godly work possible in difficult contexts. Jesus himself counseled his disciples to be "as shrewd as snakes and harmless as doves" (Matt. 10:16 NLT). The Bible often commends shrewdness in the pursuit of noble purposes (Prov. 1:4; 8:5, 12).

Joseph's shrewdness had the intended effect of testing his brothers' integrity, and they returned the silver Joseph had secretly packed in the baggage (Gen. 43:20–21). When he tested them further by treating the youngest, Benjamin, more generously than the others, they proved they

---

[19] Waltke, 545.

had learned not to fall into animosity among themselves the way they had done when they sold Joseph into slavery.

It would be superficial to read into Joseph's actions the claim that thinking you are on God's side is always a justification for deceit. But Joseph's long career of service and suffering in God's service gave him a deeper understanding of the situation than his brothers had. Seemingly, the promise that God would make them into a large nation hung in the balance. Joseph knew that it was not in his human power to save them, but he took advantage of his God-given authority and wisdom to serve and help. Two important factors differentiate Joseph in making the decision to use means that otherwise would not be commendable. First, he gained nothing from these machinations for himself. He had received a blessing from God, and his actions were solely in the service of *becoming* a blessing to others. He could have exploited his brothers' desperate predicament and spitefully exacted a greater sum of silver, knowing they would have given anything to survive. Instead, he used knowledge to save them. Second, his actions were necessary if he was to be able to offer the blessings. If he had dealt with his brothers more openly, he could not have tested their trustworthiness in the matter.

Judah's Transformation to a Man of God (Genesis 44:1–45:15)

In the final episode of Joseph's testing of his brothers, Joseph framed Benjamin for an imaginary crime and claimed Benjamin as a slave in recompense. When he demanded that the brothers return home to Isaac without Benjamin (Gen. 44:17), Judah emerged as the group's spokesman. What gave him the standing to take on this role? He had broken faith with his family by marrying a Canaanite (Gen. 38:2), had raised such wicked sons that the Lord put two of them to death (Gen. 38:7, 10), had treated his daughter-in-law as a prostitute (Gen. 38:24), and had hatched the plan to sell his own brother as a slave (Gen. 37:27). But the story Judah told Joseph showed a changed man. He exhibited unexpected compassion in telling of the family's heart-wrenching experience of starvation, of his father's undying love for Benjamin, and of Judah's own promise to his father that he would bring Benjamin back home, lest Jacob literally die from grief. Then, in an ultimate expression of compassion, Judah offered to substitute *himself* in place of Benjamin! He proposed that he be retained in Egypt for the rest of his life as the governor's slave if only the governor would let Benjamin go home to his father (Gen. 44:33–34).

Seeing the change in Judah, Joseph was able to bless them as God intended. He disclosed to them the full truth: "I am Joseph" (Gen. 45:3). It appears that Joseph finally saw that his brothers could be trusted. In our own dealings with those who would exploit and deceive us, we must tread carefully, to be as wise as serpents and as innocent as doves, as Jesus instructed the disciples (Matt. 10:16). As one writer put it, "Trust requires trustworthiness." All of the planning Joseph had done in his discussions with his brothers reached this culmination, allowing him to enter into a right relationship with them. He calmed his terrified brothers by pointing to the work of God who was responsible for placing Joseph in charge of all Egypt (Gen. 45:8). Waltke spells out the importance of the interaction between Joseph and his brothers:

> This scene exposes the anatomy of reconciliation. It is about loyalty to a family member in need, even when he or she looks guilty; giving glory to God by owning up to sin and its consequences; overlooking favoritism; offering up oneself to save another; demonstrating true love by concrete acts of sacrifice that create a context of trust; discarding control and the power of knowledge in favor of intimacy; embracing deep compassion, tender feelings, sensitivity, and forgiveness; and talking to one another. A dysfunctional family that allows these virtues to embrace it will become a light to the world.[20]

God is more than able to bring his blessings to the world through deeply flawed people. But we must be willing to continually repent of the evil we do and turn to God for transformation, even if we are never perfectly purged of our errors, weaknesses, and sins in this life.

Contrary to the values of the societies around Israel, the willingness of leaders to offer themselves in sacrifice for the sins of others was intended to be a signature trait of leadership among the people of God. Moses would show it when Israel sinned regarding the golden calf. He prayed, "Alas, this people has sinned a great sin; they have made for

---

[20] Waltke, 565–66.

themselves gods of gold. But now, if you will only forgive their sin—but if not, blot me out of the book that you have written" (Exod. 32:31–32). David would show it when he saw the angel of the Lord striking down the people. He prayed, "What have they done? Let your hand, I pray, be against me and against my father's house" (2 Sam. 24:17). Jesus, the Lion of the tribe of Judah, would show it when he said, "For this reason the Father loves me, because I lay down my life in order to take it up again. No one takes it from me, but I lay it down of my own accord" (John 10:17–18).

Jacob's Family's Move to Egypt (Genesis 45:16–47:12)

Joseph and Pharaoh lavishly gave Joseph's brothers "the best of all the land of Egypt" (Gen. 45:20) and supplied them for their return to Canaan and transportation of the family. This apparently happy ending, however, has a dark side. God had promised Abraham and his descendants the land of *Canaan*, not Egypt. Long after Joseph passed from the scene, Egypt's relationship with Israel turned from hospitality to hostility. Seen this way, how does Joseph's benevolence to the family fit with his role as mediator of God's blessing to all families of the earth (Gen. 12:3)? Joseph was a man of insight who planned for the future, and he did bring about the portion of God's blessing assigned to him. But God did not reveal to him the future rise of a "new king . . . who did not know Joseph" (Exod. 1:8). Each generation needs to remain faithful to God and receive God's blessings in their own time. Regrettably, Joseph's descendants forgot God's promises and drifted into faithlessness. Yet God did not forget his promise to Abraham, Isaac, Jacob, and their descendants. Among their descendants God would raise up new men and women to impart God's promised blessings.

God Meant All for Good (Genesis 50:15–21)

The penitent words of the brothers led Joseph to one of the finest theological points of his life and, indeed, much of Genesis. He told them not to be afraid, for he would not retaliate for their mistreatment of him. "Even though you intended to do harm to me," he told them, "God intended it for good, in order to preserve a numerous people, as he is doing today. So have no fear; I myself will provide for you and your little ones" (Gen. 50:20–21). Joseph's reference to "numerous people" echoes God's covenantal promise to bless "all families of the earth" (Gen. 12:3). From our vantage point today, we can see that God sent far more blessing than Joseph could have ever asked or imagined (see Eph. 3:20).

God's work in and through Joseph had real, practical, serious value—to preserve lives. If we ever have the impression that God wants us in the workplace only so we can tell others about him, or if we get the impression that the only part of our work that matters to God is building relationships, Joseph's work says otherwise. The things we make and do in our work are themselves crucial to God and to other people. Sometimes this is true because our work is a piece of a bigger whole, and we lose sight of the result of the work. Joseph took a larger perspective on his work, and he was not discouraged by its inevitable ups and downs.

This is not to say that relationships at work aren't also of the highest importance. Perhaps Christians have the special gift of offering forgiveness to people in our workplaces. Joseph's reassurance to his brothers is a model of forgiveness. Following the instruction of his father, Joseph forgave his brothers and thus verbally released them from guilt. But his forgiveness—like all true forgiveness—was not just verbal. Joseph used the extensive resources of Egypt, which God had placed under his control, to support them materially so that they could prosper. He acknowledged that judgment was not his role. "Am I in the place of God?" (Gen. 50:19). He did not usurp God's role as judge but helped his brothers to connect with God who had saved them.

The relationship Joseph had with his brothers was both familial and economic. There is no clearly defined boundary between these areas; forgiveness is appropriate to both. We may be tempted to think that our most cherished religious values are primarily meant to function in identifiably religious spheres, such as the local church. Of course, much of our work life does take place in the public realm, and we must respect the fact that others do not share our Christian faith. But the neat division of life into separate compartments labeled "sacred" and "secular" is something foreign to the worldview of Scripture. It is not sectarian, then, to affirm that forgiveness is a sound workplace practice.

There will always be plenty of hurt and pain in life. No company or organization is immune from that. It would be naive to assume generally that nobody deliberately means to cause harm by what they say or do. Just as Joseph acknowledged that people *did* intend to harm him, we can do likewise. But in the same sentence lives the larger truth about God's intention for good. Recalling that point when we feel hurt both helps us to bear the pain and to identify with Christ.

Joseph saw himself as an agent of God who was instrumental in effecting the work of God with his people. He knew the harm that people were capable of and accepted that sometimes people are their own worst enemies. He knew the family stories of faith mixed with doubt, of faithful service mingled with self-preservation, of both truth and deceit. He also knew of the promises God made to Abraham, of God's commitment to bless this family, and of God's wisdom in working with his people as he refined them through the fires of life. He did not paint over their sins; rather, he absorbed them into his awareness of God's grand work. Our awareness of the inevitable, providential successfulness of God's promises makes our labor worthwhile, no matter the cost to us.

Of the many lessons about work in the book of Genesis, this one in particular endures and even explains redemption itself—the crucifixion of the Lord of glory (1 Cor. 2:8–10). Our places of work provide contexts in which our values and character are brought to light as we make decisions that affect ourselves and those around us. In his wise power, God is capable of working with our faithfulness, mending our weakness, and forging our failures to accomplish what he himself has prepared for us who love him.

Conclusions from Genesis 12–50

Genesis 12–50 tells the story of the first three generations of the family through whom God chose to bring his blessings to the whole world. Having no particular power, position, wealth, fame, ability, or moral superiority of their own, they accepted his call to trust him to provide for them and fulfill the great vision he had for them. Although God proved faithful in every way, their own faithfulness was often fitful, timid, foolish, and precarious. They proved to be as dysfunctional as any family, yet they maintained, or at least kept returning to, the seed of faith he placed in them. Functioning in a broken world, surrounded by hostile people and powers, by faith they "invoked blessings for the future" (Heb. 11:20) and lived according to God's promises. "Therefore God is not ashamed to be called their God; indeed, he has prepared a city for them" (Heb. 11:16), the same city in which we also work as followers of "Jesus the Messiah, the son of David, the son of Abraham" (Matt. 1:1).

Exodus and Work

The theology of work does not begin with our understanding of what God wants us to do or even how to do it. It begins with the God who has revealed himself to us as Creator and Redeemer, and who shows us how to follow him by being formed in his character. We do what God wants us to do by becoming more like God. Through reading Exodus, we hear God describe his own character, and we see this particular God actively forming his people. As his people, Christians cannot settle for doing our work according to godly principles unless we apprehend these truths as uniquely rooted in *this certain* God, who does *this particular kind* of redemptive work, through the *unique* person of his Son, by the power of *his* Holy Spirit. In essence, we learn that God's character is revealed in his work, and his work shapes our work. Following God in our work is thus a major topic in Exodus, even though work is not the primary point of the book.

We find much in Exodus that speaks to everyday work. But these instructions and rules take place in a work context that existed over three thousand years ago. Time has not stood still, and our workplaces have changed. Some passages, such as "You shall not murder" (Exod. 20:13), seem to fit today's context much as they did in Moses' time. Others, such as "If someone's ox hurts the ox of another, so that it dies, then they shall sell the live ox and divide the price of it" (Exod. 21:35), seem less directly applicable to most modern workplaces. How can we honor, obey, and apply God's word in Exodus without falling into the traps of legalism or misapplication?

To answer these questions, we start with the understanding that this book is a narrative. Just as it helped Israel to locate itself in God's story, it helps us to find out how we fit into the fuller expression of the narrative that is our Bible today. The purpose and shape of God's work not only frames our identity as his people, but it also directs the work God has called us to do.

Introduction to Exodus

The book of Exodus opens and closes with Israel at work. At the onset, the Israelites are at work for the Egyptians. By the book's end, they have finished the work of building the tabernacle according to the Lord's instructions (Exod. 40:33). God did not deliver Israel *from* work. He set Israel free *for* work. God released them from oppressive work under the ungodly king of Egypt and led them to a new kind of work under his gracious and holy kingship. Although the book's title in Christian Bibles, "Exodus," means "the way out,"[1] the forward-leaning orientation of Exodus could legitimately lead us to conclude that the book is really about the way *in*, for it recounts Israel's entrance to the Mosaic covenant that will frame their existence, not only in the wilderness wanderings around the Sinai Peninsula but also in their settled life in the Promised Land. The book conveys how Israel ought to understand their God, and how this nation should work and worship in their new land. On all counts, Israel must be mindful of how their life under God would be distinct from and better than life for those who followed the gods of Canaan. Even today, *what* we do in work flows from *why* we do it and for *whom* we are ultimately working. We usually don't have to look very far in society to find examples of harsh and oppressive work. Certainly, God wants us to find better ways to conduct our business and to treat others. But the way *into* that new way of acting depends on seeing ourselves as recipients of God's salvation, knowing what God's work is, and training ourselves to follow his words.

The book of Exodus begins about four hundred years after the point where Genesis ends. In Genesis, Egypt had been a hospitable place where God providentially elevated Joseph so that he could save the lives of Abraham's descendants (Gen. 50:20). This accords well with God's promises to make Abraham into a great nation, to bless him and make him a blessing to others, to make his name great, and to bless all families of the earth through him (Gen. 12:2–3). In the book of Exodus, however, Egypt was an oppressive place where Israel's growth raised the

---

[1] In Hebrew, the title is simply *shemot*, the word for "names of," which appears in the first sentence.

specter of death. The Egyptians hardly saw Israel as a divine blessing, though they did not want to let go of their slave labor. In the end, Israel's deliverance at the Red Sea cost Pharaoh and his people many lives. In light of God's promises to Abraham's chosen family and God's intentions to bless the nations, the people of God in the book of Exodus are very much in transition. The magnitude of Israel's numbers indicated God's favor, yet the next generation of male children faced immediate extinction (Exod. 1:15–16). The nation as a whole was still not in the land God had promised to them.

The entire Pentateuch echoes this theme of partial fulfillment. God's promises to Abraham of descendants, favored relationship with God, and a land in which to live all express God's intentions, yet they are all in some state of jeopardy throughout the narrative.[2] Among the five books of the Pentateuch, Exodus in particular takes up the element of relationship with God, both in terms of God's deliverance of his people from Egypt and the establishment of his covenant with them at Sinai.[3] This is especially significant for how we read the book for insights about our work today. We value the shape and content of this book as we remember that our relationship with God through Jesus Christ flows from what we see here, and it orients all of our life and work around God's intentions.

To capture Israel's character as a nation in transition, we outline the book and assess its contribution to the theology of work according to the geographical stages of its journey beginning in Egypt, then at the Red Sea and on the way to Sinai, and finally at Sinai itself.

Israel in Egypt (Exodus 1:1–13:16)

Israel's mistreatment by the Egyptians provides the background and impetus for their redemption. Pharaoh did not allow them to follow Moses into the wilderness to worship the Lord and thus denied a measure of their religious freedom. But their oppression as workers in the Egyptian economic system is what really gets our attention. God

---

[2] David J. A. Clines, *Theme of the Pentateuch*, 2nd ed. (London: T&T Clark, 1997), 29.

[3] Clines, 47.

hears the cry of his people and does something about it. But we must re-member that the people of Israel do not groan because of work in general, but because of the harshness of their work. In response, God does not deliver them into a life of total rest, but a release from oppressive work.

The Harshness of the Israelites' Slave Labor in Egypt (Exodus 1:8–14)

The work that the Egyptians forced on the Israelites was evil in mo-tive and cruel in nature. The opening scene presents the land as filled with Israelites who had been fruitful and multiplied. This echoes God's creational intent (Gen. 1:28; 9:1) as well as his promise to Abraham and his chosen descendants (Gen. 17:6; 35:11; 47:27). As a nation, they were destined to bless the world. Under a previous administration, the Isra-elites had royal permission to live in the land and to work it. But here the new king of Egypt sensed in their numbers a threat to his national security and thus decided to deal "shrewdly" with them (Exod. 1:10). We are not told whether or not the Israelites were a genuine threat. The emphasis falls on Pharaoh's destructive fear that led him first to de-grade their working environment and then to use infanticide to curb the growth of their population.

Work may be physically and mentally taxing, but that does not make it wrong. What made the situation in Egypt unbearable was not only the slavery but also its extreme harshness. The Egyptian masters worked the Israelites "ruthlessly" (*befarekh*, Exod. 1:13, 14) and made their lives "bitter" (*marar*, Exod. 1:14) with "hard" (*qasheh*, in the sense of "cruel," Exod. 1:14; 6:9) service. As a result, Israel languished in "misery" and "suffering" (Exod. 3:7) and a "broken spirit" (Exod. 6:9). Work, one of the chief purposes and joys of human existence (Gen. 1:27–31; 2:15), was turned into a misery by the harshness of oppression.

The Work of Midwifery and Mothering (Exodus 1:15–2:10)

In the midst of harsh treatment, the Israelites remained faithful to God's command to be fruitful and multiply (Gen. 1:28). That entailed bearing children, which in turn depended on the work of midwives.

In addition to its presence in the Bible, the work of midwifery is well-attested in ancient Mesopotamia and Egypt. Midwives assisted women in childbearing, cut the infant's umbilical cord, washed the baby, and presented the child to the mother and father.

The midwives in this narrative possess a fear of God that led them to disobey the royal order to kill all of the male children born to the Hebrew women (Exod. 1:15–17). Generally speaking, the "fear of the Lord" (and related expressions) in the Bible refer to a healthy and obedient relationship with the covenant-making God of Israel (Hebrew, *YHWH*). Their "fear of God" was stronger than any fear that Pharaoh of Egypt could put them under. In addition, perhaps their courage arose from their work. Would those who shepherd new life into birth every day come to value life so highly that murder would become unthinkable, even if commanded by a king?

Moses' mother, Jochebed (Exod. 6:20), was another woman who faced a seemingly impossible choice and forged a creative solution. One can hardly imagine her relief at secretly and successfully bearing a male child, followed by her pain at having to place him into the river, and to do so in a way that would actually *save* his life. The parallels to Noah's ark—the Hebrew word for "basket" is used only one other place in the Bible, namely for Noah's "ark"—let us know that God was acting not only to save one baby boy, or even one nation, but also to redeem the whole creation through Moses and Israel. Parallel to his reward to the midwives, God showed kindness to Moses' mother. She recovered her son and nursed him until he was old enough to be adopted as the son of Pharaoh's daughter. The godly work of bearing and raising children is well-known to be complex, demanding, and praiseworthy (Prov. 31:10–31). In Exodus, we read nothing of the inner struggles experienced by Jochebed, the unsung heroine. From a narrative point of view, Moses' life is the main issue. But the Bible later commended both Jochebed and Amram, Moses' father, for how they put their faith into action (Heb. 11:23).

Too often the work of bearing and raising children is overlooked. Mothers, especially, often get the message that childrearing is not as important or praiseworthy as other work. Yet when Exodus tells the story of how to follow God, the first thing it has to tell us is the incomparable importance of bearing, raising, protecting, and helping children.

The first act of courage, in this book filled with courageous deeds, is the courage of a mother, her family, and her midwives in saving her child.

God's Call to Moses (Exodus 2:11–3:22)

Although Moses was a Hebrew, he was raised in Egypt's royal family as the grandson of Pharaoh. His revulsion to injustice erupted into a lethal attack on an Egyptian man he found beating a Hebrew worker. This act came to Pharaoh's attention, so Moses fled for safety and became a shepherd in Midian, a region several hundred miles east of Egypt on the other side of the Sinai Peninsula. We do not know exactly how long he lived there, but during that time he married and had a son. In addition, two important things happened. The king in Egypt died, and the Lord heard the cry of his oppressed people and remembered his covenant with Abraham, Isaac, and Jacob (Exod. 2:23–25). This act of remembering did not mean that God had forgotten about his people. It signaled that he was about to act on their behalf.[4] For that, he would call Moses.

God's call to Moses came while Moses was at work. The account of how this happened comprises six elements that form a pattern evident in the lives of other leaders and prophets in the Bible. It is therefore instructive for us to examine this call narrative and to consider its implications for us today, especially in the context of our work.

First, God *confronted* Moses and arrested his attention at the scene of the burning bush (Exod. 3:2–5). A brushfire in the semi-desert is nothing exceptional, but Moses was intrigued by the nature of this particular one. Moses heard his name called and responded, "Here I am" (Exod. 3:4). This is a statement of availability, not location. Second, the Lord *introduced* himself as the God of the patriarchs and communicated his intent to rescue his people from Egypt and to bring them into the land he had promised to Abraham (Exod. 3:6–9). Third, God *commissioned* Moses to go to Pharaoh to bring God's people out of Egypt (Exod. 3:10). Fourth, Moses *objected* (Exod. 3:11). Although he had just heard a powerful revelation of who was speaking to him in this moment, his immediate concern was, "Who am I?" In response to this, God *reassured*

---

[4] Brevard S. Childs, *Memory and Tradition in Israel* (London: SCM Press, 1962).

Moses with a promise of God's own presence (Exod. 3:12a). Finally, God spoke of a *confirming sign* (Exod. 3:12b).

These same elements are present in a number of other call narratives in Scripture—for example in the callings of Gideon, Isaiah, Jeremiah, Ezekiel, and some of Jesus' disciples. This is not a rigid formula, for many other call narratives in Scripture follow a different pattern. But it does suggest that God's call often comes via an extended series of encounters that guide a person in God's way over time.

	The Judge Gideon	The Prophet Isaiah	The Prophet Jeremiah	The Prophet Ezekiel	Jesus' Disciples in Matthew
Confrontation	6:11b–12a	6:1–2	1:4	1:1–28a	28:16–17
Introduction	6:12b–13	6:3–7	1:5a	1:28b–2:2	28:18
Commission	6:14	6:8–10	1:5b	2:3–5	28:19–20a
Objection	6:15	6:11a	1:6	2:6, 8	—
Reassurance	6:16	6:11b–13	1:7–8	2:6–7	28:20b
Confirming Sign	6:17–21	—	1:9–10	2:9–3:2	Possibly the book of Acts

Notice that these callings are *not* primarily to priestly or religious work in a congregation. Gideon was a military leader; Isaiah, Jeremiah, and Ezekiel social critics; and Jesus a king (although not in the traditional sense). In many churches today, the term "call" is limited to religious occupations, but this is not so in Scripture, and certainly not in Exodus. Moses himself was not a priest or religious leader (those were Aaron's and Miriam's roles), but a shepherd, statesman, and governor. The

Lord's question to Moses "What is that in your hand?" (Exod. 4:2) repurposes Moses' ordinary tool of sheep-keeping for uses he would never have imagined possible (Exod. 4:3–5).

God's Work of Redemption for Israel (Exodus 5:1–6:28)

In the book of Exodus, God is the essential worker. The nature and intent of that divine work set the agenda for Moses' work and through him, the work of God's people. God's initial call to Moses included an explanation of God's work. This drove Moses to speak in the name of the Lord to Pharaoh saying, "Let my people go" (Exod. 5:1). Pharaoh's rebuttal was not merely verbal; he oppressed the Israelites more harshly than before. By the end of this episode, even the Israelites themselves had turned against Moses (Exod. 5:20–21). It is at this crucial point that in response to Moses' questioning God about the entire enterprise, God clarified the design of his work. What we read here in Exodus 6:2–8 pertains not only to the immediate context of Israel's oppression in Egypt. It frames an agenda that embraces all of God's work in the Bible.[5] It is important for all Christians to be clear about the scope of God's work, because it helps us to understand what it means to pray for God's kingdom to come and for his will to be done on earth as it is in heaven (Matt. 6:10). The fulfillment of these intentions is God's business. To accomplish them, he will involve the full range of his people, not merely those who do "religious" work. Coming to a clearer understanding of God's work equips us to consider better not only the nature of our work but the manner in which God intends for us to do it.

In order to better appreciate this key text, we will make some brief observations about it and then suggest how it is relevant to the theology of work. After an initially assuring response to Moses' accusatory question about God's mission (Exod. 5:22–6:1), God frames his more extended response with the words "I am the LORD" at the beginning and the end (Exod. 6:2, 8). This key phrase demarcates the paragraph and gives the content especially high priority. English readers must be care-

---

[5] Elmer Martens, *God's Design: A Focus on Old Testament Theology*, 3rd ed. (Grand Rapids: Baker, 1994). This section follows Martens's analysis of the four-part outline of God's design.

ful to note that this phrase does not communicate *what* God is in terms of a title. It reveals God's own name and therefore speaks to *who* he is.[6] He is the covenant-making, promise-keeping God who appeared to the patriarchs. The work God is about to do for his people is therefore grounded in the intentions that God has expressed to them. Namely, these are to multiply Abraham's descendants, to make his name great, and to bless him so that through Abraham, God would bless all the families of the earth (Gen. 12:2–3).

God's work then appears in four parts. These four redemptive purposes of God reappear in various ways throughout the Old Testament and even give shape to the pinnacle of God's redemptive work in Jesus Christ. First is the work of *deliverance*. "I will free you from the burdens of the Egyptians and deliver you from slavery to them. I will redeem you with an outstretched arm and with mighty acts of judgment" (Exod. 6:6). Inherent in this work of liberation is the frank truth that the world is a place of manifold oppression. Sometimes we use the word *salvation* to describe this activity of God, but we must be careful to avoid understanding it either in terms of rescue from earth to heaven (and certainly not from matter to spirit) or as merely forgiveness of sin. The God of Israel delivered his people by stepping into their world and effecting a change "on the ground," so to speak. Exodus not only shows God's deliverance of Israel from Pharaoh in Egypt, but it also sets the stage for the messianic king, Jesus, to *deliver* his people from their sins and conquer the devil, the ultimate evil tyrant (Matt. 1:21; 12:28).

Second, the Lord will form a *godly community*. "I will take you as my people, and I will be your God" (Exod. 6:7a). God did not deliver his people so they could live however they pleased, nor did he deliver them as isolated individuals. He intended to create a qualitatively different kind of community in which his people would live with him and one another in covenantal faithfulness. Every nation in ancient times had their "gods," but Israel's identity as God's people entailed a lifestyle of obedience to all of God's decrees, commands, and laws (Deut. 26:17–18).

---

[6] English Bibles employ the convention of using the word "Lᴏʀᴅ" (in small capital letters as distinct from "Lord") to represent the Hebrew name of God, YHWH.

As these values and actions would saturate their dealings with God and each other (and even those outside the covenant), Israel would increasingly demonstrate what it genuinely means to be God's people. Again, this forms the background for Jesus who would build his "church," not as a physical structure of brick or stone, but as a new *community* with disciples from all nations (Matt. 16:18; 28:19).

Third, the Lord will create an ongoing *relationship* between himself and his people. "You shall know that I am the LORD your God, who has freed you from the burdens of the Egyptians" (Exod. 6:7b). All of the other statements of God's purpose begin with the word *I* except this one. Here, the focus is on *you*. God intends *his people* to have a certain experience of their relationship with God who graciously rescued them. To us, knowledge seems practically equivalent to information. The biblical concept of knowledge embraces this notion, but it also includes interpersonal experience of knowing others. To say that God did not make himself "known" as "LORD" to Abraham does not mean that Abraham was unaware of the divine name "*YHWH*" (Gen. 13:4; 21:33). It means that Abraham and family had not yet personally experienced the significance of this name as descriptive of their promise-keeping God who would fight on behalf of his people to deliver them from slavery on a national scale.[7] Ultimately, this is taken up by Jesus, whose name "Emmanuel" means God "with us" in *relationship* (Matt. 1:23).

Fourth, God intends for his people to experience the *good life*. "I will bring you into the land that I swore to give to Abraham, Isaac, and Jacob; I will give it to you for a possession" (Exod. 6:8). God promised to give Abraham the land of Canaan, but it is not accurate to simply equate this "land" with our concept of a "region." It is a land of promise and provision. The regular and positive description of it as "flowing with milk and honey" (Exod. 3:8) highlights its symbolic nature as a place in which to live with

---

[7]The literature in Old Testament theology on this point is immense both in scope and depth of analysis. This is understandable, given the pivotal importance of God's self-revelation. Providing even a summary of the issues and approaches to this matter exceeds the scope of this article. For an able discussion of what is at stake and a fuller understanding of the position taken in this article, see Bruce K. Waltke and Charles Yu, *An Old Testament Theology: An Exegetical, Canonical, and Thematic Approach* (Grand Rapids: Zondervan, 2007), 359–69.

God and God's people in ideal conditions, something we understand as the "abundant life."[8] Here again we see that God's work of salvation is a setting to right of his entire creation—physical environment, people, culture, economics, everything. This is also the mission of Jesus as he initiates the kingdom of God coming to earth, where the meek inherit the earth (the land) and experience eternal life (Matt. 5:5; John 17:3).[9] This comes to completion in the New Jerusalem of Revelation 21 and 22. Exodus thus sets the path for the entirety of the Bible that follows.

Consider how our work today may express these four redemptive purposes. First, God's will is to *deliver* people from oppression and the harmful conditions of life. Some of that work rescues people from physical dangers; other work focuses on the alleviation of psychological and emotional trauma. The work of healing touches people one by one; those who forge political solutions to our needs can bless whole societies and classes of people. Workers in law enforcement and in the judicial system should aim to restrain and punish those who do evil, to protect people, and to care for victims. Given the pervasive extent of oppression in the world, there will always be manifold opportunities and means to work for deliverance.

The second and third purposes (*community* and *relationship*) are closely related to each other. Godly work that promotes peace and true harmony in heaven will enhance mercy and justice on earth. This is the gist of Paul's address to the Corinthians: through Christ, God has reconciled us to himself and thus given us the message and ministry of reconciliation (2 Cor. 5:16–20). Christians have experienced this reconciliation and therefore have motive and means to do this kind of work. The work of evangelism and spiritual development honors one dimension of the area; the work of peace and justice honors the interpersonal dimension. In essence, the two are inseparable and those who work in these fields do well to remember the holistic nature of what God is doing. Jesus taught that because we *are* the light of the world, we should let our light shine before others (Matt. 5:14–16).

Building community and relationships can be the *object* of our job, as in the case of community organizers, youth workers, social directors, event

---

[8] Martens, 10.

[9] For more on the land in the New Testament, see Waltke and Yu, 558–87.

planners, social media workers, parents and family members, and many others. But they can also be *elements* of our job, whatever our occupation. When we welcome and assist new workers, ask and listen as others talk about matters of significance, take the trouble to meet someone in person, send a note of encouragement, share a memorable photo, bring good food to share, include someone in a conversation, or myriad other acts of camaraderie, we are fulfilling these two purposes of work, day by day.

Finally, godly work promotes the *good life.* God led his people *out* of Egypt in order to bring them *in* to the Promised Land where they could settle, live, and develop. Yet, what Israel experienced there was far less than God's ideal. Likewise, what Christians experience in the world is not ideal either. The promise of entering God's rest is still open (Heb. 4:1). We still wait for a new heaven and a new earth. But many of the laws of the covenant that God gave through Moses have to do with ethical treatment of one another. It is vital, then, that God's blessing be worked out in the way we live and work with one another. Seen from the negative side, how can we reasonably expect all families of the earth to experience God's blessing through us (the people of Abraham through faith in Christ), if we ourselves ignore God's instructions about how to live and do our work? As Christopher Wright has noted, "The people of God in both testaments are called to be a light to the nations. But there can be no light to the nations that is not shining already in transformed lives of a holy people."[10] It thus becomes clear that the kind of "good life" in view here has nothing to do with unbridled selfish prosperity or conspicuous consumption, for it embraces the wide spectrum of life as God intends it to be: full of love, justice, and mercy.

Moses and Aaron Announce God's Judgment to Pharaoh (Exodus 7:1–12:51)

God began the first step—deliverance—by sending Moses and Aaron to tell Pharaoh "to let the Israelites go out of his land" (Exod. 7:2). For this task, God made use of Aaron's natural skill in public speaking (Exod. 4:14; 7:1). He also equipped Aaron with skill surpassing that of the high

---

[10] Christopher J. H. Wright, *The Mission of God: Unlocking the Bible's Grand Narrative* (Downers Grove, IL: IVP Academic, 2006), 358.

officials of Egypt (Exod. 7:10–12). This reminds us that God's mission requires both word and action.

Pharaoh refused to listen to God's demand, through Moses, to release Israel from slavery. In turn, Moses announced God's judgment to Pharaoh through an increasingly severe series of ecological disasters (Exod. 7:17–10:29). These disasters caused personal misery. More significantly, they drastically impaired the productive capacity of Egypt's land and people. Disease caused livestock to die (Exod. 9:6). Crops failed and forests were ruined (Exod. 9:25). Pests invaded multiple ecosystems (Exod. 8:6, 24; 10:13–15). In Exodus, ecological disaster is the retribution of God against the tyranny and oppression of Pharaoh. In the modern world, political and economic oppression is a major factor in environmental degradation and ecological disaster. We would be fools to think we can assume Moses' authority and declare God's judgment in any of these. But we can see that when economics, politics, culture, and society are in need of redemption, so is the environment.

Each of these warnings-in-action convinced Pharaoh to release Israel, but as each passed, he reneged. Finally, God brought on the disaster of slaying every firstborn son among the people and animals of the Egyptians (Exod. 12:29–30). The appalling effect of slavery is to "harden" the heart against compassion, justice, and even self-preservation, as Pharaoh soon discovered (Exod. 11:10). Pharaoh then accepted God's demand to let Israel go free. The departing Israelites "plundered" the Egyptians' jewelry, silver, gold, and clothing (Exod. 12:35–36). This reversed the effects of slavery, which was the legalized plunder of exploited workers. When God liberates people, he restores their right to labor for fruits they themselves can enjoy (Isa. 65:21–22). Work, and the conditions under which it is performed, is a matter of the highest concern to God.

Israel at the Red Sea and on the Way to Sinai (Exodus 13:17–18:27)

The foundational expression of God's work came to dramatic fruition when God decisively led his people through the Red Sea, releasing them from Egypt's tyrannical hold. The God who had separated the waters of chaos and created dry land, the God who had brought Noah's family through the deluge to dry land, "divided" the waters of the Red Sea and led Israel across on "dry ground" (Exod. 14:21–22). Israel's journey from Egypt to Sinai is thus the continuation of the story of God's creation and redemption. Moses, Aaron, and others work hard, yet God is the real worker.

The Work of Justice among the People of Israel (Exodus 18:1–27)

While on the journey from Egypt to Sinai, Moses reconnected with his father-in-law Jethro. This former outsider to the Israelites offered much-needed counsel to Moses concerning justice in the community. God's work of redemption *for* his people was expanded into the work of justice *among* his people. Israel had already experienced unjust treatment at the hand of the Egyptian taskmasters. Out on their own, they rightly sought for *God's* answers to their own disputes. Walter Brueggemann has observed that biblical faith is not just about telling the story of what God has done. It is also "about the hard, sustained work of nurturing and practicing the daily passion of healing and restoring, and the daily rejection of dishonest gain."[11]

One of the first things we learned earlier about Moses was his desire to mediate between those embroiled in a dispute. Initially, when Moses tried to intervene, he was rebuked with the words, "Who made you a ruler and a judge over us?" (Exod. 2:14). In the current episode, we see just the opposite. Moses is in such demand as the ruler-judge that a multitude of people in need of his decisions gathered around him "from morning until evening" (Exod. 18:14; see also Deut. 1:9–18). Moses' work apparently has two aspects. First, he rendered legal decisions for people in dispute. Second, he taught God's statutes and instructions for those seeking moral and religious guidance.[12] Jethro observed that Moses was the sole agent in this noble work, but deemed the entire process to be unsustainable. "What you are doing is not good" (Exod. 18:17). Further-

---

[11] Walter Brueggemann, "The Book of Exodus," in vol. 1, *The New Interpreter's Bible: Genesis to Leviticus* (Nashville: Abingdon Press, 1994), 829.

[12] Umberto Moshe David Cassuto, *A Commentary on the Book of Exodus* (Skokie, IL: Varda Books, 2005), 219.

more, it was detrimental to Moses and unsatisfying for the people he was trying to help. Jethro's solution was to let Moses continue doing what he was uniquely qualified to do as God's representative: intercede with God for the people, instruct them, and decide the difficult cases. All of the other cases were to be delegated to subordinate judges who would serve in a four-tiered system of judicial administration.

The qualification of these judges is the key to the wisdom of the plan, for they were not selected according to the tribal divisions of the people or their religious maturity. They must meet four qualifications (Exod. 18:21). First, they must be capable. The Hebrew expression "men of *hayil*" connotes ability, leadership, management, resourcefulness, and due respect.[13] Second, they must "fear God." Third, they must be "trustworthy." Because truth is an abstract concept as well as a way of acting, these people must have a public track record of truthful character as well as conduct. Finally, they must be haters of unjust gain. They must know how and why corruption occurs, despise the practice of bribery and all kinds of subversion, and actively guard the judicial process from these infections.

Delegation is essential to the work of leadership. Though Moses was *uniquely* gifted as a prophet, statesman, and judge, he was not *infinitely* gifted. Anyone who imagines that only he or she is capable of doing God's work well has forgotten what it means to be human. Therefore, the gift of leadership is ultimately the gift of giving away power appropriately. The leader, like Moses, must discern the qualities needed, train those who are to receive authority, and develop means to hold them accountable. The leader also needs to be held accountable. Jethro performed this task in Moses' case, and the passage is remarkably frank in showing how even the greatest of all the Old Testament prophets had to be confronted by someone with the power to hold him accountable. Wise, decisive, compassionate leadership is a gift from God that every human community needs. Yet Exodus shows us that it is not so much a matter of a gifted leader assuming authority over people, as it is God's

---

[13] For more on the word *hayil*, see Bruce Waltke and Alice Matthews, *Proverbs and Work*, Proverbs 31:10–31, beginning with the section "The Valiant Woman" at www.theologyofwork.org.

process for a community to develop structures of leadership in which gifted people can succeed. Delegation is the only way to increase the capacity of an institution or community, as well as the way to develop future leaders.

The fact that Moses accepted this counsel so quickly and thoroughly may be evidence of how personally desperate he was. But on a wider scale, we also can see that Moses (the Hebrew and heir of the Abrahamic promises) was completely open to God's wisdom mediated to him through a Midianite priest. This observation may encourage Christians to receive and respect input from a wide range of traditions and religions, notably in matters of work. Doing so is not necessarily a mark of disloyalty to Christ, nor does it expose a lack of confidence in our own faith. It is not an improper concession to religious pluralism. On the contrary, it may even be a poor witness to produce biblical quotes of wisdom too frequently, for in so doing, outsiders may perceive us as narrow and possibly insecure. Christians do well to be discerning about the specifics of the counsel we adopt, whether it comes from within or without. But in the final analysis, we are confident that "all truth is God's truth."[14]

Israel at Mount Sinai (Exodus 19:1–40:38)

At Mount Sinai, Moses received the Ten Commandments from the Lord. As the *NIV Study Bible* puts it, "The Ten Commandments are the central stipulations of God's covenant with Israel made at Sinai. It is almost impossible to exaggerate their effect on subsequent history. They constitute the basis of the moral principles found throughout the Western world and summarize what the one true God expects of his people in terms of faith, worship and conduct."[15] As we will see, the role of the Israelite law for Christians is the subject of a great deal of controversy. For these reasons, we will be attentive to what the text of Exodus actually says, for this is what we hold in common. At the same time, we hope to

---

[14] Arthur Holmes, *All Truth is God's Truth* (Downers Grove, IL: InterVarsity Press, 1983).
[15] Kenneth Barker, ed., *The NIV Study Bible* (Grand Rapids: Zondervan, 1999), 269.

be aware and respectful of the variety of ways that Christians may wish to draw lessons from this part of the Bible.

The Meaning of Law in Exodus (Exodus 19:1–24:18)

We begin by recognizing that Exodus is an integral part of the whole of Scripture, not a stand-alone legal statue. Christopher Wright has written:

> The common opinion that the Bible is a moral code book for Christians falls far short, of course, of the full reality of what the Bible is and does. The Bible is essentially the story of God, the earth and humanity; it is the story of what has gone wrong, what God has done to put it right, and what the future holds under the sovereign plan of God. Nevertheless, within that grand narrative, moral teaching does have a vital place. The Bible's story is the story of the mission of God. The Bible's demand is for the appropriate response from human beings. God's mission calls for and includes human response. And our mission certainly includes the ethical dimension of that response.[16]

The English word *law* is a traditional yet inaccurate rendering of the key Hebrew word *Torah*. Because this term is so central to the entire discussion at hand, it will help us to clarify how this Hebrew word actually works in the Bible. The word *Torah* appears once in Genesis in the sense of instructions from God that Abraham followed. It can refer to instructions from one human to another (Ps. 78:1). But as something from God, the word *Torah* throughout the Pentateuch and the rest of the Old Testament designates a standard of conduct for God's people pertaining to ceremonial matters of formal worship, as well as statutes for civil and social conduct.[17] The biblical notion of Torah conveys the sense of "divinely authoritative instruction." This concept is far from our modern ideas of law as a body of codes crafted and enacted by legislators or "natural" laws.

---

[16] Wright, 357–58.

[17] Peter Enns, "Law of God," in *New International Dictionary of Old Testament Theology and Exegesis*, ed. Willem A. VanGemeren (Grand Rapids: Zondervan, 1997), 4:893. The word also refers to a body of literature in that the historical core of the book of Deuteronomy is called "the Book of the Law" (Deuteronomy 31:26). Traditionally, the entire Pentateuch is called "the Torah."

To highlight the rich and instructive nature of law in Exodus, we shall sometimes refer to it as Torah with no attempt at translation.

In Exodus, it is clear that Torah in the sense of a set of specific instructions is part of the covenant and not the other way around. In other words, the covenant as a whole describes the relationship that God has established between himself and his people by virtue of his act of deliverance on their behalf (Exod. 20:2). As the people's covenantal king, God then specifies how he desires Israel to worship and behave. Israel's pledge to obey is a *response* to God's gift of the covenant (Exod. 24:7). This is significant for our understanding of the theology of work. The way we discern God's will for our behavior at work and the way we put that into practice in the workplace are enveloped by the relationship that God has established with us. In Christian terms, we love God because he first loved us and we demonstrate that love in how we treat others (1 John 4:19–21). The categorical nature of God's command for us to love our neighbors means that God intends for us to apply it everywhere, regardless of whether we find ourselves in a church, café, home, civic venue, or place of work.

The Role of the Law for Christians (Exodus 20:1–24:18)

It can be a challenge for a Christian to draw a point from a verse in the book of Exodus or especially Leviticus, and then suggest how that lesson should be applied today. Anyone who tries this should be prepared for the comeback, "Sure, but the Bible also permits slavery and says we can't eat bacon or shrimp! Plus, I don't think God really cares if my clothes are a cotton-polyester blend" (Exod. 21:2–11; Lev. 11:7, 12; and 19:19, respectively). Since this happens even within Christian circles, we should not be surprised to find difficulties when applying the Bible to the subject of work in the public sphere. How are we to know what applies today and what doesn't? How do we avoid the charge of inconsistency in our handling of the Bible? More importantly, how do we let God's word truly transform us in every area of life? The diversity of laws in Exodus and the Pentateuch presents one type of challenge. Another comes from the variety of ways that Christians understand and apply Torah and the Old Testament in relationship to Christ and the New Testament. Still, the issue of Torah in Christianity is crucial and must be addressed in order for us to glean anything about what this part of the Bible says concerning our work. The following brief treatment aims to be helpful without being overly narrow.

The New Testament's relationship to the law is complex. It includes both Jesus' saying that "Not one letter, not one stroke of a letter, will pass from the law" (Matt. 5:18), and Paul's statement that "we are discharged from the law . . . not under the old written code but in the new life of the Spirit" (Rom. 7:6). These are not two opposing statements, but two ways of saying a common reality—that the Torah continues to reveal God's gift of justice, wisdom, and inner transformation to those he has brought to new life in Christ. God gave the Torah as an expression of his holy nature and as a consequence of his great deliverance. Reading the Torah makes us aware of our inherent sinfulness and of our need for a remedy in order for us to live at peace with God and one another. God expects his people to obey his instructions by applying them to real issues of life both great and small. The specific nature of some laws does not mean God is an unrealistic perfectionist. These laws help us to understand that no issue we face is too small or insignificant for God. Even so, the Torah is not just about outward behavior, for it addresses matters of the heart such as coveting (Exod. 20:17). Later, Jesus would condemn not just murder and adultery, but the roots of anger and lust as well (Matt. 5:22, 28).

However, obeying the Torah by applying it to the real issues of life today does not equate to repeating the actions that Israel performed thousands of years ago. Already in the Old Testament we see hints that some parts of the law were not intended to be permanent. The tabernacle certainly was not a permanent structure and even the temple was demolished at the hands of Israel's enemies (2 Kgs. 25:9). Yet Jesus spoke of his own sacrificial death and resurrection when he said he would raise the destroyed "temple" in three days (John 2:19). In some important sense, he embodied all that the temple, its priesthood, and its activities stood for. Jesus' declaration about food—that it is not what goes into people that makes them unclean—meant that the specific food laws of the Mosaic Covenant were no longer in force (Mark 7:19).[18] Moreover, in

---

[18] Tim Keller, "Keller on Rules of the Bible: Do Christians Apply them Inconsistently?" The Gospel Coalition, http://thegospelcoalition.org/blogs/tgc/2012/07/09/making-sense-of-scriptures-inconsistency/.

the New Testament the people of God live in various countries and cultures around the world where they have no legal authority to apply the sanctions of the Torah. The apostles considered such issues and, under the Holy Spirit's guidance, decided that the particulars of the Jewish law did not in general apply to Gentile Christians (Acts 15:28–29).

When asked about which commandments were most important, Jesus' answer was not controversial in light of the theology of his time. "Love the Lord your God with all your heart, and with all your soul, and with all your mind, and with all your strength" and "Love your neighbor as yourself" (Mark 12:30–31).[19]

Much in the New Testament confirms the Torah, not only in its negative commands against adultery, murder, theft, and coveting, but also in its positive command to love one another (Rom. 13:8–10; Gal. 5:14). According to Timothy Keller, "The coming of Christ changed how we worship, but not how we live."[20] This is not surprising, given that in the new covenant, God said he would put his law within his people and write it on their hearts (Jer. 31:33; Luke 22:20). Israel's faithfulness to the laws of Mosaic Covenant depended on their determination to obey them. In the end, only Jesus could accomplish this. On the other hand, new covenant believers do not work that way. According to Paul, "We serve in the new way of the Spirit" (Rom. 7:6 NIV).

For our purposes in considering the theology of work, the previous explanation suggests several points that may help us to understand and apply the laws in Exodus that relate to the workplace. The specific laws dealing with proper treatment of workers, animals, and property express abiding values of God's own nature. They are to be taken seriously but not slavishly. On the one hand, items in the Ten Commandments are worded in general terms and may be applied freely in varied contexts. On the other hand, particular laws about servants, livestock, and personal injuries exemplify applications in the specific historical and social context of ancient Israel, especially in areas that were controversial at the time. These laws are illustrative of right behavior but do not exhaust

---

[19] James Tabor and Randall Buth, *Living Biblical Hebrew for Everyone* (Pasadena, CA: Internet Language Corp., 2003).

[20] Keller, "Rules of the Bible."

every possible application. Christians honor God and his law not only by regulating our behavior, but also by allowing the Holy Spirit to transform our attitudes, motives, and desires (Rom. 12:1–2). To do anything less would amount to sidestepping the work and will of our Lord and Savior. Christians should always seek how love may guide our policies and behaviors.

Instructions about Work (Exodus 20:1–17 and 21:1–23:9)

Israel's "Book of the Covenant" (Exod. 24:7) included the Ten Commandments, also known as the Decalogue (literally, the "words," Exod. 20:1–17), and the ordinances of Exodus 21:1–23:19. The Ten Commandments are worded as general commands either to do or not do something. The ordinances are a collection of case laws, applying the values of the Decalogue in specific situations using an "if . . . then" format. These laws fit the social and economic world of ancient Israel. They are not an exhaustive legal code, but they function as exemplars, serving to curb the worst excesses and setting legal precedent for handling difficult cases.[21]

The Ten Commandments (Exodus 20:1–17)

The Ten Commandments are the supreme expression of God's will in the Old Testament and merit our close attention. They are to be thought of not as the ten most important commands among hundreds of others, but as a digest of the entire Torah. The foundation of all the Torah rests in the Ten Commandments, and somewhere within them we should be able to find *all* the law. Jesus expressed the essential unity of the Ten Commandments with the rest of the law when he summarized the law in the famous words, " 'You shall love the Lord your God with all your heart, and with all your soul, and with all your mind.' This is the greatest and first commandment. And a second is like it: 'You shall love your neighbor as yourself.' On these two commandments hang all the law and the prophets" (Matt. 22:37–40). *All* the law, as well as the prophets, is indicated whenever the Ten Commandments are expressed.

---

[21] Gordon J. Wenham, *Exploring the Old Testament, A Guide to the Pentateuch*, vol. 1 (Downers Grove, IL: IVP Academic, 2008), 71.

The essential unity of the Ten Commandments with the rest of the law, and their continuity with the New Testament, invites us to apply them to today's work broadly in light of the rest of the Scripture. That is, when applying the Ten Commandments, we will take into account related passages of Scripture in both the Old and New Testaments.

"You Shall Have No Other Gods before Me" (Exodus 20:3)

The first commandment reminds us that everything in the Torah flows from the love we have for God, which in turn is a response to the love he has for us. This love was demonstrated by God's deliverance of Israel "out of the house of slavery" in Egypt (Exod. 20:2). Nothing else in life should concern us more than our desire to love and be loved by God. If we *do* have some other concern stronger to us than our love for God, it is not so much that we are breaking God's rules, but that we are not really in relationship with God. The other concern—be it money, power, security, recognition, sex, or anything else—has become our god. This god will have its own commandments at odds with God's, and we will inevitably violate the Torah as we comply with this god's requirements. Observing the Ten Commandments is only conceivable for those who start by having no other god than God.

In the realm of work, this means that we are not to let work or its requirements and fruits displace God as our most important concern in life. "Never allow anyone or anything to threaten God's central place in your life," as David Gill puts it.[22] Because many people work primarily to make money, an inordinate desire for money is probably the most common work-related danger to the first commandment. Jesus warned of exactly this danger. "No one can serve two masters. . . . You cannot serve God and wealth" (Matt. 6:24). But almost anything related to work can become twisted in our desires to the point that it interferes with our love for God. How many careers come to a tragic end because the *means* to accomplish things for the love of God—such as political power, financial sustainability, commitment to the job, status among peers, or

---

[22] David W. Gill, *Doing Right: Practicing Ethical Principles* (Downers Grove, IL: IVP Books, 2004), 83. Gill's book contains an extended exegesis and application of the Ten Commandments in the modern world, which merits careful attention.

superior performance—become ends in themselves? When, for example, recognition on the job becomes more important than character on the job, is it not a sign that reputation is displacing the love of God as the ultimate concern?

A practical touchstone is to ask whether our love of God is shown by the way we treat people on the job. "Those who say, 'I love God,' and hate their brothers or sisters, are liars; for those who do not love a brother or sister whom they have seen, cannot love God whom they have not seen. The commandment we have from him is this: those who love God must love their brothers and sisters also" (1 John 4:20–21). If we put our individual concerns ahead of our concern for the people we work with, for, and among, then we have made our individual concerns our god. In particular, if we treat other people as things to be manipulated, obstacles to overcome, instruments to obtain what we want, or simply neutral objects in our field of view, then we demonstrate that we do not love God with all our heart, soul, and mind.

In this context, we can begin to list some work-related actions that have a high potential to interfere with our love for God. Doing work that violates our conscience. Working in an organization where we have to harm others to succeed. Working such long hours that we have little time to pray, worship, rest, and otherwise deepen our relationship with God. Working among people who demoralize us or seduce us away from our love for God. Working where alcohol, drug abuse, violence, sexual harassment, corruption, disrespect, racism, or other inhumane treatment mar the image of God in us and the people we encounter in our work. If we can find ways to avoid these dangers at work—even if it means finding a new job—it would be wise to do so. If that is not possible, we can at least be aware that we need help and support to maintain our love of God in the face of our work.

"You Shall Not Make for Yourself an Idol" (Exodus 20:4)

The second commandment raises the issue of idolatry. Idols are gods of our own creation, gods that have nothing to them that did not originate with us, gods that we feel we control. In ancient times, idolatry often took the form of worshiping physical objects. But the issue is really one of trust and devotion. On what do we ultimately pin our hope of well-being and success? Anything that is not capable of fulfilling our hope—that is, anything other than God—is an idol, whether or not it is a physical object. The story of a family forging an idol with the intent to manipulate God, and the disastrous personal, social, and economic consequences that follow, are memorably told in Judges 17–21.

In the world of work, it is common to speak of money, fame, and power as potential idols, and rightly so. They are not idolatrous, per se, and in fact may be necessary for us to accomplish our roles in God's creative and redemptive work in the world. Yet when we imagine that we have ultimate control over them, or that by achieving them our safety and prosperity will be secured, we have begun to fall into idolatry. The same may occur with virtually every other element of success, including preparation, hard work, creativity, risk, wealth and other resources, and favorable circumstances. As workers, we have to recognize how important these are. As God's people, we must recognize when we begin to idolize them. By God's grace, we can overcome the temptation to worship these good things in their own right. The development of genuinely godly wisdom and skill for any task is "*so that* your trust may be in the Lord" (Prov. 22:19; emphasis added).

The distinctive element of idolatry is the human-made nature of the idol. At work, a danger of idolatry arises when we mistake our power, knowledge, and opinions for reality. When we stop holding ourselves accountable to the standards we set for other, cease listening to others' ideas, or seek to crush those who disagree with us, are we not beginning to make idols of ourselves?

"You Shall Not Make Wrongful Use of the Name of the LORD Your God" (Exodus 20:7)

The third commandment literally prohibits God's people from making "wrongful use" of the name of God. This need not be restricted to the name "YHWH" (Exod. 3:15), but includes "God," "Jesus," "Christ," and so forth. But what is wrongful use? It includes, of course, disrespectful use in cursing, slandering, and blaspheming. But more significantly it includes falsely attributing human designs to God. This prohibits us from claiming God's authority for our own actions and decisions. Regrettably, some Christians seem to believe that following God at work consists primarily of speaking for God on the basis of their individual understanding, rather than working respectfully with others or taking responsibility for their actions. "It is God's will that . . ." or "God is punishing you for . . ." are very dangerous things to say, and almost never valid when spoken by an individual without the discernment of the community of faith (1 Thess. 5:20–21). In this light, perhaps the traditional Jewish reticence to utter even the English translation "God"—let alone the divine name itself—demonstrates a wisdom Christians often lack. If we were a little more careful about bandying the word "God" about, perhaps we would be more judicious in claiming to know God's will, especially as it applies to other people.

The third commandment also reminds us that respecting human names is important to God. The Good Shepherd "calls his own sheep by name" (John 10:3) while warning us that if you call another person "you fool," then "you will be liable to the hell of fire" (Matt. 5:22). Keeping this in mind, we shouldn't make wrongful use of other people's names or call them by disrespectful epithets. We use people's names wrongfully when we use them to curse, humiliate, oppress, exclude, and defraud. We use people's names well when we use them to encourage, thank, create solidarity, and welcome. Simply to learn and say someone's name is a blessing, especially if he or she is often treated as nameless, invisible, or insignificant. Do you know the name of the person who empties your trash can, answers your customer service call, or drives your bus? If these examples do not concern the very name of the Lord, they do concern the name of those made in his image.

"Remember the Sabbath Day and Keep It Holy. Six Days You Shall Labor" (Exodus 20:8–11)

The issue of the Sabbath is complex, not only in the book of Exodus and the Old Testament, but also in Christian theology and practice. The first part of the command calls for ceasing labor one day in seven. The other references in Exodus to the Sabbath are in chapter 16 (about gathering manna), Exodus 23:10–12 (the seventh year and the goal of weekly rest), Exodus 31:12–17 (penalty for violation), Exodus 34:21 and Exodus 35:1–3. In the context of the ancient world, the Sabbath was unique to Israel. On the one hand, this was an incomparable gift to the people of Israel. No other ancient people had the privilege of resting one day in seven. On the other hand, it required an extraordinary trust in God's provision. Six days of work had to be enough to plant crops, gather the harvest, carry water, spin cloth, and draw sustenance from creation. While Israel rested one day every week, the encircling nations continued to forge swords, feather arrows, and train soldiers. Israel had to trust God not to let a day of rest lead to economic and military catastrophe.

We face the same issue of trust in God's provision today. If we heed God's commandment to observe God's own cycle of work and rest, will we be able to compete in the modern economy? Does it take seven days of work to hold a job (or two or three jobs), clean the house, prepare the meals, mow the lawn, wash the car, pay the bills, finish the school work, and shop for the clothes, or can we trust God to provide for us even if we take a day off during the course of every week? Can we take time to worship God, to pray and to gather with others for study and encouragement, and, if we do, will it make us more or less productive overall? The fourth commandment does not explain how God will make it all work out for us. It simply tells us to rest one day every seven.

Christians have translated the day of rest to the Lord's Day (Sunday, the day of Christ's resurrection), but the essence of the Sabbath is not choosing one particular day of the week over another (Rom. 14:5–6). The polarity that actually undergirds the Sabbath is *work* and *rest*. Both work and rest are included in the fourth commandment. The six days of work are as much a part of the commandment as the one day of rest. Although many Christians are in danger of allowing work to squeeze the time set aside for rest, others are in danger of the opposite, of shirking work and trying to live a life of leisure and dissipation. This is even worse than neglecting the Sabbath, for "whoever does not provide for relatives, and especially for family members, has denied the faith and is worse than an unbeliever" (1 Tim. 5:8). What we need is a proper rhythm of work and rest, which together are good for us, our family, workers, and guests. The rhythm may or may not include twenty-four continuous hours of rest falling on Sunday (or Saturday). The proportions may change due to temporary necessities (the modern equivalent of pulling an ox out of the well on the Sabbath, see Luke 14:5) or the changing needs of the seasons of life.

If overwork is our main danger, we need to find a way to honor the fourth commandment without instituting a false, new legalism pitting the spiritual (worship on Sunday worship) against the secular (work on Monday through Saturday). If avoiding work is our danger, we need to learn how to find joy and meaning in working as a service to God and our neighbors (Eph. 4:28).

"Honor Your Father and Your Mother" (Exodus 20:12)

There are many ways to honor—or dishonor—your father and mother. In Jesus' day, the Pharisees wanted to restrict this to speaking well of them. But Jesus pointed out that obeying this commandment requires working to provide for your parents (Mark 7:9–13). We honor people by working for their good.

For many people, good relationships with parents are one of the joys of life. Loving service to them is a delight, and obeying this commandment is easy. But we are put to the test by this commandment when we find it burdensome to work on behalf of our parents. We may have been ill-treated or neglected by them. They may be controlling and meddlesome. Being around them may undermine our sense of self, our commitment to our spouses (including our responsibilities under the third commandment), even our relationship with God. Even if we have good relationships with our parents, there may come a time when caring for them is a major burden simply because of the time and work it takes. If aging or dementia begins to rob them of their memory, capabilities, and good nature, caring for them can become a deep sorrow.

Yet the fifth commandment comes with a promise, "that your days may be long in the land that the Lord your God is giving you" (Gen. 20:12). Somehow, honoring our father and mother in such practical ways has the practical benefit of giving us longer (perhaps in the sense of more fulfilling) life in God's kingdom. We are not told how this will occur, but we are told to expect it, and to do that we must trust God (see the first commandment).

Because this is a command to work for the benefit of parents, it is inherently a workplace command. The place of work may be where we earn money to support them, or it may be in the place where we assist them in the tasks of daily life. Both are work. When we take a job because it allows us to live near them, or send money to them, or make use of the values and gifts they developed in us, or accomplish things they taught us are important, we are honoring them. When we *limit* our careers so that we can be present with them, clean and cook for them, bathe and embrace them, take them to the places they love, or diminish their fears, we are honoring them.

We must also recognize that in many cultures, the work people do is dictated by the choices of their parents and needs of their families rather than their own decisions and preferences. At times this gives rise to serious conflict for Christians who find the demands of the first commandment (to follow God's call) and fifth commandment competing with each other. They find themselves forced to make hard choices that parents don't understand. Even Jesus experienced such parental misunderstanding when Mary and Joseph could not understand why he remained behind in the temple while his family departed Jerusalem (Luke 2:49).

In our workplaces, we can help other people fulfill the fifth commandment, as well as obeying it ourselves. We can remember that employees, customers, co-workers, bosses, suppliers, and others also have families, and then can adjust our expectations to support them in honoring their families. When others share or complain about their struggles with parents, we can listen to them compassionately, support them practically (for example, by offering to take a shift so they can be with their parents), perhaps offer a godly perspective for them to consider, or simply reflect the grace of Christ to those who feel they are failing in their parent-child relationships.

"You Shall Not Murder" (Exodus 20:13)

Sadly, the sixth commandment has an all-too-practical application in the modern workplace, where 10 percent of all job-related fatalities (in the United States) are homicides.[23] However, admonishing readers of this article, "Don't murder anyone at work," isn't likely to change this statistic much.

---

[23] "Fact Sheet: Workplace Shootings 2010," United States Department of Labor, *Bureau of Labor Statistics*, http://www.bls.gov/iif/oshwc/cfoi/osar0014.htm.

But murder isn't the only form of workplace violence, just the most extreme. Jesus said that even anger is a violation of the sixth commandment (Matt. 5:21–22). As Paul noted, we may not be able to prevent the feeling of anger, but we can learn how to cope with it. "Be angry but do not sin; do not let the sun go down on your anger" (Eph. 4:26). The most significant implication of the sixth commandment for work then may be, "If you get angry at work, get help in anger management." Many employers, churches, state and local governments, and nonprofit organizations offer classes and counseling in anger management, and availing yourself of these may be a highly effective way of obeying the sixth commandment.

Murder is intentional killing, but the case law that stems from the sixth commandment shows that we also have the duty to prevent unintended deaths. A particularly graphic case is when an ox (a work animal) gores a man or woman to death (Exod. 21:28–29). If the event was predictable, the ox's owner is to be treated as a murderer. In other words, owners/managers are responsible for ensuring workplace safety within reason. This principle is well established in law in most countries, and workplace safety is the subject of significant government policing, industry self-regulation, and organizational policy and practice. Yet workplaces of all kinds continue to require or allow workers to work in needlessly unsafe conditions. Christians who have any role in setting the conditions of work, supervising workers, or modeling workplace practices are reminded by the sixth commandment that safe working conditions are among their highest responsibilities in the world of work.

"You Shall Not Commit Adultery" (Exodus 20:14)

The workplace is one of the most common settings for adultery, not necessarily because adultery occurs in the workplace itself, but because it arises from the conditions of work and relationships with co-workers. The first application to the workplace, then, is literal. Married people should not have sex with people other than their spouses at, in, or because of their work. Obviously this rules out sex professions such as prostitution, pornography, and sex surrogacy, at least in most cases. But any kind of work that erodes the bonds of marriage infringes the seventh commandment. There are many ways this can occur. Work that encourages strong emotional bonds among co-workers without adequately supporting their commitments to their spouses, as can happen in hospitals, entrepreneurial ventures, academic institutions and churches, among other places. Working conditions that bring people into close physical contact for extended periods or that fail to encourage reasonable limits to off-hour encounters, as could happen on extended field assignments. Work that subjects people to sexual harassment and pressure to have sex with those holding power over them. Work that inflates people's egos or exposes them to adulation, as could occur with celebrities, star athletes, business titans, high-ranking government officials, and the super-rich. Work that demands so much time away (physically, mentally, or emotionally) that it frays the bonds between spouses. All of these may pose dangers that Christians would do well to recognize and avoid, ameliorate, or guard against. Yet the seriousness of the seventh commandment arises not so much because adultery is illicit sex, as because it breaks a covenant ordained by God. God created husband and wife to become "one flesh" (Gen. 2:24), and Jesus' commentary on the seventh commandment highlights God's role in the marriage covenant. "What God has joined together, let no one separate" (Matt. 19:6). To commit adultery, therefore, is not only to have sex with someone you shouldn't, but also to break a covenant with the Lord God. In fact, the Old Testament frequently uses the word *adultery*, and the imagery surrounding it, to refer not to sexual sin but to idolatry. The prophets often refer to Israel's faithlessness to its covenant to worship God alone as "adultery" or "whoring," as in Isaiah 57:3, Jeremiah 3:8, Ezekiel 16:38, and Hosea 2:2, among many others. Therefore, any breaking of faith with the God of Israel is figuratively adultery, whether it involves illicit sex or not. This use of the term "adultery" unites the first, second, and seventh commandments, and reminds us that the Ten Commandments are expressions of a single covenant with God, rather than some kind of top-ten list of rules.

Therefore, work that requires or leads us into idolatry or worshipping other gods is to be avoided. It's hard to imagine how a Christian could work as a tarot reader, a maker of idolatrous art or music, or a publisher of blasphemous books. Christian actors may find it difficult to perform profane, irreligious, or spiritually demoralizing roles. Everything we do in life, including work, tends in some degree either to enhance or diminish our relationship with God; over a lifetime, the constant stress of work that diminishes us spiritually may prove devastating. It's a factor we would do well to include in our career decisions, to the degree we have choices.

The distinctive aspect of covenants violated by adultery is that they are covenants with God. But isn't every promise or agreement made by a Christian implicitly a covenant with God? Paul exhorts us, "Whatever you do, in word or deed, do everything in the name of the Lord Jesus" (Col. 3:17). Contracts, promises and agreements are surely things we do in word or deed, or both. If we do them all in the name of the Lord Jesus, it cannot be that some promises must be honored because they are covenants with God, while others may be broken because they are merely human. We are to honor all our agreements, and to avoid inducing others to break theirs. Whether this is contained in Exodus 20:14 itself, or expounded in the Old and New Testament teachings that arise from it, "Keep your promises, and help others keep theirs" may serve as a fine derivation of the seventh commandment in the world of work.

"You Shall Not Steal" (Exodus 20:15)

The eighth commandment is another that takes work as its primary subject. Stealing is a violation of proper work because it dispossesses the victim of the fruits of his or her labor. It is also a violation of the commandment to labor six days a week, since in most cases stealing is intended as a shortcut around honest labor, which shows again the interrelation of the Ten Commandments. So we may take it as the word of God that we are not to steal from those we work for, with, or among.

Stealing occurs in many forms besides robbing someone. Any time we acquire something of value from its rightful owner without consent, we are engaging in theft. Misappropriating resources or funds for personal use is stealing. Using deception to make sales, gain market share, or raise prices is stealing because the deception means that whatever the buyer consents to is not the actual situation. (See the section on "Puffery/Exaggeration" in *Truth & Deception* at www.theologyofwork.org for more on this topic.) Likewise, profiting by taking advantage of people's fears, vulnerabilities, powerlessness, or desperation is a form of stealing because their consent is not truly voluntary. Violating patents, copyrights, and other intellectual property laws is stealing because it deprives owners of the ability to profit from their creation under the terms of civil law.

Regrettably, many jobs seem to include an element of taking advantage of others' ignorance or lack of alternatives to force them into transactions they otherwise wouldn't agree to. Companies, governments, individuals, unions, and other players may use their power to coerce others into unfair wages, prices, financial terms, working conditions, hours, or other factors. Although we may not rob banks, steal from our employers, or shoplift, we may very likely be participating in unfair or unethical practices that deprive others of what rights should be theirs. It can be difficult, even career-limiting, to resist engaging in these practices, but we are called to do so nonetheless.

"You Shall Not Bear False Witness against Your Neighbor" (Exodus 20:16)

The ninth commandment honors the right to one's own reputation.[24] It finds pointed application in legal proceedings where what people say depicts reality and determines the course of lives. Judicial decisions and other legal processes wield great power. Manipulating them undercuts the ethical fabric of society and thus constitutes a very serious offense. Walter Brueggemann says this commandment recognizes "that community life is not possible unless there is an arena in which there is public confidence that social reality will be reliably described and reported."[25]

Although stated in courtroom language, the ninth commandment also applies to a broad range of situations that touch practically every aspect of life. We should never say or do anything that misrepresents someone else. Brueggemann again provides insight:

> Politicians seek to destroy one another in negative campaigning; gossip columnists feed off calumny; and in Christian living rooms, reputations are tarnished or destroyed over cups of coffee served in fine china with dessert. These de facto courtrooms are conducted without due process of law. Accusations are made; hearsay allowed; slander, perjury, and libelous comments uttered without objection. No evidence, no defense. As Christians, we must refuse to participate in or to tolerate any conversa-

[24] Brueggemann, 431.
[25] Brueggemann, 848.

tion in which a person is being defamed or accused without the person being there to defend himself. It is wrong to pass along hearsay in any form, even as prayer requests or pastoral concerns. More than merely not participating, it is up to Christians to stop rumors and those who spread them in their tracks.[26]

This further suggests that workplace gossip is a serious offense. Some of it pertains to personal, off-site matters, which is evil enough. But what about cases when an employee tarnishes the reputation of a co-worker? Can truth ever truly be spoken when those being talked about are not there to speak for themselves? And what about assessments of performance? What safeguards ought to be in place to ensure that reports are fair and accurate? On a large scale, the business of marketing and advertisement operates in the public space among organizations and individuals. In the interest of presenting one's own products and services in the best possible light, to what extent may one point out the flaws and weaknesses of the competition, without incorporating their perspective? Is it possible that the rights of "your neighbor" could include the rights of other companies? The scope of our global economy suggests this command may have very wide application indeed. In a world where perception often counts for reality, the rhetoric of effective persuasion may or may not have much, if anything, to do with genuine truth. The divine origin of this command reminds us that people may not be able to detect when our representation of others is accurate or not, but God cannot be fooled. It's good to do the right thing when nobody is watching. With this command, we understand that we must *say* the right thing when *anybody* is listening. (See *Truth & Deception* at www.theologyofwork.org for a much fuller discussion of this topic, including whether the prohibition of "false witness against your neighbor" includes all forms of lying and deception.)

"You Shall Not Covet . . . Anything That Belongs to Your Neighbor" (Exodus 20:17)

Envy and acquisitiveness can arise anywhere in life, including at work where status, pay, and power are routine factors in our relation-

---

[26] Brueggemann, 432.

ships with people we spend a lot of time with. We may have many good reasons to desire achievement, advancement, or reward at work. But envy isn't one of them. Nor is working obsessively out of envy for the social standing it may enable.

In particular, we face temptation at work to falsely inflate our accomplishments at the expense of others. The antidote is simple, although hard to do at times. Make it a consistent practice to recognize the accomplishments of others and give them all the credit they deserve. If we can learn to rejoice in—or at least acknowledge—others' successes, then we cut off the lifeblood of envy and covetousness at work. Even better, if we can learn how to work so that our success goes hand-in-hand with others' success, covetousness is replaced by collaboration and envy by unity.

Leith Anderson, former pastor of Wooddale Church in Eden Prairie, Minnesota, says, "As the senior pastor, it's as if I have an unlimited supply of coins in my pocket. Whenever I give credit to a staff member for a good idea, praise a volunteer's work, or thank someone, it's like I'm slipping a coin from my pocket into theirs. That's my job as the leader, to slip coins from my pocket to others' pockets, to build up the appreciation other people have for them."[27]

Case Laws in the Book of the Covenant (Exodus 21:1–23:33)

A collection of case laws follows, flowing from the Ten Commandments. Instead of developing detailed principles, it gives examples of how to apply God's law to the kinds of cases that commonly arose in the conduct of daily life. As cases, they are all embedded in the situations faced by the people of Israel. Indeed, throughout the Pentateuch (the Torah), it can be difficult to sift out the specific laws from the surrounding narrative and exhortation. Four sections of the case law are particularly applicable to work today.

Slavery or Indentured Servitude (Exodus 21:1–11)

Although God liberated the Hebrews from slavery in Egypt, slavery is not universally prohibited in the Bible. Slavery was permissible in

---

[27] Reported by William Messenger from a conversation with Leith Anderson on October 20, 2004, in Charlotte, North Carolina.

certain situations, so long as slaves were regarded as full members of the community (Gen. 17:12), received the same rest periods and holidays as non-slaves (Exod. 23:12; Deut. 5:14–15; 12:12), and were treated humanely (Exod. 21:7, 26–27). Most importantly, slavery was not intended as a permanent condition, but a voluntary, temporary refuge for people suffering what would otherwise be desperate poverty. "When you buy a male Hebrew slave, he shall serve six years, but in the seventh he shall go out a free person, without debt" (Exod. 21:2). Cruelty on the part of the owner resulted in immediate freedom for the slave (Exod. 21:26–27). This made Hebrew slavery more like a kind of long-term labor contract among individuals, and less like the kind of permanent racial/class/ethnic exploitation that has characterized slavery in modern times.

Also in contrast to slavery in the United States, which generally forbade marriage among slaves, the regulations in Exodus aim to preserve families intact. "If he comes in single, he shall go out single; if he comes in married, then his wife shall go out with him" (Exod. 21:3). The general equality between slave owners and slaves is highlighted by the regulations about female slaves in Exodus 21:7–11. The only purpose contemplated for buying a female slave was so that she could become the wife of either the buyer or the buyer's son (Exod. 21:8–9). She became the social equal (as wife) of the slaveholder, and the purchase functioned much like the giving of a dowry. Indeed, she is even called a "wife" by the regulation (Exod. 21:10). Moreover, if the buyer failed to treat the female slave with all the rights due an ordinary wife, he was required to set her free. "She shall go out without debt, without payment of money" (Exod. 21:11). Despite these regulations, it appears that in some cases, girls or women were bought as wives for a male slave, rather than for the slave owner or a son, which resulted in a very problematic situation (Exod. 21:4).

By no means does this suggest that slavery was an idyllic situation. Slaves were, for the duration of their enslavement, property. Whatever the regulations, in practice there was probably little protection against maltreatment, and abuses undoubtedly occurred. The safeguards for foreign-born slaves were not as stringent as for Hebrews (Lev. 25:44–46). As in much of the Bible, God's word in Exodus did not demand a new form of social and economic organization, but instructed God's people how to live with justice and compassion in their present circumstances.

In any case, before we become too smug, we should take a look at the working conditions that prevail among poor people in every corner of the world, including the developed nations. Ceaseless labor for those working two or three jobs to support families, abuse and arbitrary exercise of power by those in power, and misappropriation of the fruits of labor by illicit business operators, corrupt officials, and politically connected bosses. Millions work today without so much as the regulations provided by the Law of Moses. If it was God's will to protect Israel from exploitation even in slavery, what does God expect followers of Christ to do for those who suffer the same oppression, and worse, today?

Commercial Restitution (Exodus 21:18–22:15)

The casuistic laws spelled out penalties for offenses, including many relating directly to commerce, especially in the case of liability for loss or injury. The so-called *lex talionis*, which also appears in Leviticus 24:17–21 and Deuteronomy 19:16–21, is central to the concept of retribution.[28] Literally, the law says to pay with a life for a life that is taken, as well as an eye for an eye, tooth for tooth, hand for hand, foot for foot, burn for burn, wound for wound, and stripe for stripe (Exod. 21:23–25). The list is notably specific. When Israel's judges did their work, are we really to believe they applied punishments in this way? Would a plaintiff who was burned due to someone's negligence really be satisfied to see the offender literally burned to the same degree? Interestingly, in this very part of Exodus, we do not see the *lex talionis* being applied in this manner. Instead, a man who seriously injures another in a fight must pay for the victim's lost time and cover his medical expenses (Exod. 21:18–19). The text does not go on to say he must sit still for a public and comparable beating by his former victim. It appears that the *lex talionis* did not determine the standard penalty for major offenses, but that it set an upper ceiling for damages that could be claimed. Gordon Wenham notes, "In Old Testament times there were no police or public prosecution services, so all prosecution and punishment had to be carried out by the injured party and his family. Thus it would be quite possible for injured parties

---

[28] Brueggemann, 433. The principle is also present in the Code of Hammurabi (about 1850–1750 BC), though that code does not prioritize human life as highly as the Torah does.

not to insist on their full rights under the *lex talionis*, but negotiate a lower settlement or even forgive the offender altogether."[29] This law may be perceived by some today as savage, but Alec Motyer observed, "When English law hanged a person for stealing a sheep, it was not because the principle of 'an eye for an eye' was being practiced but because it had been forgotten."[30]

This issue of interpreting the *lex talionis* illustrates that there may be a difference between doing what the Bible literally says and applying what the Bible instructs. Obtaining a biblical solution to our problems will not always be a straightforward matter. Christians must use maturity and discernment, especially in light of Jesus' teaching to forego the *lex talionis* by not resisting an evildoer (Matt 5:38–42). Was he speaking of a personal ethic, or did he expect his followers to apply this principle in business? Does it work better for small offenses than it does for big ones? Those who do evil create victims whom we are bound to defend and protect (Prov. 31:9).

The specific instructions about restitution and penalties for thievery accomplished two aims. First, they made the thief responsible for returning the original owner to his original state or fully compensating him for his loss. Second, they punished and educated the thief by causing him to experience the full pain that he had caused for the victim. These aims can form a Christian basis for the work of civil and criminal law today. Current judicial work operates according to specific statutes and guidelines set by the state. But even so, judges have a measure of freedom to set sentences and penalties. For disputes that are settled out of court, attorneys negotiate to help their clients reach a conclusive agreement. In recent times, a perspective called "restorative justice" has emerged with an emphasis on punishment that restores the victim's original condition and, to the extent possible, restores the perpetrator as a productive member of society. A full description and assessment of such approaches is beyond our scope here, but we want to note that Scripture has much to offer contemporary systems of justice in this regard.

---

[29] Wenham, 73.

[30] J. A. Motyer, *The Message of Exodus: The Days of Our Pilgrimage* (Downers Grove, IL: IVP Academic, 2005), 240.

In business, leaders sometimes must mediate between workers who have serious work-related issues with one another. Deciding the right and fair thing affects not only the ones embroiled in the dispute, it also can affect the whole atmosphere of the organization and even serve to set precedent for how workers may expect to fare in the future. The immediate stakes may be very high. On top of this, when Christians must make these kinds of decisions, onlookers draw conclusions about us as people, as well as the legitimacy of the faith we claim to live by. Clearly, we cannot anticipate every situation (and neither does the book of Exodus). But we do know that God expects us to apply his instructions, and we can be confident that asking God how to love our neighbors as ourselves is the best place to start.

Productive Opportunities for the Poor (Exodus 22:21–27 & 23:10–11)

God's intent to provide opportunities for the poor is seen in the regulations benefiting aliens, widows, and orphans (Exod. 22:21–22). What these three groups had in common was that they did not possess land on which to support themselves. Often this made left them poor, so that aliens, widows, and orphans are the main subjects whenever "the poor" are mentioned in the Old Testament. In Deuteronomy, God's concern for this triad of vulnerable people called for Israel to provide them with justice (Deut. 10:18; 27:19) and access to food (Deut. 24:19–22). Case law on this matter is also developed in Isaiah 1:17, 23; 10:1–2; Jeremiah 5:28, 7:5–7; 22:3; Ezekiel 22:6–7; Zechariah 7:8–10; and Malachi 3:5.

One of the most important of these regulations is the practice of allowing the poor to harvest, or "glean," the leftover grain active fields and to harvest all volunteer crops in fields lying fallow. The practice of gleaning was not a handout, but an opportunity for the poor to support themselves. Landowners were required to leave each field, vineyard, and orchard fallow one year in every seven, and the poor were allowed to harvest anything that might grow there (Exod. 23:10–11). Even in active fields, owners were to leave some of the grain in the field for the poor to harvest, rather than exhaustively stripping the field bare (Lev. 19:9–10). For example, an olive grove or a vineyard was to be harvested only once each season (Deut. 24:20). After that, the poor were entitled to gather what was left over, perhaps what was of lesser quality or slower to ripen. This practice was not only an expression of kindness, but it was also a matter of justice. The book of Ruth revolves around gleaning to enchanting effect (see "Ruth 2:17–23" in *Ruth and Work* at www.theologyofowork.org).

Today, there are many ways that growers, food producers, and distributors share with the poor. Many of them donate the day's leftover but wholesome food to pantries and shelters. Others work to made food more affordable by increasing their own efficiency. But most people, in developed nations at least, no longer engage in agriculture for a living, and opportunities for the poor are needed in other sectors of society. There is nothing to glean on the floor of a stock exchange, assembly plant, or programming lab. But the principle of providing productive work for vulnerable workers is still relevant. Corporations can productively employ people with mental and physical disabilities, with or without government assistance. With training and support, people from disadvantaged backgrounds, prisoners returning to society, and others who have difficulty finding conventional employment can become productive workers and earn a living.

Other economically vulnerable people may have to depend on contributions of money instead of receiving opportunities to work. Here again the modern situation is too complex for us to proclaim a simplistic application of the biblical law. But the values underlying the law may offer a significant contribution to the design and execution of systems of public welfare, personal charity, and corporate social responsibility. Many Christians have significant roles in hiring workers or designing employment policies. Exodus reminds us that employing vulnerable workers is an essential part of what it means for a people to live under God's covenant. Together with Israel of old, Christians have also experienced God's redemption, though not necessarily in identical terms. But our basic gratitude for God's grace is certainly a powerful motive for finding creative ways to serve the needy around us.

Lending and Collateral (Exodus 22:25–27)

Another set of case laws regulated money and collateral (Exod. 22:25–27). Two situations are in view. The first pertains to a needy member of God's people who requires a financial loan. This loan shall

not be made according to the usual standards of money-lending. It shall
be given without "interest." The Hebrew word *neshekh* (which in some
contexts means a "bite") has garnered a great deal of academic attention.
Did *neshek* refer to *excessive* and therefore unfair interest charged, on
top of the reasonable amount of interest required to keep the practice of
money-lending financially viable? Or did it refer to *any* interest? The text
does not have enough detail to settle this conclusively, but the latter view
seems more likely, because in the Old Testament *neshek* always pertains
to lending to those who are in miserable and vulnerable circumstances,
for whom paying any interest at all would be an excessive burden.[31] Placing the poor into a never-ending cycle of financial indebtedness will stir
Israel's compassionate God to action. Whether or not this law was good
for business is not in view here. Walter Brueggemann notes, "The law
does not argue about the economic viability of such a practice. It simply
requires the need for care in concrete ways, and it expects the community to work out the practical details."[32] The other situation envisages
a man who puts up his only coat as collateral for a loan. It should be
returned to him at night so that he can sleep without endangering his
health (Exod. 22:26–27). Does this mean that the creditor should visit
him in the morning to collect the coat for the day and to keep doing so
until the loan is repaid? In the context of such obvious destitution, a
godly creditor could avoid the near absurdity of this cycle by simply not
expecting the borrower to put up any collateral at all. These regulations
may have less application to today's banking system in general than to
today's systems of protection and assistance for the poor. For example,
microfinance in less developed countries was developed with interest
rates and collateral policies tailored to meet the needs of poor people
who otherwise have no access to credit. The goal—at least in the earli-
est years beginning in the 1970s—was not to maximize profit for the
lenders, but to provide sustainable lending institutions to help the poor
escape poverty. Even so, microfinance struggles with balancing the lend-

---

[31] Robin Wakely, "#5967 NSHK," in *New International Dictionary of Old
Testament Theology and Exegesis*, ed. Willem A. VanGemeren (Grand Rapids:
Zondervan, 1997), 3:185–89.

[32] Brueggemann, 868.

ers' need for a sustainable return and default rates with the borrowers' need for affordable interest rates and nonrestrictive collateral terms.[33]

The presence of specific regulations following the Ten Commandments means that God wants his people to honor him by putting his instructions into actual practice to serve real needs. Emotional concern without deliberate action doesn't give the poor the kind of help they need. As the Apostle James put it, "Faith without works is also dead" (James 2:26). Studying the specific applications of these laws in ancient Israel helps us to think about the particular ways we can act today. But we remember that even then, these laws were illustrations. Terence Fretheim thus concludes, "There is an open-endedness to the application of the law. The text invites the hearer/reader to extend this passage out into every sphere of life where injustice might be encountered. In other words, *one is invited by the law to go beyond the law*."[34]

A careful reading reveals three reasons why God's people should keep these laws and apply them to fresh situations.[35] First, the Israelites themselves were oppressed as foreigners in Egypt (Exod. 22:21; 23:9). Rehearsing this history not only keeps God's redemption in view, but memory becomes a motivation to treat others as we would like to be treated (Matt. 7:12). Second, God hears the cry of the oppressed and acts on it, especially when we won't (Exod. 22:22–24). Third, we are to be his holy people (Exod. 22:31; Lev. 19:2).

The Tabernacle (Exodus 25:1–40:38)

The work of building the tabernacle may seem to lie outside the scope of the Theology of Work Project because of its liturgical focus. We should note, however, that the book of Exodus does not so easily separate Israel's life in the categories of sacred and secular that we are so accustomed to. Even if we delineate between Israel's liturgical and extra-liturgical activities, nothing in Exodus suggests that one is more

---

[33] Rob Moll, "Christian Microfinance Stays on a Mission," *Christianity Today*, http://www.christianitytoday.com/ct/2011/may/stayingonmission.html.

[34] Terence E. Fretheim, *Exodus: Interpretation: A Bible Commentary for Teaching and Preaching* (Louisville: Westminster John Knox Press, 1991), 248.

[35] Motyer, 241.

important than the other. Furthermore, what actually happened at the tabernacle cannot be equated fairly with "church work" today. Certainly, its construction has no close parallel in the construction of church buildings. The chapters in Exodus dealing with the tabernacle are all about the *establishment* of a unique institution. Although the work of the tabernacle would go on from year to year and be subsumed by the temple, each of these buildings was by design central and solitary. They were not exemplars to be reproduced wherever Israelites would settle down to live. In fact, the construction and operation of local shrines throughout the land proved to be a huge detriment to Israel's national spiritual health. Finally, the purpose of the tabernacle was not to give Israel an authorized place to worship. It was about the presence of God in their midst. This is clear from the outset in God's words, "Have them make me a sanctuary, so that I may dwell among them" (Exod. 25:8). Christians today understand that God dwelt among us in the person of his Son (John 1:14). Through his work, the entire community of believers has become God's temple in which God's Spirit lives (1 Cor. 3:16). In light of these observations, we will take up two claims that relate to work. First, God is an architect. Second, God equips his people to do his work.

The large section in Exodus about the tabernacle is organized according to God's command (Exod. 25:1–31:11) and Israel's response (Exod. 35:4–40:33). But God did more than tell Israel what he wanted from them. He provided the actual design for it. This is clear from his words to Moses, "In accordance with all that I show you concerning the pattern of the tabernacle and the pattern of all its furniture, so you shall make it" (Exod. 25:9).[36] The Hebrew word for "pattern" (*tavnit*) here pertains to the building and the items associated with it. Architects today use blueprints to direct construction, but it may have been that some kind of archetypal model was in view.[37] Temples were often seen as earthy

---

[36] The translation here slightly modifies the New Revised Standard Version to show how the key word *pattern* appears twice.

[37] Victor Hurowitz, "The Priestly Account of Building the Tabernacle," *Journal of the American Oriental Society* 105 (1985): 22. The word *tavnit* describes the three-dimensional shape of idols (Deut. 4:16–18; Ps. 106:20; Isa. 44:13), a replica of an altar (Josh. 22:28; 2 Kgs. 16:10), and the form of hands (Ezek. 8:3, 10; 10:8).

replicas of celestial sanctuaries (Isa. 6:1–8). By the Spirit, King David received such a pattern for the temple and gave it to his son Solomon, who sponsored the temple's construction (1 Chr. 28:11–12, 19). From the descriptions that follow, it is clear that God's architectural design is exquisite and artful. The principle that God's design precedes God's building is true of Israel's sanctuaries, as well as the New Testament worldwide community of Christians (1 Cor. 3:5–18). The future New Jerusalem is a city only God could design (Rev. 21:10–27). God's work as architect does give dignity to that particular career. But in a general sense, the people of God may engage in their work (whatever it is) with the awareness that God has a design for it too. As we will see next, there are many details to work out within the contours of God's plan, but the Holy Spirit helps with even that.

The accounts of Bezalel, Oholiab, and all of the skilled workers on the tabernacle are full of work-related terms (Exod. 31:1–11; 35:30–36:5). Bezalel and Oholiab are important not only for their work on the taber-nacle, but also as role models for Solomon and Huram-abi who built the temple.[38] The comprehensive set of crafts included metalwork in gold, silver, and bronze as well as stonework and woodwork. The fabrication of garments would have required getting wool, spinning it, dyeing it, weaving it, designing clothes, manufacturing and tailoring them, and the work of embroidery. The craftsmen even prepared anointing oil and fra-grant incense. What unites all of these practices is God filling the work-ers with his Spirit. The Hebrew word for "ability" and "skill" in these texts (*hokhmah)* is usually translated as "wisdom," which causes us to think about the use of words and decision-making. Here, it describes work that is clearly hands-on yet spiritual in the fullest theological sense (Exod. 28:3; 31:3, 6; 35:26, 31, 35; 36:1–2).

The wide range of construction activities in this passage illustrates, but does not exhaust, what building in the ancient Near East entailed. Since God inspired them, we can safely assume he desired them and blessed them. But do we really need texts like these to assure us that God approves of these kinds of work? What about related skills that are

---

[38] Raymond B. Dillard, *2 Chronicles*, vol. 15, *Word Biblical Commentary* (Dallas: Word, 1998), 4–5.

not mentioned? Somewhat facetiously, had the tabernacle needed an air-conditioning system, we assume God would have given plans for a good one. Robert Banks wisely recommends, "In the biblical writings, we should not interpret comparisons with the [modern] process of construction in too narrow or job-specific a fashion. Occasionally this may be justified, but generally not."[39] The point here is not that God cares more about certain types of labor than others. The Bible does not have to name every noble profession for us to see it as a godly thing to do. Just as people were not made for the Sabbath but the Sabbath for people (Mark 2:27), building and cities are made for people too. The law that ancient houses be built with a protective parapet around the flat roof (Deut. 22:8) illustrates God's concern for responsible construction that truly serves and protects people. The point about the Spirit-gifting of the tabernacle-workers is that God cared about *this particular* project for *these particular* purposes. Based on that truth, perhaps the enduring lesson for us in our work today is that whatever God's work is, he does not leave his great work in our unskilled hands. The ways in which he equips us for his work may be as varied as are those many tasks. In divine faithfulness, the spiritual gifts God gives to us will strengthen us in doing God's work to the very end (1 Cor. 1:4–9). He provides us with every blessing in abundance so that we may share abundantly in every good work (2 Cor. 9:8).

Conclusions from Exodus

In Exodus, we see God bring his people out of oppressive labor into the glorious freedom of the children of God. It is not a freedom from working, but a freedom to love and serve the Lord through work in every aspect of life. God provides guidance for life and labor that will glorify him and bless Israel. And he provides a place for his presence to bless all they do.

---

[39] Robert Banks, *God the Worker: Journeys into the Mind, Heart, and Imagination of God* (Eugene, OR: Wipf & Stock, 2008), 349.

Leviticus and Work

Introduction—Does Leviticus Have Anything to Tell Us about Our Work?

Leviticus is a great source for people seeking guidance about their work. It is filled with direct, practical instructions, even though the action takes place in a workplace different from what most of us experience today. Moreover, Leviticus is one of the central places where God reveals himself and his aims for our life and work. The book is at the physical center of the Pentateuch, the third of the five books of Moses that form the narrative and theological foundation of the Old Testament. The second book, Exodus, tells what God took his people *out of*. Leviticus tells what God leads his people *into*,[1] a life full of the God's own presence. In Leviticus, work is one of the most important arenas where God is present with Israel, and God is still present with his people in our work today.

Leviticus is also central to Jesus' teaching and the rest of the New Testament. The Great Commandment that Jesus taught (Mark 12:28–31) comes directly from Leviticus 19:18: "You shall love your neighbor as yourself." The "Year of Jubilee" in Leviticus 25 lies at the center of Jesus' mission statement: "The Spirit of the Lord is upon me, because he has anointed me to . . . proclaim the year of the Lord's favor [the Jubilee]" (Luke 4:18–19). When Jesus said that "not one letter, not one stroke" of the law would pass away (Matt. 5:18), many of those letters and strokes are found in Leviticus. Jesus offered a new take on the law—that the way to fulfill the law is not found in complying with regulations, but in cooperating with the purposes for which God created the law. We are to fulfill the law in a "more excellent way" (1 Cor. 12:31) that surpasses,

---

[1]Nine times the book of Leviticus refers to the Lord having brought Israel out of Egypt, often as a motive for Israel's future obedience (11:45; 19:36; 22:33; 23:43; 25:38, 42, 55; 26:13, 45).

not ignores, the letter of the law. If we wish to fulfill the Spirit of the law, as Jesus did, then we must begin by learning what the law actually says. Much of it is found in Leviticus, and much of it applies to work.

Because Leviticus is central to Jesus' teaching about work, as followers of Jesus we are right to go to the book for guidance about God's will for our work. Of course, we must keep in mind that the codes in Leviticus must be understood and applied to the different economic and social situations today. Current society does not stand in a close parallel to ancient Israel, either in terms of our societal structure or our covenant relationship. Most workers today, for example, have little need to know what to do with an ox or sheep that has been torn apart by wild animals (Lev. 7:24). The Levitical priesthood to whom much of the book is addressed—priests performing animal sacrifice to the God of Israel—no longer exists. Moreover, in Christ we understand the law to be an instrument of God's grace in a way different from how ancient Israel did. So we cannot simply quote Leviticus as if nothing has changed in the world. We cannot read a verse and proclaim "Thus says the Lord" as a judgment against those we disagree with. Instead, we have to understand the meaning, purposes, and mind of God revealed in Leviticus, and then ask God's wisdom to apply Leviticus today. Only so will our lives reflect his holiness, honor his intentions, and enact the rule of his heavenly kingdom on earth.

The Foundational Concept of Holiness in Leviticus

The book of Leviticus is grounded in the truth that God is holy. The word *qodesh* occurs over a hundred times in the Hebrew text of Leviticus. To say that God is holy means that he is completely separate from all evil or defect. Or to put it in another way, God is completely and perfectly good. The Lord is worthy of total allegiance, exclusive worship, and loving obedience.

Israel's identity arises because by God's actions they *are* holy, yet also because the Lord expects Israel to *act* holy in practical ways. Israel is called to be holy because the Lord himself is holy (Lev. 11:44–45; 19:2; 20:7; 21:8). The seemingly disparate laws of Leviticus that deal with the ritual, ethical, commercial, and penal aspects of life all rest on this core notion of holiness.

Alexander Hill, then, is following Leviticus's central principle when he grounds his discussion of Christian business ethics on God's holiness, justice, and love. "A business act is ethical if it reflects God's holy-just-loving character."[2] Hill claims that Christians in business reflect divine holiness when they have zeal for God who is their ultimate priority, and who then behave with purity, accountability, and humility. These, rather than trying to reproduce the commercial code designed for an agrarian society, are what it means to put Leviticus into practice today. This does not mean ignoring the specifics of the law, but discerning how God is guiding us to fulfill it in today's context.

Holiness in Leviticus is not separation for separation's sake, but for the sake of a thriving community of the people of God and the reconciliation of each person to God. Holiness is not only about individuals' behavior following regulations, but about how what each person does affects the whole people of God in their life together and their work as agents of God's kingdom. In this light, Jesus' call for his people to be "salt" and "light" to outsiders (Matt. 5:13–16) makes complete sense. To be holy is to go beyond the law to love your neighbor, to love even your enemy, and to "be perfect, therefore, as your heavenly Father is perfect" (Matt. 5:48, echoing Lev. 19:2).

In short, ancient Israel did not obey Leviticus as a peculiar set of regulations, but as an expression of God's presence in their midst. This is as relevant to God's people today as it was then. In Leviticus, God is taking a collection of nomadic tribes and shaping their culture as a people. Likewise today, when God's people enter their places of work, through them God is shaping the cultures of their work units, organizations, and communities. God's call to be holy, even as he is holy, is a call to shape our cultures for the good.

Israel's Sacrificial System (Leviticus 1–10)

The book of Leviticus opens with regulations for Israel's sacrificial system, conveyed from two perspectives. The first perspective is that

---

[2] Alexander Hill, *Just Business: Christian Ethics for the Marketplace*, 2nd ed. (Downers Grove, IL: IVP Academic, 2008), 15.

of the laypersons who bring the sacrifice and participate in its offering (chapters 1–5). The second perspective is that of the priests who officiate (chapters 6–7). After this, we learn how the priests were ordained and began their ministry at the tabernacle (chapters 8–9), followed by further regulations for the priests in light of how God put the priests Nadab and Abihu to death for violating God's command about their ritual responsibilities (chapter 10). We should not assume that this material is empty liturgy irrelevant to the world of modern work. Instead, we must look through the way the people of Israel coped with their problems in order to explore how we, as people in Christ, may cope with ours—including the challenges we face in business and work.

The Dwelling of God in the Community (Leviticus 1–10)

The purpose of sacrifice was not merely to remedy occasional lapses of purity. The Hebrew verb for "offering" a sacrifice means literally to "bring (it) near." Bringing a sacrifice near to the sanctuary brought the worshipper near to God. The worshipper's individual degree of misbehavior was not the main issue. The pollution caused by impurity is the consequence of the entire community, comprised of the relative few who have committed either brazen or inadvertent sins *together with* the silent majority that has allowed the wicked to flourish in their midst. The people as a whole bear collective responsibility for corrupting society and thus giving God legitimate reason to depart his sanctuary, an event tantamount to destruction of the nation.[3] Drawing near to God is still the aim of those who call Jesus "Immanuel" ("God with us"). The dwelling of God with his people is a serious matter indeed.

Christians in their workplaces should look beyond finding godly tips for finding whatever the world defines as "success." Being aware that God is holy and that he desires to dwell at the center of our lives changes our orientation from success to holiness, whatever work God has called us to do. This does not mean doing religious activities at work, but doing all our work as God would have us do it. Work is not primarily a way to enjoy the fruit of our labor, but a way to experience God's presence. Just

---

[3] Jacob Milgrom, *Leviticus: A Book of Ritual and Ethics, A Continental Commentary* (Minneapolis: Fortress Press, 2004), 15.

as Israel's sacrifices were a "pleasing odor" to the Lord (Lev. 1:9 and six-teen other instances), Paul called Christians to "lead lives worthy of the Lord, fully pleasing to him" (Col. 1:10), "for we are the aroma of Christ to God" (2 Cor. 2:15).

What might result if we walked through our workplaces and asked the fundamental question, "How could this be a place for God's holy presence?" Does our workplace encourage people to express the best of what God has given them? Is it a place characterized by the fair treat-ment of all? Does it protect workers from harm? Does it produce goods and services that help the community to thrive more fully?

The Whole People of God at Work (Leviticus 1–10)

Leviticus brings together the perspectives of two groups who were often at odds against each other—the priests and the people. Its pur-pose is to bring the whole people of God together, without regard to distinctions of status. In today's workplace, how are Christians to handle offenses between people regardless of their wealth or position in the company? Do we tolerate abuses of power when the result seems expe-dient to our careers? Do we participate in judging co-workers by gossip and innuendo, or do we insist on airing grievances through unbiased systems? Do we pay attention to the harm that bullying and favoritism do at work? Do we promote a positive culture, foster diversity, and build a healthy organization? Do we enable open and trustworthy communica-tion, minimize backdoor politicking, and strive for top performance? Do we create an atmosphere where ideas are surfaced and explored, and the best ones put into action? Do we focus on sustainable growth?

Israel's sacrificial system addressed not only the religious needs of the people, but their psychological and emotional ones as well, thus em-bracing the whole person and the whole community. Christians under-stand that businesses have aims that are not usually religious in nature. Yet we also know that people are not equivalent to what they do or pro-duce. This does not reduce our commitment to work at being productive, but it reminds us that because God has embraced us with his forgiveness, we have even more reason than others to be considerate, fair, and gra-cious to all (Luke 7:47; Eph. 4:32; Col. 3:13).

The Workplace Significance of the Guilt Offering (Leviticus 6:1–7)

Each offering in Israel's sacrificial system has its place, but there is a special feature of the guilt offering (also known as the reparation offering) that makes it particularly relevant to the world of work. The guilt offering of Leviticus is the seed of the biblical doctrine of repentance.[4] (Numbers 5:5–10 is directly parallel.) According to Leviticus, God required offerings whenever a person deceived another with regard to a deposit or a pledge, committed robbery or fraud, lied about lost property that had been found, or swore falsely about a matter (Lev. 6:2–3). It was not a fine imposed by a court of law, but a reparation offered by perpetrators who got away with the offense, but who then felt guilty later when they came to "realize" their guilt (Lev. 6:4–5). Repentance by the sinner, not prosecution by the authorities, is the basis of the guilt offering.

Often such sins would have been committed in the context of commerce or other work. The guilt offering calls for the remorseful sinner to return what was wrongfully taken plus 20 percent (Lev. 6:4–5). Only after settling the matter on a human level may the sinner receive forgiveness from God by presenting an animal to the priest for sacrifice (Lev. 6:6–7).

The guilt offering uniquely emphasizes several principles about healing personal relationships that have been damaged by financial abuse.

1. Mere apology is not enough to right the wrong, and neither is full restoration for what was taken. In addition, something akin to today's concept of punitive damages was added. But with guilt offerings—unlike court-ordered punitive damages—offenders willingly take on a share of the harm themselves, thereby sharing in the distress they caused the victim.

2. Doing all that is required to right a wrong against another person is not only fair for the offended, but it is also good for the offender. The guilt offering recognizes the torment that seizes the conscience of those who become aware of their crime and its damaging effects. It then provides a way for the guilty to deal more fully with the

---

[4] Jacob Milgrom, *Leviticus 1–16* (New Haven: Yale University Press, 1998), 345.

matter, bringing a measure of closure and peace. This offering expresses God's mercy in that the pain and hurt is neutralized so as not to fester and erupt into violence or more serious offenses. It also extinguishes the need for the victim (or the victim's family) to take matters into their own hands to exact restitution.

3. Nothing in Jesus' atoning work on the cross releases the people of God today from the need for making restitution. Jesus taught his disciples, "So when you are offering your gift at the altar, if you remember that your brother or sister has something against you, leave your gift there before the altar and go; first be reconciled to your brother or sister, and then come and offer your gift" (Matt. 5:23–24). Loving our neighbors as ourselves lies at the heart of the law's requirements (Lev. 19:18 as quoted in Rom. 13:9), and making restitution is an essential expression of any genuine kind of love. Jesus granted salvation to the rich tax collector Zacchaeus who offered more restitution than the law required, lifting him up as an example of those who truly understood forgiveness (Luke 19:1–10).

4. Jesus' words in Matthew 5:23–24 also teach us that settling matters with people is a necessary prerequisite for making things right with God. Forgiveness from God is a stage of redemption that goes beyond, but does not replace, restitution.

The guilt offering is a potent reminder that God does not exercise his right of forgiveness at the expense of people harmed by our misdeeds. He does not offer us psychological release from our guilt as a cheap substitute for making right the damage and hurt we have caused.

The Unclean and the Clean (Leviticus 11–16)

At the heart of it, Leviticus 11:45 explains the thematic logic of this entire section. "I am the Lord who brought you up from the land of Egypt, to be your God; you shall be holy, for I am holy" (Lev. 11:45). God calls Israel to mirror his holiness in every aspect of life. Leviticus 11–16 deals with the classification of "clean" and "unclean" food (chapter 11) and rites of cleansing (chapters 12–15). It closes with the procedure for celebrating the Day of Atonement to cleanse the people and God's sanctuary (chapter 16).

Christians also recognize that every aspect of our lives is meant to be a response to God's holy presence among us. But the subjects and scope of the laws in Leviticus tend to baffle us today. Are there enduring ethical principles to be found in these particular regulations? For example, it's hard to understand the rationale for why God permitted Israel to eat some animals and not others. Why is there such concern for particular skin diseases (which we cannot even identify today with certainty) and not other, more serious diseases? Of all the ills facing society, is the issue of mold really all that important? Narrowing our focus to matters of work, should we expect these texts to tell us anything we can apply to the food industry, medicine, or environmental contamination of homes and workspaces? As noted before, we will find answers not by asking whether to obey regulations made for a different situation, but by looking for how the passages guide us to serve the welfare of the community.

The Permissibility of Eating Particular Animals (Leviticus 11)

There are several plausible theories about the rules governing animals for human consumption in Leviticus 11. Each cites supporting evidence, yet none enjoys a general consensus. Sorting them out is beyond our scope here, but Jacob Milgrom offers a perspective directly related to the workplace.[5] He notes three dominant elements: God severely limited Israel's choice of animal food, gave them specific rules for slaughter, and prohibited them from eating blood that represents life and therefore belongs to God alone. In light of these, Milgrom concludes that Israel's dietary system was a method of controlling the human instinct to kill. In short, "Though they may satisfy their appetite for food, they must curb their hunger for power. Because life is inviolable it may not be tampered with indiscriminately."[6] If God chooses to get involved in the details of

---

[5] Milgrom, *Leviticus*, 704–42.
[6] Milgrom, *Leviticus 1–16*, 105.

which animals may be killed and how it is to be done, how could we miss the point that the killing of humans is even more restricted and subject to God's scrutiny? This view suggests more applicability to the present day. For example, if every agricultural, animal, and food service facility practiced daily accountability to God for the treatment and condition of its animals, wouldn't it be all the more attentive to the safety and working conditions of its people?

In spite of the extensive details in Leviticus that initiate the ongoing discussion of food in the Bible, it would be inappropriate for any Christian to try to dictate what all believers must do and avoid doing regarding the provision, preparation, and consumption of food. Nonetheless, whatever we eat or don't eat, Derek Tidball rightly reminds Christians of the centrality of holiness. Whatever one's stance on these complex issues, it cannot be divorced from the Christian's commitment to holiness. Holiness calls upon us even to eat and drink "for the glory of God."[7] The same applies to the work of producing, preparing, and consuming food and drink.

Dealing with Skin Diseases and Mold Infections (Leviticus 13–14)

In contrast to the dietary laws, the laws about diseases and environmental contamination *do* seem to be primarily concerned with health. Health is a critical issue today as well, and even if the book of Leviticus were not in the Bible, it would still be a noble and godly concern. But it would be unwise to assume that Leviticus provides instructions for coping with contagious diseases and environmental contamination that we can directly apply today. At our distance of thousands of years from that time period, it is difficult even to be certain exactly what diseases the passages refer to. The enduring message of Leviticus is that the Lord is the God of life and that he guides, honors, and ennobles all those who bring healing to people and the environment. If the particular rules of Leviticus do not dictate the way we perform the work of healing and environmental protection, then certainly this greater point does.

---

[7] Derek Tidball, *The Message of Leviticus* (Downers Grove, IL: InterVarsity Press, 1996), 15.

Holiness (Leviticus 17–27)

Some of the instructions in the holiness code seem relevant only in Israel's ancient world, while others seem timeless. On the one hand, Leviticus tells men not to mar the edges of their beards (Lev. 19:27), but on the other hand, judges must not render unfair judgments in court but show justice to all (Lev. 19:15). How do we know which ones apply directly today? Mary Douglas helpfully explains how a clear understanding of holiness as moral *order* both grounds these instructions in God and makes sense of their variety.

> Developing the idea of holiness as order, not confusion, upholds rectitude and straight-dealing as holy, and contradiction and double-dealing as against holiness. Theft, lying, false witness, cheating in weights and measures, all kinds of dissembling such as speaking ill of the deaf (and presumably smiling to their faces), hating your brother in your heart (while presumably speaking kindly to him), these are clearly contradictions between what seems and what is.[8]

Some aspects of what leads to good order (e.g., the trimming of beards) may be important in one context but not in another. Others are essential in all situations. We can sort them out by asking what contributes to good order in our particular contexts. Here we shall explore passages that touch directly on matters of work and economics.

Gleaning (Leviticus 19:9–10)

Although ancient methods of harvesting were not as efficient as today, Leviticus 19:9–10 instructs Israelites to make them even *less* so. First, they were to leave the margins of their grain fields unharvested. The width of this margin appears to be up to the owner to decide. Second, they were not to pick up whatever produce fell to the ground. This would apply when a harvester grasped a bundle of stalks and cut them with the sickle, as well as when grapes fell from a cluster just cut from the vine. Third, they were to harvest their vineyards just once, presumably taking

---

[8] Mary Douglas, *Purity and Danger: An Analysis of the Concepts of Pollution and Taboo* (London: Routledge, 1966), 53–54.

only the ripe grapes so as to leave the later ripening ones for their poor and the immigrants living among them.⁹ These two categories of people— the poor and resident foreigners—were unified by their lack of owning land and thus were dependent on their own manual labor for food. Laws benefiting the poor were common in the ancient Near East, but only the regulations of Israel extended this treatment to the resident foreigner. This was yet another way that God's people were to be distinct from the surrounding nations. Other texts specify the widow and the orphan as members of this category. (Other biblical references to gleaning include Exod. 22:21–27; Deut. 24:19–21; Judg. 8:2; Ruth 2:17–23; Job 24:6; Isa. 17:5–6; 24:13; Jer. 6:9, 49:9; Obad. 1:5; Mic. 7:1.)

We might classify gleaning as an expression of compassion or justice, but according to Leviticus, allowing others to glean on our property is the fruit of holiness. We do it because God says, "I am the LORD your God" (Lev. 19:10). This highlights the distinction between charity and gleaning. In charity, people voluntarily give to others who are in need. This is a good and noble thing to do, but it is not what Leviticus is talking about. Gleaning is a process in which landowners have an *obligation* to provide poor and marginalized people access to the means of production (in Leviticus, the land) and to work it *themselves*. Unlike charity, it does not depend on the generosity of landowners. In this sense, it was much more like a tax than a charitable contribution. Also unlike charity, it was not given to the poor as a transfer payment. Through gleaning, the poor earned their living the same way as the landowners did, by working the fields with their own labors. It was simply a command that everyone had a right to access the means of provision created by God.

In contemporary societies, it may not be easy to discern how to apply the principles of gleaning. In many countries, land reform is certainly needed so that land is securely available to farmers, rather than being controlled by capricious government officials or landowners who ob- tained it corruptly. In more industrialized and knowledge-based econo- mies, land is not the chief factor of production. Access to education, capital, product and job markets, transport systems, and nondiscrimina- tory laws and regulations may be what poor people need to be productive.

---

⁹ Milgrom, *Leviticus 1–16*, 225.

As Christians may not be more capable than anyone else of determining precisely what solutions will be most effective, solutions need to come from across society. Certainly Leviticus does not contain a system ready-made for today's economies. But the gleaning system in Leviticus does place an obligation on the owners of productive assets to ensure that marginalized people have the opportunity to work for a living. No individual owner can provide opportunities for every unemployed or underemployed worker, of course, no more than any one farmer in ancient Israel could provide gleanings for the entire district. But owners are called to be the point people in providing opportunities for work. Perhaps Christians in general are also called to appreciate the service that business owners do in their role as job creators in their communities.

(For more on gleaning in the Bible, see "Exodus 22:21–27" in *Exodus and Work* above and "Ruth 2:17–23" in *Ruth and Work* at www.theologyofwork.org.)

Behaving Honestly (Leviticus 19:11–12)

The commands in Leviticus against stealing, dealing falsely, lying, and violating God's name by swearing to false oaths all find more familiar expression among the Ten Commandments of Exodus 20. (For more on honesty, see "Truth-telling in the Bible" and "There May Be Exceptions to Truth-telling in the Workplace," in the article *Truth & Deception* at www.theologyofwork.org.) Unique to Leviticus, however, is the Hebrew wording behind "you shall not lie *to one another*" (Lev. 19:11; emphasis added). Literally, it says that "a person shall not lie to his *amit*," meaning "companion," "friend," or "neighbor." This surely includes fellow members of Israel's community; but based on Leviticus 24:19 in the context of Leviticus 24:17–22, it also seems to take in the resident alien. Israel's ethics and morality were to be distinctly better than the nations around them, even to the point of treating immigrants from other nations the same way they treated native-born citizens.

In any case, the point here is the relational aspect of telling the truth versus lying. A lie is not only a misstatement of cold fact, but it is also a betrayal of a companion, friend, or neighbor. What we say to each other must truly flow out of God's holiness in us, not merely out of a technical analysis of avoiding blatant lies. When U.S. president Bill Clinton said, "I did not have sexual relations with that woman," he may have had some tortuous logic in mind under which the statement was not technically a lie. But his fellow citizens rightly felt that he had broken trust with them, and he later recognized and accepted this assessment. He had violated the duty not to lie *to another*.

In many workplaces, there is a need to promote either the positive or negative aspects of a product, service, person, organization, or situation. Christians need not refuse to communicate vigorously to make a point. But they must not communicate in such a way that what they convey *to another* is false. If technically true words add up to a false impression in the mind of *another*, then the duty to tell the truth is broken. As a practical matter, whenever a discussion of truthfulness descends into a technical debate about wording, it's wise to ask ourselves if the debate is about whether to lie *to another* in this sense.

Treating Workers Fairly (Leviticus 19:13)

"You shall not defraud your neighbor; you shall not steal; and you shall not keep for yourself the wages of a laborer until morning" (Lev. 19:13). Day laborers were generally poorer people who lacked land to farm themselves. They were especially dependent on immediate payment for their work, and thus needed to be paid at the close of each day (cf. Deut. 24:14–15). In our world, a comparable situation occurs when employers have the power to dictate terms and conditions of labor that take advantage of workers' vulnerabilities. This occurs, for example, when employees are pressed to contribute to their bosses' favored political candidates or expected to continue working after clocking out. These practices are illegal in most places, but unfortunately remain common.

A more controversial state of affairs concerns day laborers who lack documentation for legal employment. This situation occurs around the world, applying to refugees, internally displaced persons, rural citizens lacking urban residency permits, illegal immigrants, children under the age of legal employment, and others. Such people often work in agriculture, landscaping, piecework manufacturing, food service, and small projects, in addition to illegal occupations. Because both employers and employees are working outside the law, such workers seldom receive the protections of employment agreements and government regulations. Employers may take advantage of their situation by paying them less per hour than legal workers, by denying benefits, and by providing poor or dangerous working conditions. They may be subject to abuse and sexual harassment. In many cases, they are completely at the mercy of the employer. Is it legitimate for employers to treat them this way? Surely not.

But what if people in such situations offer themselves for substandard employment apparently willingly? In many places, undocumented workers are available outside garden and building supply stores, at agricultural markets, and other gathering places. Is it right to employ them? If so, is it the employers' responsibility to provide the things legal workers get by rights, such as the minimum wage, health benefits, retirement plans, sick pay, and termination benefits? Must Christians be strict about the legality of such employment, or should we be flexible on the grounds that legislation has not yet caught up with reality? Thoughtful Christians will inevitably differ in their conclusions about this, and so it is difficult to justify a "one size fits all" solution. However a Christian processes these issues, Leviticus reminds us that holiness (and not practical expediency) must be at the core of our thinking. And holiness in labor matters arises out of a concern for the needs of the most vulnerable workers.

Rights of People with Disabilities (Leviticus 19:14)

"You shall not revile the deaf or put a stumbling block before the blind; you shall fear your God: I am the Lord" (Lev. 19:14). These commands paint a vivid picture of cruel treatment of people with disabilities. A deaf person could not hear such a curse, nor could a blind person see the block. For these reasons, Leviticus 19:14 reminds Israelites to "fear your God" who hears and sees how *everyone* is treated in the workplace. For example, workers with disabilities do not necessarily need the same office furniture and equipment as those without disabilities. But they *do* need to be offered the opportunity for employment to the full extent of their productivity, like everyone else. In many cases, what people with disabilities most need is not to be *prevented* from working in jobs they are capable of doing. Again, the command in Leviticus is not that the people of God ought to be charitable to others, but that the holiness of God gives all people created in his image the *right* to appropriate opportunities for work.

Doing Justice (Leviticus 19:15–16)

"You shall not render an unjust judgment; you shall not be partial to the poor or defer to the great: with justice you shall judge your neighbor. You shall not go around as a slanderer among your people, and you shall not profit by the blood of your neighbor: I am the LORD." (Lev. 19:15–16)

This short section upholds the familiar biblical value of justice and then broadens considerably. The first verse begins with an application for judges, but ends with an application for everyone. Do not judge court cases with partiality, and don't judge your neighbor unfairly. The wording of the Hebrew highlights the temptation to judge the external appearance of a person or issue. Woodenly rendered, Leviticus 19:15 says, "Do not do injustice in judgment. Do not lift up the face of the poor one and do not honor the face of the great one. With rightness you shall judge your neighbor." Judges must look through their preconceptions (the "face" they perceive) in order to understand the issue impartially. The same is true of our social relationships at work, school, and civic life. In every context, some people are privileged and others oppressed because of social biases of every kind. Imagine the difference Christians could make if we simply waited to make judgments until knowing people and situations in depth. What if we took the time to know the annoying person on our team before complaining behind his or her back? What if we dared to spend time with people outside our comfort zone at school, university, or civic life? What if we sought out newspaper, TV, and media that offer a different perspective from what we are comfortable with? Would digging below the surface give us greater wisdom to do our work well and justly?

The latter part of Leviticus 19:16 reminds us that social bias is no light matter. Literally, the Hebrew says, "Do not stand by the blood of your neighbor." In the language of the courtroom in the previous verse, biased testimony ("slander") endangers the life ("blood") of the accused.

In that case, not only would it be wrong to speak biased words, but it would be wrong even to stand idly by without volunteering to testify on behalf of the falsely accused.

Leaders in workplaces must often act in the role of an arbiter. Workers may witness an injustice in the workplace and legitimately question whether or not it is appropriate to get involved. Leviticus claims that proactively standing in favor of the mistreated is an essential element of belonging to God's holy people.

On a larger level, Leviticus brings its theological vision of holiness to bear on the whole community. The health of the community and the economy we share is at stake. Hans Küng points out the necessary interrelationship of business, politics, and religion:

> It should not be forgotten that economic thought and actions, too, are not value-free or value-neutral. . . . Just as the social and ecological responsibility of business cannot simply be foisted onto politicians, so moral and ethical responsibility cannot simply be foisted onto religion. . . . No, ethical action should not be just a private addition to marketing plans, sales strategies, ecological bookkeeping and social balance-sheets, but should form the natural framework for human social action.[10]

Every kind of workplace—home, business, government, academia, medicine, agriculture, and all the rest—have a distinctive role to play. Yet all of them are called to be holy. In Leviticus 19:15–16, holiness begins by seeing others with a depth of insight that gets beneath face value.

Loving Your Neighbor as Yourself (Leviticus 19:17–18)

The most famous verse in Leviticus may be the command, "Love your neighbor as yourself" (Lev. 19:18). This imperative is so sweeping that both Jesus and the rabbis regarded it as one of the two "great" commandments, the other being "Hear, O Israel: the LORD our God, the LORD is one" (Mark 12:29–31; cf. Deut. 6:4). In quoting Leviticus 19:18, the Apostle Paul wrote that "love is the fulfilling of the law" (Rom. 13:10).

---

[10] Hans Küng, *Global Responsibility: In Search of a New World Ethic* (New York: Continuum, 1993), 32–33, quoted in Roy Gane, *The NIV Application Commentary: Leviticus, Numbers* (Grand Rapids: Zondervan, 2004), 352.

Working for Others as Much as for Ourselves

The crux of the command lies in the words "as yourself." At least to some degree, most of us work to provide for ourselves. There is a strong element of self-interest in working. We know that if we don't work, we won't eat. Scripture commends this motivation (2 Thess. 3:10), yet the "as yourself" aspect of Leviticus 19:18 suggests that we should be equally motivated to serve others through our work. This is a high call—to work as much to serve others as to meet our own needs. If we had to work twice as long to accomplish it—say one shift a day for ourselves and another shift for our neighbor—it would be nearly impossible.

Providentially, it is possible to love ourselves and our neighbors through the same work, at least to the degree that our work provides something of value to customers, citizens, students, family members, and other consumers. A teacher receives a salary that pays the bills, and at the same time imbues students with knowledge and skills that will be equally valuable to them. A hotel housekeeper receives wages while providing guests with a clean and healthy room. In most jobs, we would not stay employed for long if we don't provide a value to others at least equal to what we draw in pay. But what if we find ourselves in a situation where we can skew the benefits in favor of ourselves? Some people may have enough power to command salaries and bonuses in excess of the value they truly provide. The politically connected or corrupt may be able to wring large rewards for themselves in the form of contracts, subsidies, bonuses, and make-work jobs, while providing little of value for others. Nearly all of us have moments when we can shirk our duties yet still get paid.

Thinking more broadly, if we have a wide range of choices in our work, how much of a role does serving others make in our job decisions, compared to making the most for ourselves? Almost every kind of work can serve others and please God. But that does not mean that every job or work opportunity is of equal service to others. We love ourselves when we make work choices that bring us high pay, prestige, security, comfort, and easy work. We love others when we choose work that provides needed goods and services, opportunities for marginalized people, protection for God's creation, justice and democracy, truth, peace, and beauty. Leviticus 19:18 suggests that the latter should be as important to us as the former.

Be Nice?

Instead of striving to meet this high calling, it is easy to relax our understanding of "love your neighbor as yourself" into something banal like "be nice." But being nice is often nothing more than a facade and an excuse for disengaging from the people around us. Leviticus 19:17 commands us to do the opposite. "Reprove your neighbor, or you will incur guilt yourself" (Lev. 19:17). These two commands—both to love and to reprove your neighbor—seem like unlikely fellows, but they are brought together in the proverb, "Better is open rebuke than hidden love" (Prov. 27:5).

Regrettably, too often the lesson we absorb at church is always to be nice. If this becomes our rule in the workplace, it can have disastrous personal and professional effects. Niceness can lull Christians into allowing bullies and predators to abuse and manipulate them and to do the same to others. Niceness can lead Christian managers to gloss over workers' shortcomings in performance reviews, depriving them of a reason to sharpen their skills and keep their jobs in the long run. Niceness may lead anyone into holding onto resentment, bearing a grudge, or seeking revenge. Leviticus tells us that loving people sometimes means making an honest rebuke. This is not a license for insensitivity. When we rebuke, we need to do so with humility—we may also need to be rebuked in the situation—and compassion.

Who Is My Neighbor? (Leviticus 19:33–34)

Leviticus teaches that Israelites must not "oppress" resident foreigners (Lev. 19:33). (The same Hebrew verb appears in Lev. 25:17, "You shall not cheat one another.") The command continues, "The alien who resides with you shall be to you as the citizen among you; you shall love the alien as yourself, for you were aliens in the land of Egypt: I am the LORD your God" (Lev. 19:34). This verse is a particularly strong example of the unbreakable connection in Leviticus between the moral force of the law ("love the alien as yourself") and the very being of God, "I am the LORD your God." You do not oppress foreigners because you belong to a God who is holy.

Resident aliens, along with widows and the poor (see Lev. 19:9–10 above), typify outsiders lacking power. In today's workplaces, power differentials arise not only from nationality and gender differences, but also from a variety of other factors. Whatever the cause, most workplaces develop a hierarchy of power that is well known to everyone, regardless of whether it is openly acknowledged. From Leviticus 19:33–34, we may conclude that Christians should treat other people fairly in business as an expression of genuine worship of God.

Trading Fairly (Leviticus 19:35–36)

This passage prohibits cheating in business by falsely measuring length, weight, or quality, and is made more specific by reference to scales and stones, the standard equipment of trade. The various measurements mentioned indicate that this rule would apply across a wide spectrum, from tracts of land to the smallest measure of dry and wet goods. The Hebrew word *tsedeq* (NRSV "honest") that appears four times in Leviticus 19:36 denotes character that is right in terms of having integrity and being blameless. All weights and measures should be accurate. In short, buyers should get what they have paid for.

Sellers possess a vast array of means to deliver less than what buyers think they are getting. These are not limited to falsified measurements of weight, area, and volume. Exaggerated claims, misleading statistics, irrelevant comparisons, promises that can't be kept, "vaporware," and hidden terms and conditions are merely the tip of the iceberg. (For applications in various workplaces, see "Truth-telling in the Workplace" at www.theologyofwork.org.)

A woman who works for a large credit card issuer tells a disturbing story along these lines.

> Our business is providing credit cards to poor people with bad credit histories. Although we charge high interest rates, our customers' default rate is so high that we can't make a profit simply by charging interest. We have to find a way to generate fees. One challenge is that most of our customers are afraid of debt, so they pay their monthly balance on time. No fees for us that way. So we have a trick for catching them off-guard. For the first six months, we send them a bill on the 15th of the month, due the 15th of the following month. They learn the pattern and diligently send us the payment on the 14th every month. On the seventh month, we send their bill on the 12th, due on the 12th of the next month. They don't notice the

change, and they send us the payment on the 14th as usual. Now we've got them. We charge them a $30 service charge for the late payment. Also, because they are delinquent, we can raise their interest rate. Next month they are already in arrears and they're in a cycle that generates fees for us month after month.[11]

It is hard to see how any trade or business that depends on deceiving or misleading people to make a profit could be a fit line of work for those who are called to follow a holy God.

The Sabbath Year and the Year of Jubilee (Leviticus 25)

Leviticus 25 ordains a sabbath year, one in every seven (Lev. 25:1–7), and a jubilee year, one in every fifty (Lev. 25:8–17), to sanctify Israel's internal economy. In the sabbath year, each field was to lie fallow, which appears to be a sound agricultural practice. The year of jubilee was much more radical. Every fiftieth year, all leased or mortgaged lands were to be returned to their original owners, and all slaves and bonded laborers were to be freed (Lev. 25:10). This naturally posed difficulties in banking and land transactions, and special provisions were designed to ameliorate them (Lev. 25:15–16), which we will explore in a moment. The underlying intent is the same as seen in the law of gleaning (Lev. 19:9–10), to ensure that everyone had access to the means of production, whether the family farm or simply the fruits of their own labor.

There is no clear evidence that Israel ever actually observed the jubilee year or the antislavery provisions associated with it (e.g., Lev. 25:25–28, 39–41). Regardless, the sheer detail of Leviticus 25 strongly suggests that we treat the laws as something that Israel potentially could have implemented. Rather than see the jubilee year as a utopian literary fiction, it seems better to believe that Israel neglected it not because it was unfeasible, but because the wealthy were unwilling to accept the social and economic implications that would have been costly and disruptive to them.

---

[11]Name withheld by request, as told to TOW Project editor William Messenger at a meeting of the Fordham Consortium at Seattle Pacific University, August 5, 2011.

Protection for the Destitute

After Israel conquered Canaan, the land was assigned to Israel's clans and families as described in Numbers 26 and Joshua 15–22. This land was never to be sold in perpetuity for it belonged to the Lord, not the people (Lev. 25:23–24).[12] The effect of the jubilee was to prevent any family from becoming permanently landless through sale, mortgage, or permanent lease of its assigned land. In essence, any sale of land was really a term lease that could last no longer than the next year of jubilee (Lev. 25:15). This provided a means for the destitute to raise money (by leasing the land) without depriving the family's future generations of the means of production. The rules of Leviticus 25 are not easy to figure out, and Milgrom makes good sense of them as he defines three progressive stages of destitution.[13]

1. The first stage is depicted in Leviticus 25:25–28. A person could simply become poor. The presumed scenario is that of a farmer who borrowed money to buy seed but did not harvest enough to repay the loan. He therefore must sell some of the land to a buyer in order to cover the debt and buy seed for the next planting. If there was a person who belonged to the farmer's clan who wished to act as a "redeemer," he could pay the buyer according to the number of remaining annual crops until the jubilee year when it reverted to the farmer. Until that time, the land belonged to the redeemer, who allowed the farmer to work it.

2. The second stage was more serious (Lev. 25:35–38). Assuming that the land was not redeemed and the farmer again fell into debt from which he could not recover, he would forfeit all of his land to the creditor. In this case, the creditor must lend the farmer the funds necessary to continue working as a tenant farmer on his own land, but must not charge him interest. The farmer would amortize this loan with the profit made from the crops, perhaps

---

[12] Christopher J. H. Wright, *The Mission of God: Unlocking the Bible's Grand Narrative* (Downers Grove, IL: IVP Academic, 2006), 296.

[13] Bruce K. Waltke and Charles Yu, *An Old Testament Theology: An Exegetical, Canonical, and Thematic Approach* (Grand Rapids: Zondervan, 2007), 528.

eliminating the debt. If so, the farmer would regain his land. If the loan was not fully repaid before the jubilee, then at that time the land would revert back to the farmer or his heirs.

3. The third stage was more serious still (Lev. 25:39–43). Assuming that the farmer in the previous stage could neither pay on the loan or even support himself and his family, he would become temporarily bound to the household of the creditor. As a bound laborer he would work for wages, which were entirely for reduction of the debt. At the year of jubilee, he would regain his land and his freedom (Lev. 25:41). Throughout these years, the creditor must not work him as a slave, sell him as a slave, or rule over him harshly (Lev. 25:42–43). The creditor must "fear God" by accepting the fact that all of God's people are God's slaves (NRSV "servants") whom he graciously brought out from Egypt. No one else can own them because God already does.

The point of these rules is that Israelites were never to become slaves to other Israelites. It was conceivable, though, that impoverished Israelites might sell themselves as slaves to wealthy resident aliens living in the land (Lev. 25:47–55). Even if this happened, the sale must not be permanent. People who sold themselves must retain the right to buy themselves out of slavery if they prospered. If not, a near relative could intervene as a "redeemer" who would pay the foreigner according to the number of years left until the jubilee when the impoverished Israelites were to be released. During that time, they were not to be treated harshly but be regarded as hired workers.

What Does the Year of Jubilee Mean for Today?

The year of jubilee operated within the context of Israel's kinship system for the protection of the clan's inalienable right to work their ancestral land, which they understood to be owned by God and to be enjoyed by them as a benefit of their relationship with him. These social and economic conditions no longer exist, and from a biblical point of view, God no longer administers redemption through a single political state. We must therefore view the jubilee from our current vantage point.

A wide variety of perspectives exists about the proper application, if any, of the jubilee to today's societies. To take one example that engages seriously with contemporary realities, Christopher Wright has written extensively on the Christian appropriation of Old Testament laws.[14] He identifies principles implicit in these ancient laws in order to grasp their ethical implications for today. His treatment of the jubilee year thus considers three basic angles: the theological, the social, and the economic.[15]

Theologically, the jubilee affirms that the Lord is not only the God who owns Israel's land; he is sovereign over all time and nature. His act of redeeming his people from Egypt committed him to provide for them on every level because they were his own. Therefore, Israel's observance of the Sabbath day and year and the year of jubilee was a function of obedience and trust. In practical terms, the jubilee year embodies the trust all Israelites could have that God would provide for their immediate needs and for the future of their families. At the same time, it calls on the rich to trust that treating creditors compassionately will still yield an adequate return.

Looking at the *social* angle, the smallest unit of Israel's kinship structure was the household that would have included three to four generations. The jubilee provided a socioeconomic solution to keep the family whole even in the face of economic calamity. Family debt was a reality in ancient times as it is today, and its effects include a frightening list of social ills. The jubilee sought to check these negative social consequences by limiting their duration so that future generations would not have to bear the burden of their distant ancestors.[16]

The *economic* angle reveals the two principles that we can apply today. First, God desires just distribution of the earth's resources. According to God's plan, the land of Canaan was assigned equitably among the people. The jubilee was not about redistribution but restoration. According to

---

[14] Milgrom, *Leviticus*, 299–303.

[15] Christopher J. H. Wright, *Old Testament Ethics for the People of God* (Downers Grove, IL: InterVarsity Press, 2004), chapter 9.

[16] The following discussion of these three angles is indebted to Wright's exposition in *Mission of God*, 296–300. Chapter 5, "Economics and the Poor," in *Old Testament Ethics* is also helpful and relevant, but ranges far beyond the jubilee concerns of Leviticus 25.

Wright, "The jubilee thus stands as a critique not only of massive private accumulation of land and related wealth but also of large-scale forms of collectivism or nationalization that destroy any meaningful sense of personal or family ownership."[17] Second, family units must have the opportunity and resources to provide for themselves.

In most modern societies, people cannot be sold into slavery to pay debts. Bankruptcy laws provide relief to those burdened with unpayable debts, and descendants are not liable for ancestors' debts. The basic property needed for survival may be protected from seizure. Nonetheless, Leviticus 25 seems to offer a broader foundation than contemporary bankruptcy laws. It is founded not on merely protecting personal liberty and a bit of property for destitute people, but on ensuring that everyone has access to the means of making a living and escaping multigenerational poverty. As the gleaning laws in Leviticus show, the solution is neither handouts nor mass appropriation of property, but social values and structures that give every person an opportunity to work productively. Have modern societies actually surpassed ancient Israel in this regard? What about the millions of people enslaved or in bonded labor today in situation where anti-slavery laws are not adequately enforced? What would it take for Christians to be capable of offering real solutions?

Conclusions from Leviticus

The single most important conclusion we can draw from Leviticus is that our call as God's people is to reflect God's holiness in our work. This calls us to separate ourselves from the actions of any around us who oppose God's ways. When we reflect God's holiness, we find ourselves in God's presence, whether at work, home, church, or society. We reflect God's holiness not by hanging up Scripture verses, reciting prayers, wearing crosses, or even by being nice. We do it by loving our co-workers, customers, students, investors, competitors, rivals, and everyone we encounter as much as we love ourselves. In practical terms, this means doing as much good for others through our work as we do for ourselves.

---

[17] Wright, *Mission of God*, 296–97.

This enlivens our motivation, our diligence, our exercise of power, our skill development, and perhaps even our choice of work. It also means working for the benefit of the entire community and working in harmony with the rest of society, so far as it depends on us. And it means working to change the structures and systems of society to reflect God's holiness as the one who delivered Israel from slavery and oppression. When we do this, we find by God's grace that his words are fulfilled: "I will place my dwelling in your midst, and I shall not abhor you. And I will walk among you, and will be your God, and you shall be my people" (Lev. 26:11–12).

Numbers and Work

Introduction to Numbers

The book of Numbers contributes significantly to our understanding and practice of work. It shows us God's people, Israel, struggling to work in accordance with God's purposes in challenging times. In their struggles, they experience conflicts about identity, authority, and leadership as they work their way across the wilderness toward God's Promised Land. Most of the insight we can gain for our work comes by example, where we see what pleases God and what does not, rather than by a series of commands.

The book is called "Numbers" in English because it records a series of censuses that Moses took of the tribes of Israel. Censuses were taken to quantify the human and natural resources available for the economic and governmental affairs, including military service (Num. 1:2–3; 26:2–4), religious duties (Num. 4:2–3, 22–23), taxation (Num. 3:40–48), and agriculture (Num. 26:53–54). Effective resource allocation depends on good data. But these censuses serve as a framework for a narrative that goes beyond merely reporting the numbers. In the narratives, the statistics are often misused leading to dissent, rebellion, and social unrest. Quantitative reasoning itself is not the problem—God himself orders censuses (Num. 1:1–2). But when numerical analysis is used as a pretext for deviating from the word of the Lord, disaster follows (Num. 14:20–25). A distant echo of this manipulation of numbers as a substitute for genuine moral reasoning can be heard in today's accounting scandals and financial crises.

Numbers takes place in that wilderness region that is neither Egypt nor the Promised Land. The Hebrew title of the book, *bemidbar,* is shorthand for the phrase "in the wilderness of Sinai" (Num. 1:1), which describes the main action in the book—Israel's journey through the wilderness. The nation progresses from Sinai toward the Promised Land, concluding with Israel in the region east of the Jordan River. They came to be in this location because God's "mighty hand" (Exod. 6:1) had liberated them from slavery in Egypt, the story told in the book of Exodus. Getting the people out of slavery was one matter; getting the slavery out of the people would prove to be quite another. In short, the book of Numbers is about life with God during the journey to the destination of his promises, a journey we as God's people are still undertaking. From Israel's experience in the wilderness, we find resources for challenges in our life and work today, and we can draw encouragement from God's ever-present help.

God Numbers and Orders the Nation of Israel (Numbers 1:1–2:34)

Prior to the Exodus, Israel had never been a nation. Israel began as the family of Abraham and Sarah and their descendants, prospered as a clan under Joseph's leadership, but fell into bondage as an ethnic minority in Egypt. The Israelite population in Egypt grew to become nation-sized (Exod. 12:37) but, as an enslaved people, they were permitted no national institutions or organizations. They had departed Egypt as a barely organized refugee mob (Exod. 12:34–39) who now had to be organized into a functioning nation.

God directs Moses to enumerate the population (the first census, Num. 1:1–3) and create a provisional government headed by tribal leaders (Num. 1:4–16). Under God's further direction, Moses appoints a religious order, the Levites, and equips them with resources to build the tabernacle of the covenant (Num. 1:48–54). He lays out camp housing for all the people, then regiments the men of fighting age into military echelons, and appoints commanders and officers (Num. 2:1–9). He creates a bureaucracy, delegates authority to qualified leaders, and institutes a civil judiciary and court of appeal (this is told in Exodus 18:1–27, rather than in Numbers). Before Israel can come into possession of the Promised Land (Gen. 28:15) and fulfill its mission to bless all the nations (Gen. 18:18), the nation had to be ordered effectively.

Moses' activities of organization, leadership, governance, and resource development are closely paralleled in virtually every sector of
society today—business, government, military, education, religion, non-
profits, neighborhood associations, even families. In this sense, Moses
is the godfather of all managers, accountants, statisticians, economists,
military officers, governors, judges, police, headmasters, community
organizers, and myriad others. The detailed attention Numbers gives
to organizing workers, training leaders, creating civic institutions,
developing logistical capabilities, structuring defenses, and developing accounting systems suggests that God still guides and empowers
the ordering, governing, resourcing, and maintaining of social structures today.

The Levites and the Work of God (Numbers 3–8)

Numbers 3 through 8 focuses on the work of the priests and Levites.
(The Levites are the tribe whose men serve as priests—to a large degree
the terms are interchangeable in Numbers.) They have the essential role
of mediating God's redemption to all the people (Num. 3:40–51). Like
other workers, they are enumerated and organized into work units, although they are exempted from military service (Num. 4:2–3; 22–23). It
may seem that their work is singled out as higher than the work of others, as it "concerns the most holy things" (Num. 4:4). It's true that the
uniquely detailed attention given to the tent of meeting and its utensils
seems to elevate the priests' role above those of the rest of the people.
But the text actually portrays how intricately their work is related to the
work of *all* Israelites. The Levites assist *all* people in bringing their life
and work into line with God's law and purposes. Moreover, the work
performed by the Levites in the tent is quite similar to the work of most
Israelites—breaking, moving and setting up camp, kindling fire, washing
linens, butchering animals, and processing grain. The emphasis, then,
is on the integration of the Levites' work with everyone else's. Numbers
pays careful attention to the priests' work of mediating God's presence,
not because religious work is the most important occupation, but because *God* is the center point of *every* occupation.

Offering God the Products of Human Labor (Numbers 4 and 7)

The Lord gives detailed instructions for setting up the tent of meeting, the location of his presence with Israel. The tent of meeting requires materials produced by a wide variety of workers—fine leather, blue cloth, crimson cloth, curtains, poles and frames, plates, dishes, bowls, flagons, lamp stands, snuffers, trays, oil and vessels to hold it, a golden altar, fire pans, forks, shovels, basins, and fragrant incense (Num. 4:5–15). (For a similar description, see "The Tabernacle" in Exodus 31:1–12 above.) In the course of worship, the people bring into it further products of human labor, such as offerings of drink (Num. 4:7, et al.), grain (4:16, et al.), oil (7:13, et al.), lambs and sheep (6:12, et al.), goats (7:16, et al.), and precious metals (7:25, et al.). Virtually every occupation—indeed nearly every person—in Israel is needed to make it possible to worship God in the tent of meeting.

The Levites fed their families largely with a portion of the sacrifices. These were allotted to the Levites because, unlike the other tribes, they were not given land to farm (Num. 18:18–32). The Levites did not receive sacrifices because *they* were holy men, but because by presiding at sacrifices, they brought *everyone* into a holy relation with God. The people, not the Levites, were the prime beneficiaries of the sacrifices. In fact, the sacrificial system itself was a component in Israel's food supply system. Aside from some portions burned on the altar and the Levites' allotment mentioned above, the main parts of the grain and animal offerings were designated for consumption by those who brought them.[1] Everyone in Israel was thus fed in part by the system. Overall, the sacrificial system did not serve to isolate a few holy things from the rest of human production, but to mediate God's presence in the entire life and work of the nation.

Likewise today, the products and services of all God's people are expressions of God's power at work in human beings, or at least they

[1] David P. Wright, "The Disposal of Impurity: Elimination Rites in the Bible and in Hittite and Mesopotamian Literature," *Society of Biblical Literature Dissertation Studies* 101 (1987): 34–36.

should be. The New Testament develops this theme from the Old Testament explicitly. "You are a chosen race, a royal priesthood, a holy nation, God's own people, in order that you may proclaim the mighty acts of him who called you out of darkness into his marvelous light" (1 Pet. 2:9). All the work we do is priestly work when it proclaims God's goodness. The items we produce—leather and cloth, dishes and plates, construction materials, lesson plans, financial forecasts, and all the rest—are priestly items. The work we do—washing clothes, growing crops, raising children, and every other form of legitimate work—is priestly service to God. All of us are meant to ask, "How does my work reflect the goodness of God, make him visible to those who do not recognize him and serve his purposes in the world?" All believers, not just clergy, are descendants of the priests and Levites in Numbers, doing God's work every day.

Confession and Restitution (Numbers 5:5–10)

An essential role of the people of God is bringing reconciliation and justice to scenes of conflict and abuse. Although the people of Israel bound themselves to obey God's commandments, they routinely fell short, as we do today. Often this took the form of mistreating other people. "When a man or a woman wrongs another, breaking faith with the LORD, that person incurs guilt" (Num. 5:6). Through the work of the Levites, God provides a means of repentance, restitution, and reconciliation in the aftermath of such wrongs. An essential element is that the guilty party not only repays the loss he or she caused, but also adds 20 percent (Num. 5:7), presumably as a way of suffering loss in sympathy with the victim. (This passage is parallel with the guilt offering described in Leviticus; see "The Workplace Significance of the Guilt Offering" in *Leviticus and Work* above.)

The New Testament gives a vivid example of this principle at work. When the tax collector Zacchaeus comes to salvation in Christ, he offers to pay back four times the amount he overcharged his fellow citizens. A more modern example—though not explicitly grounded in the Bible—is the growing practice of hospitals admitting mistakes, apologizing, and offering immediate financial restitution and assistance to patients and families involved.[2] But you don't have to be a tax collector or a medical worker to make mistakes. All of us have ample opportunities to confess our mistakes and offer to make up for them, and more. It is in the workplace where much of this challenge takes place. Yet do we actually do it, or do we try to cover up our shortcomings and minimize our responsibility?

Aaron's Blessing for the People (Numbers 6:22–27)

One of the chief roles of the Levites is invoking God's blessing. God ordains these words for the priestly blessing:

> The LORD bless you and keep you;
> the LORD make his face to shine upon you, and be gracious to you;
> the LORD lift up his countenance upon you, and give you peace.
>   (Num. 6:24–26)

God blesses people in countless ways—spiritual, mental, emotional, and material. But the focus here is on blessing people with words. Our good words become the moment of God's grace in the lives of people. "So they shall put my name on the Israelites, and I will bless them," God promises (Num. 6:27).

The words we use in our places of work have the power either to bless or curse, to build up others or to tear them down. Our choice of words often has more power than we realize. The blessings in Numbers 6:24–26 declare that God will "keep" you, be "gracious" to you and give you "peace." At work our words can "keep" another person—that is, reassure, protect, and support. "If you need help, come to me. I won't hold it against you." Our words can be full of grace, making the situation better than it otherwise would be. We can accept responsibility for a shared error, for example, rather than shifting the blame by minimizing our

---

[2] Steve S. Kraman and Ginny Hamm, "Risk Management: Extreme Honesty May Be the Best Policy," *Annals of Internal Medicine* 131 (Dec. 1999): 963–67. Further coverage is found in Pauline Chen, "When Doctors Admit Their Mistakes," *New York Times*, Aug. 19, 2010.

role. Our words can bring peace by restoring relationships that have been broken. "I realize that things have gone wrong between us, but I want to find a way to have a good relationship again," for example. Of course, there are times we have to object, critique, correct, and perhaps punish others at work. Even so, we can choose whether to criticize the faulty action or whether to damn the whole person. Conversely, when others do well, we can choose to praise instead of keeping silent, despite the slight risk to our reputation or cool reserve.

Retirement from Regular Service (Numbers 8:23–26)

Numbers contains the only passage in the Bible that specifies an age limit for work. The Levites entered their service as young men who would be strong enough to erect and transport the tabernacle with all of its sacred elements. The censuses of Numbers 4 did not include names of any Levites over the age of fifty, and Numbers 8:25 specifies that at age fifty Levites must retire from their duties. In addition to the heavy lifting of the tabernacle, Levites' job also included inspecting skin diseases closely (Lev. 13). In a time before reading glasses, virtually no one over the age of fifty would be able to see anything at close range. The point is not that fifty is a universal retirement age, but that a time comes when an aging body performs with less effectiveness at work. The process varies highly among individuals and occupations. Moses was eighty when he began his duties as Israel's leader (Exod. 7:7).

Retirement, however, was not the end of the Levites work. The purpose was not to remove productive workers from service, but to redirect their service in a more mature direction, given the conditions of their occupation. After retirement they could still "assist their brothers in the tent of meeting in carrying out their duties" (Num. 8:26). Sometimes, some faculties—judgment, wisdom, and insight, perhaps—may actually improve with increasing age. By "assisting their brothers," older Levites transitioned to different ways of serving their communities. Modern notions of retirement that consist of ceasing work and devoting time exclusively to leisure are not found in the Bible.

Like the Levites, we should not seek a total cessation of meaningful work in old age. We may want or need to relinquish our positions, but our abilities and wisdom are still valuable. We may continue to serve others in our occupations by leadership in trade associations, civic organizations, boards of directors, and licensing bodies. We may consult, train, teach, or coach. We may finally have the time to serve to our fullest in church, clubs, elective office, or service organizations. We may be able to invest more time with our families, or if it is too late for that, in the lives of other children and young people. Often our most valuable new service is coaching and encouraging (blessing) younger workers (see Num. 6:24–27).

Given these possibilities, old age can be one of the most satisfying periods in a person's life. Sadly, retirement sidelines many people just at the moment when their gifts, resources, time, experience, networks, influence, and wisdom may be most beneficial. Some choose to pursue only leisure and entertainment or simply give up on life. Others find that age-related regulations and social marginalization prevent them from working as fully as they desire. There is too little material in Scripture to derive a specific theology of retirement. But as we age, each of us can prepare for retirement with as much, or more, care as we have prepared for work. When young, we can respect and learn from more experienced colleagues. At every age, we can work toward retirement policies and practices that are fairer and more productive for both younger and older workers.

The Challenge to Moses' Authority (Numbers 12)

In Numbers 12, Moses' brother and sister, Aaron and Miriam, try to launch a revolt against his authority. They appear to have a reasonable complaint. Moses teaches that Israelites are not to marry foreigners (Deut. 7:3), yet he himself has a foreign wife (Num. 12:1). If this complaint had been their true concern, they could have brought it to Moses or to the council of elders he had recently formed (Num. 11:16–17) for resolution. Instead, they agitate to put themselves in Moses' place as leaders of the nation. In reality, their complaint was merely a pretext to launch a general rebellion with the aim of elevating themselves to positions of ultimate power.

God punishes them severely on Moses' behalf. He reminds them he has chosen Moses as his representative to Israel, speaking "face to face" with Moses, and entrusts him with "all my house" (Num. 12:7–8). "Why then were you not afraid to speak against my servant Moses?" he demands (Num. 12:8). When he hears no answer, Numbers tells us that "the anger of the LORD was kindled against them" (Num. 12:9). His punishment falls first on Miriam who becomes leprous to the point of death, and Aaron begs Moses to forgive them (Num. 12:10–12). The authority of God's chosen leader must be respected, for to rebel against such a leader is to rebel against God himself.

When We Have Grievances against Those in Authority

God was uniquely present in Moses' leadership. "Never since then has there arisen a prophet in Israel like Moses, whom the LORD knew face to face" (Deut. 34:10). Today's leaders do not manifest God's authority face to face as Moses did. Yet God commands us to respect the authority of all leaders, "for there is no authority except from God" (Rom. 13:1–3). This does not mean that leaders must never be questioned, held accountable, or even replaced. It does mean that whenever we have a grievance against those in legitimate authority—as Moses was—our duty is to discern the ways in which their leadership is a manifestation of God's authority. We are to respect them for whatever portion of God's authority they truly bear, even as we seek to correct, limit, or even remove them from power.

A telling detail in the story is that Aaron and Miriam's purpose was to thrust themselves into positions of power. A thirst for power can never be a legitimate motivation for rebelling against authority. If we have a grievance against our boss, our first hope should be to resolve the grievance with him or her. If the boss's abuse of power or incompetence prevents this, our next aim would be to have him or her replaced by someone of integrity and ability. But if our purpose is to magnify our own power, then our aim is untrue, and we have even lost the standing to perceive whether the boss is acting legitimately or not. Our own cravings have made us incapable of discerning God's authority in the situation.

When Others Oppose Our Authority

Although Moses was both powerful and in the right, he responds to the leadership challenge with gentleness and humility. "The man Moses was very humble, more so than anyone else on the face of the earth" (Num. 12:3). He remains with Aaron and Miriam throughout the episode, even when they begin to receive their deserved punishment. He intervenes with God to restore Miriam's health, and succeeds in reducing her punishment from death to seven days banishment from camp (Num. 12:13–15). He retains them in the senior leadership of the nation.

If we are in positions of authority, we are likely to face opposition as Moses did. Assuming that we, like Moses, have come to authority legitimately, we may be offended by opposition and even recognize it as an offense against God's purpose for us. We may well be in the right if we attempt to defend our position and defeat those who are attacking it. Yet, like Moses, we must care first for the people over whom God has placed us in authority, including those who are opposing us. They may have legitimate grievances against us, or they may be aspiring to tyranny. We may succeed in resisting them, or we may lose. We may or may or not continue in the organization, and they also may or may not continue. We may find common ground, or we may find it impossible to restore good working relationships with our opponents. Nonetheless, in every situation we have a duty of humility, meaning that we act for the good of those God has entrusted to us, even at the expense of our comfort, power, prestige, and self-image. We will know we are fulfilling this duty when we find ourselves advocating for those who oppose us, as Moses did with Miriam.

When Leadership Leads to Unpopularity
(Numbers 13 and 14)

Another challenge to Moses' authority arises in Numbers 13 and 14. The Lord tells Moses to send spies into the land of Canaan to prepare for the conquest. Both military and economic intelligence are to be collected, and spies are named from every tribe (Num. 13:18–20). This means the spies' report could be used not only to plan the conquest, but also to begin discussions about allocating territory among the Israelite tribes. The spies' report confirms that the land is very good, that "it flows with milk and honey" (Num. 13:27). However, the spies also report that "the people who live in the land are strong, and the towns are fortified and very large" (Num. 13:28). Moses and his lieutenant, Caleb, use the intelligence to plan the attack, but the spies become fearful and declare that the land cannot be conquered (Num. 13:30–32). Following the spies' lead, the people of Israel rebel against the Lord's plan and resolve to find a new leader to take them back to slavery in Egypt. Only Aaron, Caleb, and a young man named Joshua remain with him.

But Moses stands fast, despite the plan's unpopularity. The people are on the verge of replacing him, yet he sticks to what the Lord has revealed to him as right. He and Aaron plead with the people to cease their rebellion, but to no avail. Finally, the Lord chastises Israel for its lack of faith and declares he will strike them with a deadly pestilence (Num. 14:5–12). By abandoning the plan, they thrust themselves into an even worse situation—imminent, utter destruction. Only Moses, steadfast in his original purpose, knows how to avert disaster. He appeals to the Lord to forgive the people, as he has done before. (We have seen in Numbers 12 how Moses is always ready to put his peoples' welfare first, even at his own expense.) The Lord relents, but declares there are inescapable consequences for the people. None of those who joined the rebellion will be allowed to enter the Promised Land (Num. 14:20–23).

Moses' actions demonstrate that leaders are chosen for the purpose of decisive commitment, not for blowing in the wind of popularity. Leadership can be a lonely duty, and if we are in positions of leadership, we may be severely tempted to acquiesce to popular opinion. It is true that good leaders do listen to others' opinions. But when a leader knows the best course of action, and has tested that knowledge to the best of his or her ability, the leader has a responsibility to do what is best, not what is most popular.

In Moses' situation, there was no doubt about the right course of action. The Lord commanded Moses to occupy the Promised Land. As we have seen, Moses himself remained humble in demeanor, but he did not waver in direction. He did not, in fact, succeed in carrying out the Lord's command. If people will not follow, the leader cannot accomplish the mission alone. In this case, the consequence for the people was the disaster of an entire generation missing out on the land God had chosen for them. At least Moses himself did not contribute to the disaster by changing his plan in response to their opinions.

The modern era is filled with examples of leaders who *did* give in to popular opinion. British Prime Minister Neville Chamberlain's capitulation to Hitler's demands in Munich in 1938 comes readily to mind. In contrast, Abraham Lincoln became one of America's greatest presidents by steadfastly refusing to give in to popular opinion to end the American Civil War by accepting the nation's division. Although he had the humility to acknowledge the possibility that he might be wrong ("as God gives us to see the right"), he also had the fortitude to do what he knew was right despite enormous pressure to give in. The book *Leadership on the Line* by Ronald Heifetz and Martin Linsky[3] explores the challenge of remaining open to others' opinions while maintaining steadfast leadership in times of challenge. (For more on this episode, see "Israel Refuses to Enter the Promised Land" in Deuteronomy 1:19–45 above.)

Offering God Our Firstfruits
(Numbers 15:20–21; 18:12–18)

Building on the sacrificial system described in Numbers 4 and 7, two passages in Numbers 15 and 18 describe the offering of the *first* produce of labor and the land to God. In addition to the offerings described earlier, the Israelites are to offer to God "the first fruits of all that is in their land" (Num. 18:13). Because God is the sovereign in possession of all things, the *entire* produce of the land and people actually belong to God already. When the people bring the firstfruits to the altar, they acknowledge God's ownership of everything, not merely what is left over after they meet their own needs. By bringing the firstfruits *before* making use of the rest of the increase themselves, they express respect for God's sovereignty, as well as the urgent hope that God will bless the continuing productivity of their labor and resources.[4]

[3] Martin Linsky and Ronald A. Heifetz, *Leadership on the Line: Staying Alive Through the Dangers of Leading* (Boston: Harvard Business Press, 2002).

[4] Richard O. Rigsby, "First Fruits," in *The Anchor Yale Bible Dictionary,* ed. David Noel Freedman (New York: Doubleday, 1992), 797.

The offerings and sacrifices in Israel's sacrificial system are different from the gifts and offerings we make today to God's work, but the concept of giving our firstfruits to God is still applicable. By giving first to God, we acknowledge God to be the owner of everything we have. Therefore, we give him our first and best. In this way, offering our firstfruits becomes a blessing for us as it was for ancient Israel.

Reminders of the Covenant (Numbers 15:37–41)

A short passage in Numbers 15 commands the Israelites to make fringes or tassels on the corners of their garments, with a blue cord at each corner, "so that, when you see it, you will remember all the commandments of the LORD and do them." In work, as elsewhere, there is always the temptation to "follow the lust of your own heart and your own eyes" (Num. 15:39). In fact, the more diligently you pay attention to your work (your "eyes"), the greater the chance that things in your workplace that are not of the Lord will influence you (your "heart"). The answer is not to stop paying attention at work or to take it less seriously. Instead, it could be a good thing to plant reminders that will remind you of God and his way. It may not be tassels, but it could be a Bible that will come across your eyesight, an alarm reminding you to pray momentarily from time to time, or a symbol worn or carried in a place that will catch your attention. The purpose is not to show off for others, but to draw "your own heart" back to God. Although this is a small thing, it can have a significant effect. By doing so, "you shall remember and do all my commandments, and you shall be holy to your God" (Num. 15:40).

Moses' Unfaithfulness at Meribah (Numbers 20:2–13)

Moses' moment of greatest failure came when the people of Israel resumed complaining, this time about food and water (Num. 20:1–5). Moses and Aaron decided to bring the complaint to the Lord, who commanded them to take their staff, and in the people's presence command a rock to yield water enough for the people and their livestock (Num. 20:6–8). Moses did as the Lord instructed but added two flourishes of his own. First he rebuked the people, saying, "Listen, you rebels, shall we bring water for you out of this rock?" Then he struck the rock twice with his staff. Water poured out in abundance (Num. 20:9–11), but the Lord was extremely displeased with Moses and Aaron.

God's punishment was harsh. "Because you did not trust in me, to show my holiness before the eyes of the Israelites, therefore you shall not bring this assembly into the land that I have given them" (Num. 20:12). Moses and Aaron, like all the people who rebelled against God's plan earlier (Num. 14:22–23), will not be permitted to enter the Promised Land.

Scholarly arguments about the exact action Moses was punished for may be found in any of the general commentaries, but the text of Numbers 20:12 names the underlying offense directly, "You did not trust in me." Moses' leadership faltered in the crucial moment when he stopped trusting God and started acting on his own impulses.

Honoring God in leadership—as all Christian leaders in every sphere must attempt to do—is a terrifying responsibility. Whether we lead a business, a classroom, a relief organization, a household, or any other organization, we must be careful not to mistake our authority for God's. What can we do to keep ourselves in obedience to God? Meeting regularly with an accountability (or "peer") group, praying daily about the tasks of leadership, keeping a weekly Sabbath to rest in God's presence, and seeking others' perspective on God's guidance are methods some leaders employ. Even so, the task of leading firmly while remaining wholly dependent on God is beyond human capability. If the most humble man on the face of the earth (Num. 12:3) could fail in this way, so can we. By God's grace, even failures as great as Moses' at Meribah, with disastrous consequences in this life, do not separate us from the ultimate fulfillment of God's promises. Moses did not enter the Promised Land, yet the New Testament declares him "faithful in all God's house" and reminds us of the confidence that all in God's house have in the fulfillment of our redemption in Christ (Heb. 3:2–6).

When God Speaks through Unexpected Sources (Numbers 22–24)

In Numbers 22 and 23, the protagonist is not Moses but Balaam, a man residing near the path Israel was slowly taking toward the Promised Land. Although he was not an Israelite, he was a priest or prophet of the Lord. The king of Moab recognized God's power in Balaam's words, saying, "I know that whomever you bless is blessed, and whomever you curse is cursed." Fearing the strength of the Israelites, the king of Moab sent emissaries asking Balaam to come to Moab and curse the Israelites to rid him of the perceived threat (Num. 22:1–6).

God informs Balaam that he has chosen Israel as a blessed nation and commands Balaam neither to go to Moab nor to curse Israel (Num. 22:12). However, after multiple embassies from the king of Moab, Balaam agrees to go to Moab. His hosts try to bribe him to curse Israel, but Balaam warns them that he will do only what the Lord commands (Num. 22:18). God seems to agree with this plan, but as Balaam rides his donkey toward Moab, an angel of the Lord blocks his way three times. The angel is invisible to Balaam, but the donkey sees the angel and turns aside each time. Balaam becomes infuriated at the donkey and begins to beat the animal with his staff. "Then the Lord opened the mouth of the donkey, and it said to Balaam, 'What have I done to you, that you have struck me these three times?'" (Num. 22:28). Balaam converses with the donkey and comes to realize that the animal has perceived the Lord's guidance far more clearly than Balaam has. Balaam's eyes are opened; he sees the angel and receives God's further instructions about dealing with the king of Moab. "Go with the men; but speak only what I tell you," the Lord reminds him (Num. 22:35). Over the course of chapters 23 and 24, the king of Moab continues to entreat Balaam to curse Israel, but each time Balaam replies that the Lord declares Israel blessed. Eventually he succeeds in dissuading the king from attacking Israel (Num. 24:12–25), thus sparing Moab from immediate destruction by the hand of the Lord.

Balaam is similar to Moses because he manages to follow the Lord's guidance despite personal failings at times. Like Moses he plays a significant role in fulfilling God's plan to bring Israel to the Promised Land. But Balaam is also very unlike Moses and most of the other heroes of the

Hebrew Bible. He is not an Israelite himself. And his primary accomplishment is to save Moab, not Israel, from destruction. For both of these reasons, the Israelites would be quite surprised to read that God spoke to Balaam as clearly and directly as to Israel's own prophets and priests. Even more surprising—both to Israel and to Balaam himself—is that God's guidance at the crucial moment came to him through the mouth of an animal, a lowly donkey. In two surprising ways, we see that God's guidance comes not from the sources most favored by people, but from the sources God chooses himself. If God chooses to speak through the words of a potential enemy or even a beast of the field, we should pay attention.

The passage does not tell us that the best source of God's guidance is necessarily foreign prophets or donkeys, but it does give us some insight about listening for God's voice. It is easy for us to listen for God's voice only from sources we know. This often means listening only to those people who think like we do, belong to our social circles, or speak and act like us. This may mean we never pay attention to others who would take a different position from us. It becomes easy to believe that God is telling us exactly what we already thought. Leaders often reinforce this by surrounding themselves with a narrow band of like-minded deputies and advisors. Perhaps we are more like Balaam than we would like to believe. But by God's grace, could we somehow learn to listen to what God might be saying to us, even through people we don't trust or sources we don't agree with?

Land Ownership and Property Rights (Numbers 26–27; 36:1–12)

As time passes and demographics change, another new census is needed (Num. 26:1–4). A crucial purpose of this census is to begin developing socioeconomic structures for the new nation. Economic production and governmental organization is to be organized around tribes, with their subunits of clans and household. The land is to be divided among the clans in proportion to their population (Num. 26:52–56), and the assignment is to be made randomly. The result is that each household (extended family) receives a plot of land sufficient to support itself.

Unlike in Egypt—and later, the Roman Empire and medieval Europe— land is not to be owned by a class of nobles and worked by a dispossessed class of commoners or slaves. Instead, each family owns its own means of agricultural production. Crucially, the land can never be permanently lost to the family though debt, taxation, or even voluntary sale. (See Lev. 25 for the legal protections to keep families from losing their land.) Even if one generation of a family fails at farming and falls into debt, the next generation has access to the land needed to make a living.

The census is enumerated according to male heads of tribes and clans, whose heads of households each receive an allotment. But in cases where women are the heads of households (for example, if their fathers die be- fore receiving their allotment), the women are allowed to own land and pass it on to their descendants (Num. 27:8). This could complicate the ordering of Israel, however, because a woman might marry a man from another tribe. This would transfer the woman's land from her father's tribe to her husband's, weakening the social structure. In order to prevent this, the Lord decrees that although women may "marry whom they think best" (Num. 36:6), "no inheritance shall be transferred from one tribe to another" (Num. 36:9). This decree holds the rights of all people—women included—to own property and marry as they choose in balance with the need to preserve social structures. Tribes have to respect the rights of their members. Heads of household have to respect the needs of society.

In much of today's economy, owning land is not the chief means to make a living, and social structures are not ordered around tribes and clans. Therefore, the specific regulations in Numbers and Leviticus do not apply directly today. Conditions today require different specific solutions. Wise, just, and fairly enforced laws respecting property and economic structures, individual rights, and the common good are es- sential in every society. According to the United Nations Development Programme, "The advancement of the rule of law at the national and international levels is essential for sustained and inclusive economic growth, sustainable development, the eradication of poverty and hunger and the full realization of all human rights and fundamental freedoms."[5]

---

[5] United Nations Development Programme, *Issue Brief: Rule of Law and Development* (New York: United Nations, 2013), 3.

Christians have much to contribute to the good governance of society, not only through the law but also through prayer and transformation of life. And increasingly, Christians are discovering that by working together, we can provide effective opportunities for marginalized people to gain permanent access to the resources needed to thrive economically. One example is Agros International, which is guided by a Christian "moral compass" to help poor, rural families in Latin America acquire and successfully cultivate land.[6]

Succession Planning (Numbers 27:12–23)

Building a sustainable organization—in this case, the nation of Israel—requires orderly transitions of authority. Without continuity, people become confused and fearful, work structures fall apart, and workers become ineffective, "like sheep without a shepherd" (Num. 27:17). Preparing a successor takes time. Poor leaders may be afraid to equip someone capable of succeeding them, but great leaders like Moses begin developing successors long before they expect to leave office. The Bible doesn't tell us what process Moses uses to identify and prepare Joshua, except that he prays for God's guidance (Num. 27:16). Numbers does tell us that he makes sure to publicly recognize and support Joshua and to follow the recognized procedure to confirm his authority (Num. 27:17–21).

Succession planning is the responsibility of both the current executive (like Moses) and those who exercise complementary authority (like Eleazar and the leaders of the congregation), as we see in Numbers 27:21. Institutions, whether as big as a nation or as small as a work group, need effective processes for training and succession.

Daily Offering for the People (Numbers 28 and 29)

Although people make individual and family offerings at appointed times, there is also a sacrifice on behalf of the entire nation every day

---

[6]Agros International, http://www.agros.org/ag/how-we-work/frequently-asked-questions.

(Num. 28:1–8). There are additional offerings on the Sabbath (Num. 28:9–10), new moons (Num. 28:11–15), Passover (Num. 28:16–25), and the Festivals of Weeks (Num. 28:26–31), Trumpets (Num. 29:1–6), the Atonement (Num. 29:7–10), and Booths (Num. 29:12–40). Through these communal offerings, the people receive the benefits of the Lord's presence and favor even when they are not personally at worship.[7]

The Israelite sacrifice system is no longer in operation, and it is impossible to apply it directly to life and work today. But the importance of sacrificing, offering, and worshiping for the benefit of others remains (Rom. 12:1–6). Some believers—notably, certain orders of monks and nuns—spend most of their day praying for those who cannot or do not worship or pray for themselves. In our work, it would not be right to neglect our duties to pray. But in the times we do pray, we can pray for the people we work among, especially if we know no one else is praying for them. We are, after all, called to bring blessings to the world around us (Num. 6:22–27). We can certainly emulate Numbers 28:1–8 by praying on a daily basis. Praying every day, or multiple times throughout the day, seems to keep us closest to God's presence. Faith is not only for the Sabbath.

Honoring Commitments (Numbers 30)

Chapter 30 of Numbers gives an elaborate system for determining the validity of promises, oaths, and vows. The basic position, however, is simple: Do what you say you will do.

> When a man makes a vow to the LORD, or swears an oath to bind himself by a pledge, he shall not break his word; he shall do according to all that proceeds out of his mouth. (Num. 30:2)

Elaborations are given to handle exceptions to the rule when someone makes a promise that exceeds their authority. (The regulations in the text deal with situations where certain women are subject to the authority of particular men.) Although the exceptions are valid—you can't enforce the

---

[7] Phillip J. Budd, *Numbers*, vol. 5, *Word Biblical Commentary* (Dallas: Word, 1998), 319.

promise of a person who lacks the authority to make it in the first place—when Jesus commented on this passage, he proposed a much simpler rule of thumb: Don't make promises you can't or won't keep (Matt. 5:33–37).

Work-related commitments tempt us to pile up elaborations, qualifications, exceptions, and justifications for not doing what we promise. No doubt many of them are reasonable, such as *force majeure* clauses in contracts, which excuse a party from fulfilling its obligations if prevented by court orders, natural disasters, and the like. It doesn't stop at honoring the letter of the contract. Many agreements are made with a handshake. Sometimes there are loopholes. Can we learn to honor the intent of the agreement and not just the letter of the law? Trust is the ingredient that makes workplaces work, and trust is impossible if we promise more than we can deliver, or deliver less than we promise. This is not only a fact of life, but a command of the Lord.

Civic Planning for Levitical Towns (Numbers 35:1–5)

Unlike the rest of the tribes, the Levites were to live in towns scattered throughout the Promised Land where they could teach the people the law and apply it in local courts. Numbers 35:2–5 details the amount of pasture land each town should have. Measuring from the edge of town, the area for pasture was to extend outward a thousand cubits (about 1,500 feet) in each direction, east, south, west, and north.

Jacob Milgrom has shown that this geographical layout was a realistic exercise in town planning.[8] The diagram shows a town with pastureland extending beyond the town diameter in each direction. As the town diameter grows and absorbs the closest pasture, additional pasture land is added so that the pasture remains 1,000 cubits beyond the town limits in each direction. (In the diagram the shaded areas remain the same size as they move outward, but the cross-hatched areas get wider as the town center gets wider.)

---

[8] Jacob Milgrom, "Excursus 74: The Levitical Town: An Exercise in Realistic Planning," *JPS Torah Commentary: Numbers* (The Jewish Publication Society, 1990), 502–4.

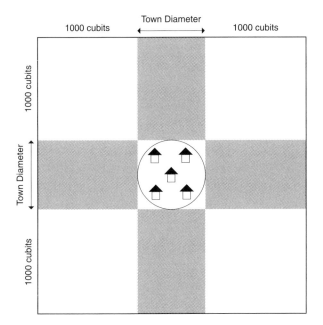

You shall measure, outside the town, for the east side two thousand cubits, for the south side two thousand cubits, for the west side two thousand cubits, and for the north side two thousand cubits, with the town in the middle. (Num. 35:5)

Mathematically, as the town grows, so does the area of its pasture land, but at a lower rate than the area of the inhabited town center. That means the population is growing faster than agricultural area. For this to continue, agricultural productivity per square meter must increase. Each herder must supply food to more people, freeing more of the population for industrial and service jobs. This is exactly what is required for economic and cultural development. To be sure, the town planning doesn't *cause* productivity to increase, but it creates a social-economic structure adapted for rising productivity. It is a remarkably sophisticated example of civic policy creating conditions for sustainable economic growth.

This passage in Numbers 35:5 illustrates again the detailed attention God pays to enabling human work that sustains people and creates economic well-being. If God troubles to instruct Moses on civic planning, based on semi-geometrical growth of pastureland, doesn't it suggest that God's people today should vigorously pursue all the professions, crafts, arts, academics, and other disciplines that sustain and prosper communities and nations? Perhaps churches and Christians could do more to encourage and celebrate its members' excellence in all fields of endeavor. Perhaps Christian workers could do more to become excellent at our work as a way of serving our Lord. Is there any reason to believe that excellent city planning, economics, childcare, or customer service bring less glory to God than heartfelt worship, prayer, or Bible study?

Conclusions from Numbers

The book of Numbers shows God at work through Moses to order and organize the new nation of Israel. The first part of the book focuses on worship, which depends on the work of priests in conjunction with laborers from every occupation. The essential work of those who represent God's people is not to perform rituals, but to bless all people with God's presence and reconciling love. All of us have the opportunity to bring blessing and reconciliation through our work, whether we think of ourselves as priests or not.

The second part of the book of Numbers traces the ordering of society as the people move towards the Promised Land. Passages in Numbers can help us gain a godly perspective on contemporary work issues such as offering the fruit of our labor to God, conflict resolution, retirement, leadership, property rights, economic productivity, succession planning, social relationships, honoring our commitments, and civic planning.

Leaders in Numbers—especially Moses—provide examples of what it means both to follow God's guidance and to fail in doing so. Leaders have to be open to wisdom from other people and from surprising sources. Yet they need to remain firm in following God's guidance as best as they can understand it. They must be bold enough to confront kings, yet humble enough to learn from the beasts of the field. No one in the book of Numbers succeeds completely in the task, but God remains faithful to his people in their successes and in their failings. Our mistakes have real—but not eternal—negative consequences, and we look for a hope beyond ourselves for the fulfillment of God's love for us. We see God's Spirit guiding Moses and hear God's promise to give the leaders who come after Moses a portion of God's Spirit too. By this, we ourselves can be encouraged in seeking God's guidance for the opportunities and challenges in our work. Whatever we do, we can be confident of God's presence with us as we work, for he tells us, "I the LORD dwell among the Israelites" (Num. 35:34) in whose steps we tread.

Deuteronomy and Work

Introduction to Deuteronomy

Work is a major subject of the book of Deuteronomy and prominent topics include the following:

- *The meaning and value of work.* God's command to work for the benefit of others, the blessings of work for the individual and the community, the consequences of failure and the dangers of success, and the responsibility that comes from representing God to others.

- *Relationships at work.* The importance of good relationships, the development of dignity and respect for others, and the requirement not to harm others or speak unjustly of them in our work.

- *Leadership.* The wise exercise of leadership and authority, succession planning and training, and the responsibility of leaders to work for the benefit of the people they lead.

- *Economic justice.* Respect for property, worker's rights, and courts of law, productive use of resources, lending and borrowing, and honesty in commercial agreements and fair trade

- *Work and rest.* The requirement to work, the importance of rest, and the invitation to trust God to provide for us whether at work or at rest.

Despite the centuries of change in commerce and vocation, Deuteronomy can help us better understand how to live in response to God's love and serve others through our work.

The book's dramatic, unified presentation makes it especially memorable. Jesus quoted from Deuteronomy at length. In fact, his first Scripture quotations were three passages from Deuteronomy (Matt. 4:4, 7, 10). The New Testament refers to Deuteronomy more than fifty times, a number exceeded only by Psalms and Isaiah.[1] And Deuteronomy contains the first formulation of the Great Commandment, "You shall love the LORD your God with all your heart, and with all your soul, and with all your might" (Deut. 6:4–5).

Underlying all the themes in Deuteronomy is Israel's covenant with the one true God. Everything in the book flows from the keystone of the covenant, "I am the LORD your God . . . you shall have no other gods before me" (Deut. 5:6–7). When people worship the Lord alone, good governance, productive work, ethical commerce, civic good, and fair treatment for all will generally result. When people put other motivations, values, and concerns ahead of God, work and life come to grief.

Deuteronomy covers the same material as the other books of the law—Exodus, Leviticus, and Numbers—but heightens the attention paid to work, most notably in the Ten Commandments. It seems as if in retelling the events and teachings of the other books, Moses feels a need to emphasize the importance of work in the life of God's people. Perhaps in some sense this foreshadows the growing attention that Christians are giving work in the present day. Looking at Scripture with fresh eyes, we discover that work is more important to God than we realized before, and that God's word gives more direction to our work than we thought.

Rebellion and Complacency (Deuteronomy 1:1–4:43)

Deuteronomy begins with a speech by Moses recounting the major events in Israel's recent history. Moses draws lessons from these events and exhorts Israel to respond to God's faithfulness by obeying him in trust (Deut. 4:40). Two sections—about violating trust in God by rebellion and complacency, respectively—are particularly important to the theology of work.

---

[1] Bruce K. Waltke and Charles Yu, *An Old Testament Theology: An Exegetical, Canonical, and Thematic Approach* (Grand Rapids: Zondervan, 2007), 479–80.

Israel Refuses to Enter the Promised Land (Deuteronomy 1:19–45)

In the wilderness, the people's fear leads to a failure to trust God. As a result they rebel against God's plan for them to enter the land he promised to Abraham, Isaac, and Jacob (Deut. 1:7–8). God had brought Israel out of slavery in Egypt, given the law at Mt. Horeb (Sinai), and brought the people swiftly to the borders of the promised land (Deut. 1:19–20). Moses then announces it is time to enter the land, but the people are fearful of the Amorites who occupy the borders. They convince Moses to send a scouting expedition as a matter of prudent planning. The scouts return with a good report of the land. At this point the people's true concern is revealed—they are afraid. "The people are stronger and taller than we; the cities are large and fortified up to heaven," they tell Moses, adding that "our hearts melt" (Deut. 1:28). The people do not trust God to fulfill his promises, so they refuse to follow his commands.

God's response is severe. "Not one of these—not one of this evil generation—shall see the good land that I swore to give to your ancestors" (Deut. 1:35). Entering Canaan had been delayed for the children and lost forever for the parents. Even Moses is barred from entering the land because he demonstrated a lack of trust in God himself, perhaps by agreeing to send scouts. Soon after, the people realize that they have condemned themselves to a lifetime of eking out an existence in the desert instead of enjoying the "good land" (Deut. 1:25) God had prepared for them. Belatedly, they make their own plans to attack the Amorites. But God declares, "Do not go up and do not fight, for I am not in the midst of you; otherwise you will be defeated by your enemies" (Deut. 1:42). A lack of trust in God's promises leads Israel to miss the blessings he had in store for them.

When we know what is right, but are tempted to violate it, trust in God is all we have to keep us in God's ways. This is not a matter of moral fiber. If even Moses failed to trust God completely, can we really imagine that we will succeed? Instead, it is a matter of God's grace. We can pray for God's Spirit to strengthen us when we stand for what is right, and we can ask for God's forgiveness when we fall. Like Moses and the people of Israel, failure to trust God can have serious consequences in life, but our failure is ultimately redeemed by God's grace. (For more on this episode, see "When Leadership Leads to Unpopularity" in Numbers 13–14 above.)

When Success Leads to Complacency (Deuteronomy 4:25–40)

In the wilderness, Israel's abandon of trust in God arises not only from fear, but also from success. At this point in his first speech, Moses is describing the prosperity that awaits the new generation about to enter the Promised Land. Moses points out that success is likely to breed a spiritual complacency far more dangerous than failure. "When you have had children and children's children, and become complacent in the land, if you act corruptly by making an idol in the form of anything . . . you will soon utterly perish from the land" (Deut. 4:25–26). We will come to idolatry, per se, in Deuteronomy 5:8, but the point here is the spiritual danger caused by complacency. In the wake of success, people cease fearing God and begin to believe success is a birthright. Instead of gratitude, we forge a sense of entitlement. The success for which we strive is not wrong, but it is a moral danger. The truth is that the success we achieve is mixed from a pinch of skill and hard work, combined with a heaping of fortunate circumstances and the common grace of God. We cannot actually provide for our own wants, desires, and security. Success is not permanent. It does not truly satisfy. A dramatic illustration of this truth is found in the life of King Uzziah in 2 Chronicles. "He was marvelously helped [by God] until he became strong. But when he had become strong he grew proud, to his destruction" (2 Chr. 26:15–16). Only in God can we find true security and satisfaction (Ps. 17:15).

It may be surprising that the result of complacency is not atheism but idolatry. Moses foresees that if the people abandon the Lord, they will not become spiritual free agents. They will bind themselves to "objects of wood and stone that neither see, nor hear, nor eat, nor smell" (Deut. 4:28). Perhaps in Moses' day the idea of religionless existence did not occur to anyone. But in our day it does. A growing tide of secularism attempts to throw off what it sees—sometimes quite correctly—as shackles of domination by corrupt religious institutions, belief, and practices. But does this result in a true freedom, or is the worship of God necessarily replaced by the worship of human-made fabrications?

Although this question sounds abstract, it has tangible effects on work and workplaces. For example, prior to the last half of the twentieth century, questions about business ethics were generally settled by reference to the Scriptures. This practice was far from perfect, but it did give serious standing to those on the losing side of power struggles related to work. The most dramatic case was probably the religiously based opposition to slavery in England and the United States of America, which ultimately succeeded in abolishing both the slave trade and slavery itself. In secularized institutions, there is no moral authority to which one can appeal. Instead, ethical decisions must be based on law and "ethical custom," as Milton Friedman put it.[2] Law and ethical custom being human constructs, business ethics becomes reduced to rule by the powerful and the popular. No one wants a workplace dominated by religious elite, but does a fully secularized workplace simply open the door for a different kind of exploitation? It is certainly possible for believers to bring the blessings of God's faithfulness to their workplaces without trying to reimpose special privileges for themselves.

All this is not to say that success must necessarily lead to complacency. If we can remember that God's grace, God's word, and God's guidance are at the root of whatever success we have, then we can be grateful, not complacent. The success we experience could then honor God and bring us joy. The caution is simply that over the course of history success seems to be spiritually more dangerous than adversity. Moses further warns Israel about the dangers of prosperity in Deuteronomy 8:11–20.

God's Law and Its Applications (Deuteronomy 4:44–30:20)

Deuteronomy continues with a second speech containing the main body of the book. This section centers on God's covenant with Israel, especially the law, or principles and rules by which Israel should live. After a narrative introduction (Deut. 4:44–49), the speech itself consists of three parts. In the first part, Moses expounds the Ten Commandments (Deut. 5:1–11:33). In the second part, he describes in detail the "statutes and ordinances" that Israel is to follow (Deut. 12:1–26:19). In the third part, Moses describes the blessings Israel will experience if they keep

---

[2] Milton Friedman, "The Social Responsibility of Business Is to Increase Its Profits," *New York Times*, September 13, 1970.

the covenant, and the curses that will destroy them if they do not (Deut. 27:1–28:68). The second speech thus has the pattern of first giving the larger, governing principles (Deut. 5:1–11:32), then the specific rules (Deut. 12:1–26:19), and then the consequences for obedience or disobedience (Deut. 27:1–28:68).

The Ten Commandments (Deuteronomy 5:6–21)

The Ten Commandments are great contributors to the theology of work. They describe the essential requirements of Israel's covenant with God and are the core principles that govern the nation and the work of its people. Moses' exposition begins with the most memorable statement of the book, "Hear, O Israel: The LORD is our God, the LORD alone. You shall love the LORD your God with all your heart, and with all your soul, and with all your might" (Deut. 6:4–5). As Jesus pointed out centuries later, this is the greatest commandment of the entire Bible. Then Jesus added a quotation from Leviticus 19:18, "And a second is like it: 'You shall love your neighbor as yourself' " (Matt. 22:37–40). Although the "second" greatest commandment is not stated explicitly in Deuteronomy, we will see that the Ten Commandments do indeed point us to love of both God and neighbor.

The passage is virtually identical to Exodus 20:1–17—grammatical variations aside—except for some differences in the fourth (keeping the Sabbath), fifth (honoring mother and father), and tenth (coveting) commandments. Intriguingly, the variations in these commandments specifically address work. We will repeat the commentary from *Exodus and Work* here, with additions exploring the variations between the Exodus and Deuteronomy accounts.

"You Shall Have No Other Gods before Me" (Deuteronomy 5:7; Exodus 20:3)

The first commandment reminds us that everything in the Torah flows from the love we have for God, which is a response to the love he has for us. This love was demonstrated by God's deliverance of Israel "out of the house of slavery" in Egypt (Deut. 5:6). Nothing else in life should concern us more than our desire to love and be loved by God. If we *do* have some other concern stronger to us than our love for God, it is not so much that we are breaking God's rules, but that we are not really in relationship with God. The other concern—be it money, power, security, recognition, sex, or anything else—has become our god. This false god will have its own commandments at odds with God's, and we will inevitably violate the Torah as we comply with this god's requirements. Observing the Ten Commandments is conceivable only for those who start by worshipping no other god than the Lord.

In the realm of work, this means that we are not to let work or its requirements and fruits displace God as our most important concern in life. "Never allow anyone or anything to threaten God's central place in your life," as David Gill puts it.[3]

Because many people work primarily to make money, an inordinate desire for money is probably the most common work-related danger to the first commandment. Jesus warned of exactly this danger: "No one can serve two masters. . . . You cannot serve God and wealth" (Matt. 6:24). But almost anything related to work can become twisted in our desires to the point that it interferes with our love for God. How many careers come to a tragic end because the *means* to accomplish things for the love of God—such as political power, financial sustainability, commitment to the job, status among peers, or superior performance—become ends in themselves? When, for example, recognition on the job becomes more important than character on the job, is this not a sign that reputation is displacing the love of God as the ultimate concern?

"You Shall Not Make for Yourself an Idol" (Deuteronomy 5:8; Exodus 20:4)

The second commandment raises the issue of idolatry. Idols are gods of our own creation, gods that we feel will give us what we want. In ancient times, idolatry often took the form of worshiping physical objects. But the issue is really one of trust and devotion. On what do we ultimately pin our hope of well-being and success? Anything that is not capable of fulfilling our hope—that is, anything other than God—is an idol, whether or not it is a physical object. The story of a family forging

---

[3] David W. Gill, *Doing Right: Practicing Ethical Principles* (Downers Grove, IL: IVP Books, 2004), 83. Gill's book contains an extended exegesis and application of the Ten Commandments in the modern world.

an idol with the intent to manipulate God, and the disastrous personal, social and economic consequences that follow, are memorably told in Judges 17–21.

In the world of work, it is common to speak of money, fame, and power as potential idols, and rightly so. They are not idols, per se, and in fact may be necessary for us to accomplish our roles in God's creative and redemptive work in the world. Yet when we imagine that by achieving them our safety and prosperity will be secured, we have begun to fall into idolatry. Idolatry begins when we place our trust and hope in these things more than in God. The same may occur with virtually every other element of success, including preparation, hard work, creativity, risk, wealth and other resources, and even luck. Are we able to recognize when we begin to idolize these things? By God's grace, we can overcome the temptation to worship them in God's place.

"You Shall Not Make Wrongful Use of the Name of the Lord Your God" (Deuteronomy 5:11; Exodus 20:7)

The third commandment literally prohibits God's people from making "wrongful use" of the name of God. This need not be restricted to the name "YHWH" (Deut. 5:11), but includes "God," "Jesus," "Christ," and so forth. But what is wrongful use? It includes, of course, disrespectful use in cursing, slandering, and blaspheming. But more significantly, it includes falsely attributing human designs to God. This prohibits us from claiming God's authority for our own actions and decisions. Regrettably, some Christians seem to believe that following God at work consists primarily of speaking for God on the basis of their individual understanding, rather than working respectfully with others or taking responsibility for their actions. "It is God's will that . . . ," or "God is punishing you for . . . ," are dangerous things to say, and almost never valid when spoken by an individual without the discernment of the community of faith (1 Thess. 5:20–21). In this light, perhaps the traditional Jewish reticence to utter even the English translation "God"—let alone the divine name itself—demonstrates a wisdom Christians often lack. If we were a little more careful about bandying the word *God* about, perhaps we would be more judicious in claiming to know God's will, especially as it applies to other people.

The third commandment also reminds us that respecting human names is important to God. The Good Shepherd "calls his own sheep by name" (John 10:3), while warning us that if you call another person "you fool," then "you will be liable to the hell of fire" (Matt. 5:22). Keeping this in mind, we shouldn't make wrongful use of other people's names or call them by disrespectful epithets. We use people's names wrongfully when we use them to curse, humiliate, oppress, exclude, and defraud. We use people's names well when we use them to encourage, thank, create solidarity, and welcome. Simply to learn and say someone's name is a blessing, especially if he or she is often treated as nameless, invisible, or insignificant. Do you know the name of the person who empties your trash can, answers your customer service call, or drives your bus? People's names are not the very name of the Lord, but they are the names of those made in his image.

"Observe the Sabbath Day and Keep It Holy" *(Deuteronomy 5:12; Exodus 20:8–11)*

The issue of the Sabbath is complex, not only in the books of Deuteronomy and Exodus and the Old Testament, but also in Christian theology and practice. The precise applicability of the fourth commandment, keeping the Sabbath, to Gentile believers has been a matter of debate since New Testament times (Rom. 14:5–6). Nonetheless, the general principle of the Sabbath applies directly to the matter of work.

The Sabbath and the Work We Do

The first part of the fourth commandment calls for ceasing labor one day in seven. On the one hand, this was an incomparable gift to the people of Israel. No other ancient people had the privilege of resting one day in seven. On the other hand, it required an extraordinary trust in God's provision. Six days of work had to be enough to plant crops, gather the harvest, carry water, spin cloth, and draw sustenance from creation. While Israel rested one day every week, the encircling nations continued to forge swords, feather arrows, and train soldiers. Israel had to trust God not to let a day of rest lead to economic and military catastrophe.

We face the same issue of trust in God's provision today. If we heed God's commandment to observe God's own cycle of work and rest, will we be able to compete in the modern economy? Does it take seven days of work to hold a job (or two or three jobs), clean the house, prepare the meals, mow the lawn, wash the car, pay the bills, finish the school work, and shop for the clothes, or can we trust God to provide for us even if we take a day off during the course of every week? Can we take time to worship God, to pray, and to gather with others for study and encouragement, and if we do, will it make us more or less productive overall? The fourth commandment does not explain how God will make it all work out for us. It simply tells us to rest one day every seven.

Christians have translated the day of rest to the Lord's Day (Sunday, the day of Christ's resurrection), but the essence of the Sabbath is not choosing one particular day of the week over another (Rom. 14:5–6). The polarity that actually undergirds the Sabbath is *work* and *rest*. Both work and rest are included in the fourth commandment: "Six days you shall labor and do all your work" (Deut. 5:13). The six days of work are as much a part of the commandment as the one day of rest. Although many Christians are in danger of allowing work to squeeze the time set aside for rest, others are in danger of the opposite—of shirking work and trying to live a life of leisure and dissipation. This is even worse than neglecting the Sabbath, for "whoever does not provide for relatives, and especially for family members, has denied the faith and is worse than an unbeliever" (1 Tim. 5:8). What we need are times and places for both work and rest, which together are good for us, our family, workers, and guests. This may or may not include twenty-four continuous hours of rest falling on Sunday (or Saturday). The proportions may change due to temporary necessities or the changing needs of the seasons of life.

If overwork is our main danger, then we need to find a way to honor the fourth commandment without instituting a false, new legalism pitting the spiritual (worship on Sunday) against the secular (work on Monday through Saturday). If avoiding work is our danger, we need to learn how to find joy and meaning in working as a service to God and our neighbors (Eph. 4:28).

The Sabbath and the Work People Do for Us

Of the few variations between the two versions of the Ten Commandments, the majority occur as additions to the fourth commandment in

Deuteronomy. First, the list of those you cannot force to work on the Sabbath is expanded to include "your ox or your donkey, or any of your livestock" (Deut. 5:14a). Second, a reason is given why you cannot force slaves to work on the Sabbath: "So that your male and female slave may rest as well as you. Remember that you were a slave in the land of Egypt" (Deut. 5:14b–15a). Finally, a reminder is added that your ability to rest securely in the midst of military and economic competition from other nations is a gift from God, who protects Israel "with a mighty hand and an outstretched arm" (Deut. 5:15b).

An important distinction between the two texts on this commandment is their grounding in creation and redemption, respectively. In Exodus, the Sabbath is rooted in the six days of creation followed by a day of rest (Gen. 1:3–2:3). Deuteronomy adds the element of God's redemption. "The LORD your God brought you out from there with a mighty hand and an outstretched arm; therefore the LORD your God commanded you to keep the sabbath day" (Deut. 5:15). Bringing the two together, we see that the foundations for keeping the Sabbath are both the way God made us and the way he redeems us.

These additions highlight God's concern for those who work under the authority of others. Not only must you rest, those who work for you— slaves, other Israelites, even animals—must be given rest. When you "remember that you were a slave in the land of Egypt," it reminds you not to take your own rest as a special privilege, but to bring rest to others just as the Lord brought it to you. It does not matter what religion they follow or what they may choose to do with the time. They are workers, and God directs us to provide rest for those who work. We may be accustomed to thinking about keeping the Sabbath in order to rest ourselves, but how much thought do we give to resting those who work to serve us? Many people work at hours that interfere with their relationships, sleep rhythms, and social opportunities in order to make life more convenient for others.

The so-called "blue laws" that once protected people—or prevented people, depending on your point of view—from working at all hours have disappeared from most developed countries. Undoubtedly this has opened many new opportunities for workers and the people they serve. But is this always something we should participate in? When we shop late at night, golf on Sunday morning, or watch sporting events that continue past midnight, do we consider how it may affect those working at these times? Perhaps our actions help create a work opportunity that wouldn't otherwise exist. On the other hand, perhaps we simply require someone to work at a miserable time who otherwise would have worked at a convenient hour.

The fast-food restaurant chain Chick-fil-A is well known for being closed on Sundays. It is often assumed this is because of founder Truett Cathy's particular interpretation of the fourth commandment. But according to the company's website, "His decision was as much practical as spiritual. He believes that all franchised Chick-fil-A Operators and Restaurant employees should have an opportunity to rest, spend time with family and friends, and worship if they choose to do so." Of course, reading the Fourth Commandment as a way to care for the people who work for you *is* a particular interpretation, just not a sectarian or legalistic one. The issue is complex, and there is no one-size-fits-all answer. But we do have choices as consumers and (in some cases) as employers that affect the hours and conditions of other people's rest and work.

"Honor Your Father and Your Mother" (Deuteronomy 5:16; Exodus 20:12)

The fifth commandment says that we must respect the most basic authority among human beings, that of parents for children. To put it another way, parenting children is among the most important kinds of work there are in the world, and it both deserves and requires the greatest respect. There are many ways to honor—or dishonor—your father and mother. In Jesus' day, the Pharisees wanted to restrict this to speaking well of them. But Jesus pointed out that obeying this commandment requires working to provide for your parents (Mark 7:9–13). We honor people by working for their good.

For many people, good relationships with parents are one of the joys of life. Loving service to them is a delight and obeying this commandment is easy. But we are put to the test by this commandment when we find it burdensome to work on behalf of our parents. We may have been ill-treated or neglected by them. They may be controlling and meddlesome. Being around them may undermine our sense of self, our commitment to our spouses (including our responsibilities under the third commandment), even our relationship with God. Even if we have good relationships with our parents, there may come a time when caring for them is a major burden simply because of the time and work it takes. If aging or dementia begins to rob them of their memory, capabilities, and good nature, caring for them can become a deep sorrow.

Yet the fifth commandment comes with a promise: "that your days may be long and that it may go well with you in the land that the LORD your God is giving you" (Deut. 5:16). Through proper honor of parents, children learn proper respect in every other kind of relationship, including those in their future workplaces. Obeying this command enables us to live long and do well because developing proper relationships of respect and authority is essential to individual success and social order.

Because this is a command to work for the benefit of parents, it is inherently a workplace command. The place of work may be where we earn money to support them, or it may be in the place where we assist them in the tasks of daily life. Both are work. When we take a job because it allows us to live near them, or send money to them, or make use of the values and gifts they developed in us, or accomplish things they taught us are important, we are honoring them. When we *limit* our careers so that we can be present with them, clean and cook for them, bathe and embrace them, take them to the places they love, or diminish their fears, we are honoring them.

Parents therefore have the duty to be worthy of trust, respect, and obedience. Raising children is a form of work, and no workplace requires higher standards of trustworthiness, compassion, justice, and fairness. As the Apostle Paul put it, "Fathers, do not provoke your children to anger, but bring them up in the discipline and instruction of the Lord" (Eph. 6:4). Only by God's grace could anyone hope to serve adequately as a parent, another indication that worship of God and obedience to his ways underlies all of Deuteronomy.

In our workplaces, we can help other people fulfill the fifth commandment, as well as obey it ourselves. We can remember that employees, customers, co-workers, bosses, suppliers, and others also have families, and then adjust our expectations to support them in honoring their families. When others share or complain about their struggles with parents, we can listen to them compassionately, support them practically (say, by offering to take a shift so they can be with their parents), or perhaps offer a godly perspective for them to consider. For example, if a career-focused colleague reveals a family crisis, we have a chance both to pray for the family and to suggest that the colleague think about rebalancing time between career and family.

"You Shall Not Murder" (Deuteronomy 5:17; Exodus 20:13)

Sadly, the sixth commandment has an all-too-practical application in the modern workplace, where 10 percent of all job-related fatalities (in the United States) are homicides.[4] However, admonishing readers of this article, "Don't murder anyone at work," isn't likely to change this statistic much.

But murder isn't the only form of workplace violence, just the most extreme. A more practical course arises when we remember that Jesus said even anger is a violation of the sixth commandment (Matt. 5:21–22). As Paul noted, we may not be able to prevent the feeling of anger, but we can learn how to cope with our anger. "Be angry but do not sin; do not let the sun go down on your anger" (Eph. 4:26). The most significant implication of the sixth commandment for work then may be, "If you get angry at work, get help in anger management." Many employers, churches, state and local governments, and nonprofit organizations offer classes and counseling in anger management. Availing yourself of these may be a highly effective way of obeying the sixth commandment.

Murder is the intentional killing of a person, but the case law that stems from the sixth commandment shows that we also have the duty to prevent unintended deaths. A particularly graphic case is when an ox (a work animal) gores a man or woman to death (Exod. 21:28–29). If the event was predictable, the ox's owner is to be treated as a murderer. In other words, owners/managers are responsible for ensuring workplace safety within reason. This principle is well established law in most countries, and workplace safety is the subject of significant government policing, industry self-regulation, and organizational policy and practice. Yet workplaces of all kinds continue to require or allow workers to work in needlessly unsafe conditions. Christians who have any role in setting the conditions of work, supervising workers, or modeling workplace

---

[4] "Fact Sheet: Workplace Shootings 2010," United States Department of Labor, *Bureau of Labor Statistics*, http://www.bls.gov/iif/oshwc/cfoi/osar0014.htm.

practices are reminded by the sixth commandment that safe working conditions are among their highest responsibilities in the world of work.

"You Shall Not Commit Adultery" (Exodus 20:14; Deuteronomy 5:18)

The workplace is one of the most common settings for adultery, not necessarily because adultery occurs in the workplace itself, but because it arises from the conditions of work and relationships with co-workers. The first application to the workplace, then, is literal. Married people should not have sex with people other than their spouses at, in, or because of their work. Some professions such as prostitution and pornography almost always violate this commandment, as they almost always require sex between people married to others. But any kind of work that erodes the bonds of marriage infringes the seventh commandment. There are many ways this can occur. Work may encourage strong emotional bonds among co-workers without adequately supporting their commitments to their spouses, as can happen in hospitals, entrepreneurial ventures, academic institutions and churches, among other places. Working conditions may bring people into close physical contact for extended periods or fail to encourage reasonable limits to off-hour encounters, as could happen on extended field assignments. Work may subject people to sexual harassment and pressure to have sex with those holding power over them. Work may inflate people's egos or expose them to adulation, as could occur with celebrities, star athletes, business titans, high-ranking government officials, and the super-rich. Work may demand so much time away—physically, mentally, or emotionally—that it frays the bond between spouses. All of these may pose dangers that Christians would do well to recognize and avoid, ameliorate, or guard against

"You Shall Not Steal" (Exodus 20:15; Deuteronomy 5:19)

The eighth commandment is another that takes work as its primary subject. Stealing is a violation of proper work because it dispossesses the victim of the fruits of his or her labor. It is also a violation of the commandment to labor six days a week, since in most cases stealing is intended as a shortcut around honest labor, which shows again the interrelation of the Ten Commandments. So we may take it as the word of God that we are not to steal from those we work for, with, or among.

The very idea that there is such a thing as "stealing" implies the existence of property and property rights. There are only three ways to acquire things—by making them ourselves, by the voluntary exchange of goods and services with others (trade or gifts), or by confiscation. Stealing is the most blatant form of confiscation, when someone grabs what belongs to another and runs away. But confiscation also occurs on a larger, more sophisticated scale, as when a corporation defrauds customers or a government imposes ruinous taxation on its citizens. Such institutions lack respect for property rights. This is not the place to explore what constitutes fair versus monopolistic commerce or legitimate versus excessive taxation. But the eighth commandment tells us that no society can thrive when property rights are violated with impunity by individuals, criminal gangs, businesses, or governments.

In practical terms, this means that stealing occurs in many forms besides robbing someone. Any time we acquire something of value from its rightful owner without consent, we are engaging in theft. Misappropriating resources or funds for personal use is stealing. Using deception to make sales, gain market share, or raise prices is stealing because the deception means that whatever the buyer consents to is not the actual situation. (See the section on "Puffery/Exaggeration" in *Truth & Deception* at www.theologyofwork.org for more on this topic.) Likewise, profiting by taking advantage of people's fears, vulnerabilities, powerlessness, or desperation is a form of stealing because their consent is not truly voluntary. Violating patents, copyrights, and other intellectual property laws is stealing because it deprives the owner of the ability to profit from their creation under the terms of civil law.

Respect for the property and rights of others means that we don't take what is theirs or meddle in their affairs. But it does not mean that we look out only for ourselves. Deuteronomy 22:1 states, "You shall not watch your neighbor's ox or sheep straying away and ignore them; you shall take them back to their owner." Saying "It's none of my business" is no excuse for callousness.

Regrettably, many jobs seem to include an element of taking advantage of others' ignorance or lack of alternatives to force them into transactions they otherwise wouldn't agree to. Companies, governments, individuals, unions, and other players may use their power to coerce others into unfair wages, prices, contract terms, working conditions, hours, or other factors. Although we may not rob banks, steal from our employers, or shoplift, we may very likely be participating in unfair or unethical practices that deprive others of what rights should be theirs. It can be difficult, even career limiting, to resist engaging in these practices, but we are called to do so nonetheless.

"You Shall Not Bear False Witness against Your Neighbor" (Exodus 20:16; Deuteronomy 5:20)

The ninth commandment honors the right to one's own reputation.[5] It finds pointed application in legal proceedings where what people say depicts reality and determines the course of lives. Judicial decisions and other legal processes wield great power. Manipulating them undercuts the ethical fabric of society and thus constitutes a serious offense. Walter Brueggemann says this commandment recognizes "that community life is not possible unless there is an arena in which there is public confidence that social reality will be reliably described and reported."[6]

Although stated in courtroom language, the ninth commandment also applies to a broad range of situations that touch practically every aspect of life. We should never say or do anything that misrepresents someone else. Brueggemann again provides insight:

> Politicians seek to destroy one another in negative campaigning; gossip columnists feed off calumny; and in Christian living rooms, reputations are tarnished or destroyed over cups of coffee served in fine china with dessert. These de facto courtrooms are conducted without due process of law. Accusations are made; hearsay allowed; slander, perjury, and libelous comments uttered without objection. No evidence, no defense. As Christians, we must refuse to participate in or to tolerate any conversation in which a person is being defamed or accused without the person being there to defend himself. It is wrong to pass along hearsay in any form, even as prayer requests or pastoral concerns. More than merely not participating, it is up to Christians to stop rumors and those who spread them in their tracks.[7]

---

[5] Walter Brueggemann, "The Book of Exodus," in vol. 1, *The New Interpreter's Bible: Genesis to Leviticus* (Nashville: Abingdon Press, 1994), 431.

[6] Brueggemann, 848.

[7] Brueggemann, 432.

This further suggests that workplace gossip is a serious offense. Some of it pertains to personal, off-site matters, which is evil enough. But what about cases when an employee tarnishes the reputation of a co-worker? Can truth ever truly be spoken when the person being talked about is not there to speak for him or herself? And what about assessments of performance? What safeguards ought to be in place to ensure that reports are fair and accurate? On a large scale, the business of marketing and advertisement operates in the public space among organizations and individuals. In the interest of presenting one's own products and services in the best possible light, to what extent may one point out the flaws and weaknesses of the competition without incorporating their perspective? Is it possible that the rights of "your neighbor" could include the rights of other companies? The scope of our global economy suggests this command may have wide application indeed.

The commandment specifically prohibits speaking falsely about another person, but it brings up the question of whether we must tell the truth in every kind of situation. Is issuing false or misleading financial statements a violation of the ninth commandment? How about exaggerated advertising claims, even if they do not falsely disparage competitors? What about assurances from management that mislead employees about impending layoffs? In a world where perception often counts for reality, the rhetoric of persuasion may care little for truth. But the divine origin of the ninth commandment reminds us that God cannot be fooled. At the same time, we recognize that deception is sometimes practiced, accepted, and even approved in the Scriptures. A complete theology of truth and deception draws on texts including, but not limited to, the ninth commandment. (See *Truth & Deception* at www.theologyofwork.org for a much fuller discussion of this topic, including whether the prohibition of "false witness against your neighbor" includes all forms of lying and deception.)

"You Shall Not Covet . . . Anything That Belongs to Your Neighbor" (Exodus 20:17; Deuteronomy 5:21)

The tenth commandment prohibits coveting "anything that belongs to your neighbor" (Deut. 5:21). It is not wrong to notice the things that belong to our neighbors, nor even to desire to obtain such things for ourselves legitimately. Coveting happens when someone sees the prosperity, achievements, or talents of another, and then *resents* it, or wants to *take it,* or wants to *punish* the successful person. It is the harm to another person, "your neighbor"—not the desire to have something—that is prohibited.

We can either take inspiration from the success of others or we can covet. The first attitude provokes hard work and prudence. The second attitude causes laziness, generates excuses for failure, and provokes acts of confiscation. We will never succeed if we convince ourselves that life is a zero-sum game and that we are somehow harmed when other people do well. We will never do great things if, instead of working hard, we fantasize that other people's achievements are our own. Here again, the ultimate grounding of this commandment is the command to worship God alone. If God is the focus of our worship, desire for him displaces all unholy, covetous desire for anything else, including that which belongs to our neighbors. As the Apostle Paul put it, "I have learned to be content with whatever I have" (Phil. 4:11).

Deuteronomy adds the words "or field" to Exodus's list of your neighbor's things you are not to covet. As in the other additions to the Ten Commandments' in Deuteronomy, this one draws attention to the workplace. Fields are workplaces, and to covet a field is to covet the productive resources another person has.

Envy and acquisitiveness are indeed especially dangerous at work where status, pay, and power are routine factors in our relationships with people we spend a lot of time with. We may have many good reasons to desire achievement, advancement, or reward at work. But envy isn't one of them. Nor is working obsessively out of envy for the social standing it may enable.

In particular, we face temptation at work to falsely inflate our accomplishments at the expense of others. The antidote is simple, although hard to do at times. Make it a consistent practice to recognize the accomplishments of others and give them all the credit they deserve. If we can learn to rejoice in—or at least acknowledge—others' successes, we cut off the lifeblood of envy and covetousness at work. Even better, if we can learn how to work so that our success goes hand in hand with others' success, covetousness is replaced by collaboration and envy by unity.

Leith Anderson, former pastor of Wooddale Church in Eden Prairie, Minnesota, says, "As the senior pastor, it's as if I have an unlimited supply of coins in my pocket. Whenever I give credit to a staff member for a good idea, praise a volunteer's work, or thank someone, it's like I'm slipping a coin from my pocket into theirs. That's my job as the leader, to slip coins from my pocket to others' pockets, to build up the appreciation other people have for them."[8]

Statues and Ordinances (Deuteronomy 4:44–28:68)

In the second part of his second speech, Moses describes in detail the "statutes and ordinances" that God charges Israel to obey (Deut. 6:1). These rules deal with a wide array of matters, including war, slavery, tithes, religious festivals, sacrifices, kosher food, prophecy, the monarchy, and the central sanctuary. This material contains several passages that speak directly to the theology of work. We will explore them in their biblical order.

The Blessings of Obeying God's Covenant (Deuteronomy 7:12–15; 28:2–12)

In case the commandments, statutes, and ordinances in God's covenant might come to seem like nothing but a burden to Israel, Moses reminds us that their primary purpose is to bless us.

> If you heed these ordinances, by diligently observing them, the LORD your God will maintain with you the covenant loyalty that he swore to your ancestors; he will love you, bless you, and multiply you; he will bless the fruit of your womb and the fruit of your ground, your grain and your wine and your oil, the increase of your cattle and the issue of your flock, in the land that he swore to your ancestors to give you. (Deut. 7:12–13)

> If you obey the LORD your God: Blessed shall you be in the city, and blessed shall you be in the field. Blessed shall be the fruit of your womb, the fruit of your ground, and the fruit of your livestock, both the increase of your cattle and the issue of your flock. Blessed shall be your basket and your kneading bowl. Blessed shall you be when you come in, and blessed shall you be when you go out. . . . The LORD will make you abound in prosperity, in the fruit

---

[8] Reported by William Messenger from a conversation with Leith Anderson on October 20, 2004 in Charlotte, North Carolina.

of your womb, in the fruit of your livestock, and in the fruit of your ground in the land that the LORD swore to your ancestors to give you. The LORD will open for you his rich storehouse, the heavens, to give the rain of your land in its season and to bless all your undertakings. (Deut. 28:2–7; 11–12)

Obeying the covenant is meant to be a source of blessing, prosperity, joy, and health for God's people. As Paul says, "The law is holy, and the commandment is holy and just and good" (Rom. 7:12), and "Love is the fulfilling of the law" (Rom. 13:10).

This is not to be confused with the so-called "Prosperity Gospel," which incorrectly claims that God inevitably brings wealth and health to individuals who gain his favor. It does mean that if *God's people* lived according to his covenant, the world would be a better place for *everyone*. Of course, the Christian witness is that we are *not* capable of fulfilling the law through any power we possess. That is why there is a new covenant in Christ, in which God's grace is made available to us through Christ's death and resurrection, rather than being limited by our own obedience. By living in Christ, we find that we *are* able to love and serve God, and that we *do* after all receive the blessings described by Moses, in part in the present day, and in full when Christ brings God's kingdom to fulfillment.

In any case, obedience to God's covenant is the overarching theme running through the book of Deuteronomy. In addition to these three extended passages, the theme is sounded on many brief occasions throughout the book, and Moses returns to it in his final speech at the end of his life in chapters 29 and 30.

The Dangers of Prosperity (Deuteronomy 8:11–20)

In contrast to joyful obedience to God is the arrogance that often accompanies prosperity. This is similar to the danger of complacency that Moses warns about in Deuteronomy 4:25–40, but with a focus on active pride rather than passive entitlement.

When you have eaten your fill and have built fine houses and live in them, and when your herds and flocks have multiplied, and your silver and gold is multiplied, and all that you have is multiplied, then do not exalt yourself, forgetting the LORD your God, who brought you out of the land of Egypt, out of the house of slavery. (Deut. 8:12–14)

When, after many years of sweat equity, a person sees a business, career, research project, child raising, or other work become a success, he or she will have a justifiable sense of pride. But we can allow joyful pride to slip into arrogance. Deuteronomy 8:17–18 reminds us, "Do not say to yourself, 'My power and the might of my own hand have gotten me this wealth.' But remember the LORD your God, for it is he who gives you power to get wealth, so that he may confirm his covenant that he swore to your ancestors, as he is doing today." As part of his covenant with his people, God gives us the ability to engage in economic production. We need to remember, however, that it *is* a gift of God. When we attribute our success entirely to our abilities and effort, we forget that God gave us those abilities as well as life itself. We are not self-created. The illusion of self-sufficiency makes us hard-hearted. As always, the proper worship and awareness of dependence on God provides the antidote (Deut. 8:18).

Generosity (Deuteronomy 15:7–11)

The topic of generosity arises in Deuteronomy 15:7–8. "If there is among you anyone in need . . . do not be hard-hearted or tight-fisted toward your needy neighbor. You should rather open your hand." Generosity and compassion are of the essence of the covenant. "Give liberally and be ungrudging when you do so, for on this account the LORD your God will bless you in all your work" (Deut. 15:10). Our work becomes fully blessed only when it blesses others. As Paul put it, "Love is the fulfilling of the law" (Rom. 13:10).

For most of us, the money earned by work gives us the means to be generous. Do we actually use it generously? Moreover, are there ways we can be generous in our work itself? The passage speaks of generosity specifically as an aspect of work ("all your work"). If a co-worker needs help developing a skill or capability, or an honest word of recommendation from us, or patience dealing with his or her shortcomings, would these be opportunities for generosity? These kinds of generosity may cost us time and money, or they may require us to reconsider our self-image, examine our complicity, and question our motives. If we could become ungrudging in making these sacrifices, would we open a new door for God's blessing through our work?

Slavery (Deuteronomy 15:12–18)

A troubling topic in Deuteronomy is slavery. The allowance of slavery in the Old Testament generates a great deal of debate, and we cannot resolve all the issues here. We should not, however, equate Israelite slavery with slavery in the modern era, including slavery in the United States. The latter involved kidnapping West Africans from their homeland for sale as slaves, followed by the perpetual enslavement of their descendants. The Old Testament condemns this kind of practice (Amos 1:6), and makes it punishable by death (Deut. 24:7; Exodus 21:16). Israelites became slaves to one another not through kidnapping or unfortunate birth, but because of debt or poverty (Deut. 15:12, NRSV footnote a). Slavery was preferable to starvation, and people might sell themselves into slavery to pay off a debt and at least have a home. But the slavery was not to be lifelong. "If a member of your community, whether a Hebrew man or a Hebrew woman, is sold to you and works for you six years, in the seventh year you shall set that person free" (Deut. 15:12). Upon release, former slaves were to receive a share of the wealth their work had created. "When you send a male slave out from you a free person, you shall not send him out empty-handed. Provide liberally out of your flock, your threshing floor, and your wine press, thus giving to him some of the bounty with which the LORD your God has blessed you" (Deut. 15:13–14).

In some parts of the world people are still sold (usually by parents) into debt bondage—a form of work that is slavery in all but name. Others may be lured into sex trafficking from which escape is difficult or impossible. Christians in some places are taking the lead in rooting out such practices, but much more could be done. Imagine the difference it would make if many more churches and individual Christians made this a high priority for mission and social action.

In more developed countries, desperate workers are not sold into involuntary labor but take whatever jobs they may be able to find. If Deuteronomy contains protections even for slaves, don't these protections also apply to workers? Deuteronomy requires that masters must abide by contract terms and labor regulations including the fixed release date, the provision of food and shelter, and the responsibility for working conditions. Work hours must be reasonably limited, including a weekly day off (Deut. 5:14). Most significantly, masters are to regard slaves as equals in God's eyes, remembering that *all* God's people are rescued slaves. "Remember that you were a slave in the land of Egypt, and the Lord your God redeemed you; for this reason I lay this command upon you today" (Deut. 15:15).

Modern employers might abuse desperate workers in ways similar to the ways ancient masters abused slaves. Do workers *lose* these protections merely because they are not actually slaves? If not, then employers have a duty at least not to treat workers worse than slaves. Vulnerable workers today may face demands to work extra hours without pay, to turn over tips to managers, to work in dangerous or toxic conditions, to pay petty bribes in order to get shifts, to suffer sexual harassment or degrading treatment, to receive inferior benefits, or to endure illegal discrimination and other forms of mistreatment. Even well-off workers may find themselves unfairly denied a reasonable share of the fruits of their labor.

To modern readers, the Bible's acceptance of temporary slavery seems difficult to accept—even though we recognize that ancient slavery was not the same as sixteenth- through nineteenth-century slavery—and we can be thankful that slavery is at least technically illegal everywhere today. But rather than regarding the Bible's teaching about slavery as obsolete, we would do well to work to abolish modern forms of involuntary servitude, and to follow and promote the Bible's protections for economically disadvantaged members of society.

Bribery and Corruption (Deuteronomy 16:18–20)

The effectiveness of property rights and workers' protections often depends on law enforcement and judicial systems. Moses' charge to judges and officials is especially important when it comes to work. "You must not distort justice; you must not show partiality; and you must not accept bribes, for a bribe blinds the eyes of the wise and subverts the cause of those who are in the right" (Deut. 16:19). Without impartial justice, it would be impossible to "live and occupy the land that the Lord your God is giving you" (Deut. 16:20).

Modern workplaces and societies are no less susceptible to bribery, corruption, and bias than ancient Israel was. According to the United Nations, the greatest impediment to economic growth in less developed countries is lapses in the impartial rule of law.[9] In places where corruption is endemic, it may be impossible to make a living, travel across town, or abide in peace without paying bribes. This statute seems to recognize that in general those who have the power to demand bribes are more at fault than those who acquiesce in paying them, for the prohibition is against accepting bribes, not against paying them. Even so, whatever Christians can do to reduce corruption—whether on the giving or the receiving end—is a contribution to the "just decisions" (Deut. 16:18) that are sacred to the Lord. (For a more in-depth exploration of economic applications of the rule of law, see "Land Ownership and Property Rights" in Numbers 26–27; 36:1–12 above.)

Obeying Decisions of Courts of Law (Deuteronomy 17:8–13)

Moses sets up a system of trial courts and courts of appeal that are surprisingly similar to the structure of modern courts of law. He commands the people to obey their decisions. "You must carry out fully the law that they interpret for you or the ruling that they announce to you; do not turn aside from the decision that they announce to you, either to the right or to the left" (Deut. 17:11).

Workplaces today are governed by laws, regulations, and customs with procedures, courts, and appeal processes to interpret and apply them appropriately. We are to obey these legal structures, as Paul also affirmed (Rom. 13:1). In some countries, laws and regulations are routinely ignored by those in power or circumvented by bribery, corruption, or violence. In other countries, businesses and other workplace institutions seldom intentionally break the law, but may try to contravene it through nuisance lawsuits, political favors, or lobbying that opposes the common good. But Christians are called to respect the rule of law, to obey it, uphold it, and seek to strengthen it. This is not to say that civil disobedience never has a place. Some laws are unjust and must be broken if change is not feasible. But these instances are rare and always involve personal sacrifice in pursuit of the common good. Subverting the law for self-interested purposes, by contrast, is not justifiable.

---

[9] United Nations Development Programme, *Issue Brief: Rule of Law and Development* (New York: United Nations, 2013), 3.

Using Governmental Authority Justly (Deuteronomy 17:14–20)

Just as people and institutions must not contravene legitimate authority, people in positions of power must not use their authority illegitimately. Moses specifically deals with the case of a king.

> He must not acquire many horses for himself . . . and he must not acquire
> many wives . . . also silver and gold he must not acquire in great quantity
> for himself. When he has taken the throne of his kingdom, he shall have a
> copy of this law written for him. . . . It shall remain with him and he shall
> read it . . . diligently observing all the words of this law and these statutes.
> (Deut. 17:16–19)

In this text we see two restrictions on the use of authority—those in authority are not above the law but must obey and uphold it, and those in authority must not abuse their power by enriching themselves.

Today, people in authority may try to put themselves above the law, as for example when police and court workers "fix" traffic tickets for themselves and their friends, or when high-ranking public servants or business employees do not obey the expense policies others are subject to. Similarly, officials may use their power to enrich themselves receiving bribes, zoning, and licensing exemptions, access to privileged information, or personal use of public or private property. Sometimes special perks are granted to those in power as a matter of policy or law, but this does not really eliminate the offense. Moses' command to kings is not to make sure to get legal authorization for their excesses, but to avoid the excesses altogether. When those in power use their authority not simply to gain special privileges but to create monopolies for their cronies, to appropriate vast lands and assets, and to jail, torture, or kill opponents, the stakes become deadly. There is no difference in kind between petty abuses of power and totalitarian oppression, merely in degree.

Employing Assets for the Common Good (Deuteronomy 23:1–24:13)

Deuteronomy requires owners of productive assets to employ them to benefit the community, and it does so in a clear-headed way. For example, landowners are to allow neighbors to use their land to help meet their immediate needs. "If you go into your neighbor's vineyard, you may eat your fill of grapes, as many as you wish, but you shall not put any in a container. If you go into your neighbor's standing grain, you may pluck the ears with your hand, but you shall not put a sickle to your neighbor's standing grain" (Deut. 23:24–25). This was the law that allowed Jesus' disciples to pluck grain from local fields as they went on their way (Matt. 12:1). Gleaners were responsible for harvesting food for themselves, and landowners were responsible for giving them access to do so. (See "Gleaning" in Leviticus 19:9–10 above for more on this practice.)

Likewise, those who lend capital must not demand terms that put the borrower's health or livelihood in jeopardy (Deut. 23:19–20; 24:6, 10–13). In some cases, they must even be willing to lend when a loss is likely, simply because the neighbor's need is so great (Deut. 15:7–9). (See "Lending and Collateral" in Exodus 22:25–27 above for more detail.)

God requires us to be open with our resources to those in need, while also exercising good stewardship of the resources he entrusts to us. On the one hand everything we have belongs to God, and his command is that we use what is his for the good of the community (Deut. 15:7). On the other hand, Deuteronomy does not treat a person's field as common property. Outsiders could not cart off as much as they pleased. The requirement for contribution to the public good is set within a system of private ownership as the primary means of production. The balance between private and public ownership, and the suitability of various economic systems for today's societies, is a matter of debate to which the Bible can contribute principles and values but cannot prescribe regulations.

Economic Justice (Deuteronomy 24:14–15; 25:19; 27:17–25)

Differences of class and wealth can create opportunities for injustice. Justice requires treating workers fairly. We read in Deuteronomy 24:14, "You shall not withhold the wages of poor and needy laborers, whether other Israelites or aliens who reside in your land in one of your towns." Neither the poor nor the aliens had the standing in the community to challenge wealthy landowners in the courts, and thus they were vulnerable to such abuse. James 5:4 contains a similar message. Employers must regard their obligations to their lowest employees as sacred and binding.

Justice also requires treating customers fairly. "You shall not have in your bag two kinds of weights, large and small" (Deut. 25:13). The weights in question are used for measuring grain or other commodities in a sale. For the seller, it would be advantageous to weigh the grain against a weight that was lighter than advertised. The buyer would profit from using a falsely heavy weight. But Deuteronomy demands that a person always use the same weight, whether buying or selling. Protection against fraud is not limited to sales made to customers, but to all kinds of dealings with all the people around us.

> Cursed be anyone who moves a neighbor's boundary marker. (Deut. 27:17)
>
> Cursed be anyone who misleads a blind person on the road. (Deut. 27:18)
>
> Cursed be anyone who deprives the alien, the orphan, and the widow of justice. (Deut. 27:19)
>
> Cursed be anyone who takes a bribe to shed innocent blood. (Deut. 27:25)

In principle, these rules prohibit every kind of fraud. As a modern analogy, a company might knowingly sell a defective product while oblivious to the moral implication. Customers might abuse store policies on returning used merchandise. Companies might issue financial statements in violation of generally accepted accounting principles. Workers might conduct personal business or ignore their work during paid time. Not only are these practices unjust, they violate the commitment to worship God alone, "for you to be a people holy to the LORD your God" (Deut. 26:19).

Moses' Final Appeal for Obedience to God (Deuteronomy 29:1–30:20)

Moses concludes with a third speech, a final appeal for obedience to God's covenant, which will result in human thriving. It reinforces his earlier exhortations in Deuteronomy 7:12–15 and 28:2–12. Deuteronomy 30:15 summarizes it well: "See, I have set before you today life and prosperity, death and adversity." Obedience to God leads to blessing and life, while disobedience leads to curses and death. In this context, "obedience to God" meant keeping the Sinai covenant and was thus an obligation that related solely to Israel. Yet obedience to God, leading to blessing, is a timeless principle not limited to ancient Israel, and it applies to work and life today. If we love God and do as he commands, we find it the best plan for our life and in work. This does not mean that following Christ never involves hardship and want (Christians may be persecuted, ostracized, or imprisoned). It does mean that those who live with genuine piety and integrity will do well not just because they have good character but also because they are under God's blessing. Even in evil times, when obedience to God may lead to persecution, the sweet fruit of God's blessing is better than the sour residue of complicity in evil. In the big picture, we are always better off in God's ways than in any other.

The End of Moses' Work (Deuteronomy 31:1–34:12)

Succession Planning (Deuteronomy 31:1–32:47)

After the speeches, Joshua succeeds Moses as leader of Israel. "Moses summoned Joshua and said to him in the sight of all Israel: 'Be strong and bold, for you are the one who will go with this people into the land'" (Deut. 31:7). Moses conducts the transition publicly for two reasons. First, Joshua has to acknowledge before the whole nation that he has accepted the duties laid upon him. Second, the whole nation has to acknowledge that Joshua is Moses' sole, legitimate successor. After this, Moses steps aside in the most complete possible way—he dies. Any organization, be it a nation, a school, a church, or a business, will be in confusion if the matter of legitimate succession is unclear or unresolved.

Notice that Joshua is not a capricious, last-minute choice. Under the Lord's direction, Moses has long been preparing Joshua to succeed him. As early as Deuteronomy 1:38, the Lord refers to Joshua as Moses' "assistant." Moses had noticed Joshua's military capability not long after the departure from Egypt, and over time delegated leadership of the army to him (Deut. 31:3). Moses observed that Joshua was able to see things from God's perspective and was willing to risk his own safety to stand up for what was right (Num. 14:5–10). Moses had trained Joshua in state-craft in the incident with the kings of the Amorites (Deut. 3:21). Praying to God on Joshua's behalf was an important element of Moses' training regimen (Deut. 3:28). By the time Joshua takes over from Moses, he is fully prepared for leadership, and the people are fully prepared to follow him (Deut. 34:9).

Moses also sings his final song (Deut. 32:1–43), a prophetic text warning that Israel will not obey the covenant, will suffer terribly, but will finally experience redemption by a mighty act of God. Finally, Moses exhorts the people one last time to take the law seriously (Deut. 32:46–47).

Moses' Last Acts (Deuteronomy 32:48–34:12)

Moses' final act before departing Israel and this world is to bless the nation tribe by tribe in the song of Deuteronomy 33:1–29. This song is analogous to Jacob's blessing of the tribes just before his death (Gen. 49:1–27). This is apt since Jacob was the biological father of the twelve tribes, but Moses is the spiritual father of the nation. Also, in this song Moses departs Israel with words of blessing and not with words of chiding and exhortation. "Then Moses, the servant of the Lord, died" (Deut. 34:5). The text honors Moses with a title both humble and exalted, "the servant of the Lord." He had not been perfect, and Israel under his leadership had not been perfect, but he had been great. Even so, he was not irreplaceable. Israel would continue, and the leaders who came after him would have their own successes and failures. When the people of any institution consider their leader irreplaceable, they are already in crisis. When a leader considers himself irreplaceable, it is a calamity for all.

Conclusions from Deuteronomy

In retelling the events of Israel's early history and God's giving of the law, Deuteronomy vividly portrays the importance of work to the fulfillment of God's covenant with his people. The overarching themes of the book are the need to trust God, to obey his commandments, and to turn to him for help. To abandon any of these pursuits is to fall into idolatry, the worship of false gods of our own making. Although these themes may initially sound abstract or philosophical, they are enacted in concrete, practical ways in daily work and life. When we trust God, we give him thanks for the good things he gives us the ability to produce. We recognize our limitations and turn to God for guidance. We treat others with respect. We observe a rhythm of work and rest that refreshes both ourselves and the people who work for our benefit. We exercise authority, obey authority diligently with an accurate sense of justice, and we exercise authority wisely for the common good. We limit ourselves to work that serves, rather than harms, others and that builds up, rather than destroys, families and communities. We make generous use of the resources God puts at our disposal, and we do not confiscate resources belonging to others. We are honest in our dealings with others. We train ourselves to be joyful in the work God gives us and not to envy other people.

Each day gives us opportunities to be thankful and generous in our work, to make our workplaces fairer, freer, and more rewarding for those we work among, and to work for the common good. In our own way, each of us has the opportunity—whether great or small—to transform ourselves, our families, our communities, and the nations of the world to eradicate idolatrous practices such as slavery and exploitation of workers, corruption and injustice, and indifference to the lack of resources suffered by the poor.

But if Deuteronomy were nothing but a long list of do's and don'ts for our work, the burden on us would be intolerable. Who could possibly fulfill the law, even if only in the sphere of work? By God's grace, Deuteronomy is not at its heart a list of rules and regulations but an invitation to a relationship with God. "Seek the LORD your God, and you will find him if you search after him with all your heart and soul" (Deut. 4:29). "For you are a people holy to the LORD your God; the LORD your God has chosen you out of all the peoples on earth to be his people, his treasured possession" (Deut. 7:6). If we find that our work falls short of the picture painted by Deuteronomy, let our response be not a grim resolve to try harder, but a refreshing acceptance of God's invitation to a closer relationship with him. A living relationship with God is our only hope for the power to live according to his word. This, of course, is the gospel

Jesus preached, and it was rooted deeply in the book of Deuteronomy. As Jesus put it, "My yoke is easy, and my burden is light" (Matt. 11:30). It is not an impossible list of demands, but an invitation to draw close to God. In this he echoes Moses: "O Israel, what does the Lord your God require of you? Only to fear the Lord your God, to walk in all his ways, to love him, to serve the Lord your God with all your heart and with all your soul" (Deut. 10:12).

BIBLIOGRAPHY

Banks, Robert. *God the Worker: Journeys into the Mind, Heart, and Imagination of God*. Eugene, OR: Wipf & Stock, 2008.

Barker, Kenneth, ed. *The NIV Study Bible*. Grand Rapids: Zondervan, 1999.

Brueggemann, Walter. "The Book of Exodus." Vol. 1, *The New Interpreter's Bible: Genesis to Leviticus*. Nashville: Abingdon Press, 1994.

———. *Reverberations of Faith: A Theological Handbook of Old Testament Themes*. Louisville: Westminster John Knox Press, 2002. See esp. "Sabbath."

Budd, Phillip J. *Numbers*. Vol. 5, *Word Biblical Commentary*. Dallas: Word, 1998.

Cassuto, Umberto Moshe David. *A Commentary on the Book of Exodus*. Skokie, IL: Varda Books, 2005.

Chen, Pauline. "When Doctors Admit Their Mistakes." *New York Times*. August 19, 2010.

Childs, Brevard S. *Memory and Tradition in Israel*. London: SCM Press, 1962.

Chisholm, Robert B., Jr. *From Exegesis to Exposition: A Practical Guide to Using Biblical Hebrew*. Grand Rapids: Baker, 1998.

Clines, David J. A. *Theme of the Pentateuch*. 2nd ed. London: T&T Clark, 1997.

Dillard, Raymond B. *2 Chronicles*. Vol. 15, *Word Biblical Commentary*. Dallas: Word, 1998.

Dostoevsky, Fyodor. *The Brothers Karamazov*. Translated by Richard Pevear and Larissa Volokhonsky. San Francisco: North Point Press, 1990.

Douglas, Mary. *Purity and Danger: An Analysis of the Concepts of Pollution and Taboo*. London: Routledge, 1966.

Enns, Peter. "Law of God." Vol. 4, *New International Dictionary of Old Testament Theology and Exegesis*. Edited by Willem A. VanGemeren. Grand Rapids: Zondervan, 1997.

Fretheim, Terence E. *Exodus: Interpretation: A Bible Commentary for Teaching and Preaching*. Louisville: Westminster John Knox Press, 1991.

Friedman, Milton. "The Social Responsibility of Business Is to Increase Its Profits." *New York Times*. September 13, 1970.

Gayne, Roy. *The NIV Application Commentary: Leviticus, Numbers*. Grand Rapids: Zondervan, 2004.

Gill, David W. *Doing Right: Practicing Ethical Principles*. Downers Grove, IL: IVP Books, 2004.

Harris, R. Laird, Gleason L. Archer, Jr., and Bruce K. Waltke. *Theological Wordbook of the Old Testament*. Chicago: Moody Press, 1999.

Harrison, Roland K. "Baker." Vol. 1, *The International Standard Bible Encyclopedia*. Edited by Geoffrey W. Bromiley. Grand Rapids: Eerdmans, 1979.

Hart, Ian. "Genesis 1:1–2:3 as a Prologue to the Book of Genesis." *TynBul* 46, no. 2 (1995): 315–37.

Hill, Alexander. *Just Business: Christian Ethics for the Marketplace*. 2nd ed. Downers Grove, IL: IVP Academic, 2008.

Holmes, Arthur. *All Truth is God's Truth*. Downers Grove, IL: InterVarsity Press, 1983.

Houston, Walter J. *Purity and Monotheism: Clean and Unclean Animals in Biblical Law*. London: Bloomsbury, 2009.

Hurowitz, Victor. "The Priestly Account of Building the Tabernacle." *Journal of the American Oriental Society* 105 (1985): 21–30.

Keller, Tim. "Keller on Rules of the Bible: Do Christians Apply Them Inconsistently?" The Gospel Coalition. http://thegospelcoalition.org/blogs/tgc/2012/07/09/making-sense-of-scriptures-inconsistency/.

Kitchen, Kenneth A. "Cupbearer." *New Bible Dictionary*. 3rd ed. Edited by I. Howard Marshall, A. R. Millard, J. I. Packer, and D. J. Wiseman. Downers Grove, IL: InterVarsity Press, 1996.

Kline, Meredith. *Kingdom Prologue: Genesis Foundations for a Covenantal Worldview*. Eugene, OR: Wipf & Stock, 2006.

Kraman, Steve S., and Ginny Hamm. "Risk Management: Extreme Honesty May Be the Best Policy." *Annals of Internal Medicine* 131 (December 1999): 963–67.

Küng, Hans. *Global Responsibility: In Search of a New World Ethic.* New York: Continuum, 1993.

Linsky, Martin, and Ronald A. Heifetz. *Leadership on the Line: Staying Alive through the Dangers of Leading.* Boston: Harvard Business Press, 2002.

Martens, Elmer. *God's Design: A Focus on Old Testament Theology.* 3rd ed. Grand Rapids: Baker, 1994.

Matthews, Victor H. "Hospitality and Hostility in Judges 4." *Biblical Theology Bulletin* 21, no. 1 (1991): 13–21.

———. "Nomadism, Pastoralism." *Eerdmans Dictionary of the Bible.* Edited by David Noel Freedman, Allen C. Myers, and Astrid B. Beck. Grand Rapids: Eerdmans, 2000.

Milgrom, Jacob. "Excursus 74: The Levitical Town: An Exercise in Realistic Planning." *Numbers.* JPS Torah Commentary. Philadelphia: Jewish Publication Society, 1990.

———. *Leviticus 1–16.* New Haven: Yale University Press, 1998.

———. *Leviticus: A Book of Ritual and Ethics, A Continental Commentary.* Minneapolis: Fortress Press, 2004.

Mitchell, T. C. "Nomads." *New Bible Dictionary.* 3rd ed. Edited by I. Howard Marshall. Downers Grove, IL: InterVarsity Press, 1996.

Moll, Rob. "Christian Microfinance Stays on a Mission." *Christianity Today.* May 27, 2011. http://www.christianitytoday.com/ct/2011/may/stayingonmission.html.

Motyer, J. A. *The Message of Exodus: The Days of Our Pilgrimage.* Downers Grove, IL: IVP Academic, 2005.

Pitt-Rivers, Julian. "The Stranger, the Guest, and the Hostile Host: Introduction to the Study of the Laws of Hospitality." *Contributions to Mediterranean Sociology.* Edited by John G. Peristiany. Paris: Mouton, 1968.

Rigsby, Richard O. "First Fruits." *The Anchor Yale Bible Dictionary.* Edited by David Noel Freedman. New York: Doubleday, 1992.

Schaeffer, Francis A. *Genesis in Space and Time.* Downers Grove, IL: InterVarsity Press, 1972.

Stevens, R. Paul. *The Other Six Days.* Grand Rapids: Wm. B. Eerdmans, 2000.

Tabor, James, and Randall Buth. *Living Biblical Hebrew for Everyone.* Pasadena, CA: Internet Language Corp., 2003.

Tidball, Derek. *The Message of Leviticus.* Downers Grove, IL: InterVarsity Press, 2005.

United Nations Development Programme. *Issue Brief: Rule of Law and Development.* New York: United Nations, 2013).

United States Department of Labor. "Fact Sheet: Workplace Shootings 2010." *Bureau of Labor Statistics.* http://www.bls.gov/iif/oshwc/cfoi/osar0014.htm.

Wakely, Robin. "#5967 NSHK." Vol. 3, *New International Dictionary of Old Testament Theology and Exegesis.* Edited by Willem A. VanGemeren. Grand Rapids: Zondervan, 1997.

Waltke, Bruce K. *Genesis: A Commentary.* Grand Rapids: Zondervan, 2001.

Waltke, Bruce K., and Charles Yu. *An Old Testament Theology: An Exegetical, Canonical, and Thematic Approach.* Grand Rapids: Zondervan, 2007.

Waltke, Bruce, and Alice Mathews. *Proverbs and Work.* Theology of Work Project. See esp. "The Valiant Woman." http://www.theologyofwork.org/old-testament/proverbs/.

Walton, John H. *Genesis.* The NIV Application Commentary. Grand Rapids: Zondervan, 2001.

Walton, John H., Victor H. Matthews, and Mark W. Chavalas. *The IVP Bible Background Commentary: Old Testament.* Downers Grove, IL: IVP Academic, 2000.

Wenham, Gordon J. *Exploring the Old Testament: A Guide to the Pentateuch.* Vol. 1. Downers Grove, IL: IVP Academic, 2008.

———. *Genesis 1–15.* Vol. 1, *Word Biblical Commentary.* Dallas: Word, 1998.

Wright, Christopher J. H. *The Mission of God: Unlocking the Bible's Grand Narrative.* Downers Grove, IL: IVP Academic, 2006.

———. *Old Testament Ethics for the People of God.* Downers Grove, IL: InterVarsity Press, 2004.

Wright, David P. "The Disposal of Impurity: Elimination Rites in the Bible and in Hittite and Mesopotamian Literature." *Society of Biblical Literature Dissertation Studies* 101 (1987): 34–36.

CONTRIBUTORS

John Alsdorf resides in New York City and is a member of the Theology of Work Project's steering committee.

Katherine Leary Alsdorf is founder and director emeritus of the Center for Faith and Work at Redeemer Presbyterian Church in New York City. She is a member of the Theology of Work Project's steering committee.

Patricia Anders is editorial director of Hendrickson Publishers in Peabody, Massachusetts. She serves as editorial director for the commentary.

Jill L. Baker is an independent researcher of ancient Near Eastern archaeology and faculty fellow at Florida International University, Honors College, in Miami, Florida. She contributed to the commentary on 1 and 2 Samuel, 1 and 2 Kings, and 1 and 2 Chronicles.

Cara Beed is a retired lecturer in sociology in the Department of Social Science, retired graduate advisor for the Faculty of Education, and retired honorary fellow at the Australian Catholic University in Melbourne, Victoria, Australia. She is a writer and researcher with works published in many international journals. She is a member of the Theology of Work Project's steering committee.

Daniel Block is the Gunther H. Knoedler Professor of Old Testament at Wheaton College in Wheaton, Illinois. He contributed to the commentary on Ruth.

Daniel T. Byrd is special assistant to the provost at the University of La Verne in La Verne, California. He served as a member of the Theology of Work Project's steering committee from 2007 to 2009.

Alice Camille is a nationally known Roman Catholic author, religious educator, and retreat leader. She resides in Desert Hot Springs, California. She contributed to the commentary on Joshua and Judges.

Darrell Cosden is professor of theological studies at Judson University in Elgin, Illinois. He served as a member of the Theology of Work Project's steering committee from 2007 to 2010.

Al Erisman is executive in residence at Seattle Pacific University in Seattle, Washington, and former director of technology at the Boeing Company. He serves as co-chair of the Theology of Work Project's steering committee. He contributed to the commentary on 2 John and 3 John.

Nancy S. Erisman volunteers as a board member of KIROS and on the leadership team at Westminster Chapel Women in the Workplace in Bellevue, Washington. She served as a contributing editor to the commentary.

Jarrett Fontenot resides in Baton Rouge, Louisiana. He served as a contributing editor to the commentary.

Larry Fowler resides in Gig Harbor, Washington. He served as a contributing editor to the commentary.

Russell Fuller is professor of Old Testament at Southern Baptist Theological Seminary in Louisville, Kentucky. He contributed to the commentary on Psalms.

Duane A. Garrett is the John R. Sampey Professor of Old Testament Interpretation at Southern Baptist Theological Seminary in Louisville, Kentucky. He contributed to the commentary on Deuteronomy, Ecclesiastes, and Song of Songs, and served as editor for the poetical books.

Mark S. Gignilliat is associate professor of divinity at Beeson Divinity School, Samford University in Birmingham, Alabama. He contributed to the commentary on Isaiah and served as editor for the prophetic books.

Michaiah Healy is youth pastor at the Greater Boston Vineyard in Cambridge, Massachusetts. She served as a contributing editor to the commentary.

Bill Heatley is the former executive director of Dallas Willard Ministries in Oak Park, California, and served as a member of the Theology of Work Project's steering committee. He contributed to the commentary on Colossians and Philemon.

Bill Hendricks is president of the Giftedness Center in Dallas, Texas. He is a member of the Theology of Work Project's steering committee.

Brian Housman is executive pastor at the Vineyard Christian Fellowship of Greater Boston in Cambridge, Massachusetts. He contributed to the commentary on 1 and 2 Samuel, 1 and 2 Kings, and 1 and 2 Chronicles.

L. T. Jeyachandran is former chief engineer (civil) at the Department of Telecommunications for the government of India in Calcutta, India, and former executive director of Ravi Zacharias International Ministries (Asia-Pacific) in Singapore. He is a member of the Theology of Work Project's steering committee.

Timothy Johnson is assistant professor of Old Testament and Hebrew at Nashotah House Theological Seminary in Nashotah, Wisconsin. He contributed to the commentary on Job.

Randy Kilgore is senior writer and workplace chaplain at Desired Haven Ministries/Made to Matter in North Beverly, Massachusetts. He is a member of the Theology of Work Project's steering committee.

Alexander N. Kirk resides in Wilmington, Delaware, and contributed to the commentary on 1 and 2 Timothy and Titus.

Aaron Kuecker is associate professor of theology and director of the Honors College at LeTourneau University in Longview, Texas. He contributed to the commentary on Luke and Acts.

Jon C. Laansma is associate professor of classical languages and New Testament at Wheaton College and Wheaton Graduate School in Wheaton, Illinois. He contributed to the commentary on Hebrews.

Clint Le Bruyns is director and senior lecturer at the Theology and Development Programme at the University of KwaZulu-Natal in Pietermaritzburg, KwaZulu-Natal, South Africa. He is a member of the Theology of Work Project's steering committee.

John G. Lewis is director of Saint Benedict's Workshop and Missioner for Christian Formation at the Episcopal Diocese of West Texas in San Antonio, Texas. He consulted on the commentary on Romans.

Kelly Liebengood is associate professor of biblical studies at LeTourneau University in Longview, Texas. He contributed to the commentary on James, 1 and 2 Peter, 1 John, and Jude.

Kerry E. Luddy is director of community relations and discipleship at Brighton Presbyterian Church in Rochester, New York. She served as a contributing editor to the commentary.

Grant Macaskill is senior lecturer in New Testament studies at the University of Saint Andrews in St. Andrews, Fife, Scotland, United Kingdom. He contributed to the commentary on Mark.

Alistair Mackenzie is senior lecturer at the School of Theology, Mission and Ministry, Laidlaw College in Christchurch, New Zealand. He is a member of the Theology of Work Project's steering committee.

Ryan P. Marshall is minister to students at Redeemer Community Church in Needham, Massachusetts. He served as a contributing editor to the commentary.

Steven D. Mason is associate provost and dean of faculty at LeTourneau University in Longview, Texas. He contributed to the commentary on Ezekiel.

Alice Mathews is the Lois W. Bennett Distinguished Professor Emerita at Gordon-Conwell Theological Seminary in South Hamilton, Massachusetts. She is a member of the Theology of Work Project's steering committee. She contributed to the commentary on Genesis 1–11, Proverbs, 1 and 2 Samuel, 1 and 2 Kings, 1 and 2 Chronicles, Introduction to the Prophets, Isaiah, Jeremiah, Lamentations, and Matthew. She also served as a consulting editor for the commentary.

Kenneth Mathews is professor of divinity at Beeson Divinity School, Samford University, in Birmingham, Alabama. He contributed to the commentary on Daniel.

Sean McDonough is professor of New Testament at Gordon-Conwell Theological Seminary in South Hamilton, Massachusetts. He is a member of the Theology of Work Project's steering committee. He contributed to the commentary on Joshua, Judges, John, and Revelation, and served as editor for biblical studies and the Epistles.

Tim Meadowcroft is senior lecturer in biblical studies at Laidlaw College in Auckland, New Zealand. He contributed to the commentary on Hosea, Joel, Amos, Obadiah, Micah, Nahum, Habakkuk, Zephaniah, Haggai, Zechariah, and Malachi.

William Messenger is executive editor of the Theology of Work Project in Boston, Massachusetts, and adjunct faculty member of

Laidlaw-Carey Graduate School in Auckland, New Zealand. He also serves on the board of directors of ArQule, Inc. He is a member of the Theology of Work Project's steering committee. He contributed to the commentary on Jonah and served as general editor.

Andy Mills is former president and CEO at Thomson Financial and Professional Publishing Group in Boston, Massachusetts. He serves as co-chair of the Theology of Work Project's steering committee.

Joshua Moon resides in Minneapolis, Minnesota. He contributed to the commentary on Jeremiah and Lamentations.

Colin R. Nicholl is an independent researcher and author in Northern Ireland, United Kingdom. He contributed to the commentary on 1 and 2 Thessalonians.

Valerie O'Connell is an independent consultant in Burlington, Massachusetts. She served as a contributing editor to the commentary.

Jane Lancaster Patterson is assistant professor of New Testament at Seminary of the Southwest in Austin, Texas. She consulted on the commentary on Romans.

Jonathan T. Pennington is associate professor of New Testament and director of Ph.D. studies at Southern Baptist Theological Seminary in Louisville, Kentucky. He contributed to the commentary on Matthew and served as editor for the Gospels and Acts.

Gordon Preece is director of Ethos: the Evangelical Alliance Centre for Christianity and Society in Melbourne, Victoria, Australia. He is a member of the Theology of Work Project's steering committee.

Mark D. Roberts is executive director of digital media at the H. E. Butt Family Foundation/The High Calling in Kerrville, Texas. He is a member of the Theology of Work Project's steering committee. He contributed to the commentary on Ezra, Nehemiah, Esther, Galatians, Ephesians, and Philippians.

Haddon Robinson is the Harold John Ockenga Distinguished Professor of Preaching, senior director of the Doctor of Ministry program, and former interim president of Gordon-Conwell Theological Seminary in South Hamilton, Massachusetts. He is president and chair emeritus of the Theology of Work Project.

Justin Schell is on the global leadership and support team with The Lausanne Movement. He served as a contributing editor to the commentary.

Andrew J. Schmutzer is professor of biblical studies at Moody Bible Institute in Chicago, Illinois. He contributed to the commentary on Genesis 1–11.

Bob Stallman is professor of Bible and Hebrew at Northwest University in Kirkland, Washington. He contributed to the commentary on Genesis 12–50, Exodus, Leviticus, and Numbers.

Christine S. Tan is director of marketing and social media at the Theology of Work Project in Boston, Massachusetts. She served as a contributing editor to the commentary.

Hanno van der Bijl resides in Mobile, Alabama. He is web editor at the Theology of Work Project and served as a contributing editor to the commentary.

Bruce Waltke is professor emeritus of biblical studies at Regent College in Vancouver, British Columbia, Canada. He has also held teaching positions at Westminster Theological Seminary in Glenside, Pennsylvania, and Knox Theological Seminary in Fort Lauderdale, Florida, where he is a distinguished professor of Old Testament. He contributed to the commentary on Proverbs and served as editor for the Pentateuch.

Joel White is lecturer in New Testament at Giessen School of Theology in Giessen, Germany. He contributed to the commentary on 1 and 2 Corinthians.

Andy Williams is program manager at HOPE International in Kigali, Rwanda. He served as a contributing editor to the commentary.

David Williamson is director emeritus of Laity Lodge in Kerrville, Texas. He is a member of the Theology of Work Project's steering committee.

Lindsay Wilson is academic dean and senior lecturer in Old Testament at Ridley Melbourne Mission and Ministry College in Melbourne, Victoria, Australia. He contributed to the commentary on Psalms.

INDEX OF NAMES AND SUBJECTS

Note: page numbers in *italics* indicate most significant occurrences.

About the Theology of Work Project

The Theology of Work Project is an independent, international organization dedicated to researching, writing, and distributing materials with a biblical perspective on work. The Project's primary mission is to produce resources covering every book of the Bible plus major topics in today's workplaces. Wherever possible, the Project collaborates with other faith-and-work organizations, churches, universities and seminaries to help equip people for meaningful, productive work of every kind.

Theology of Work Bible Commentary
By the Theology of Work Project

William Messenger, Executive Editor, Theology of Work Project
Sean McDonough, Biblical Editor, Theology of Work Project
Patricia Anders, Editorial Director, Hendrickson Publishers

Contributors to Volume 1:

Andrew Schmutzer and Alice Mathews, "Genesis 1–11 and Work"
Bob Stallman, "Genesis 12–50 and Work," "Exodus and Work," "Leviticus and Work," and "Numbers and Work"
Duane Garrett, "Deuteronomy and Work"